SAX EXPAT

American Made Music Series
Advisory Board

David Evans, General Editor
Barry Jean Ancelet
Edward A. Berlin
Joyce J. Bolden
Rob Bowman
Curtis Ellison
William Ferris
John Edward Hasse
Kip Lornell
Bill Malone
Eddie S. Meadows
Manuel H. Peña
Wayne D. Shirley
Robert Walser

SAX EXPAT

Don Byas

CON CHAPMAN

University Press of Mississippi / Jackson

The University Press of Mississippi is the scholarly publishing agency of the Mississippi Institutions of Higher Learning: Alcorn State University, Delta State University, Jackson State University, Mississippi State University, Mississippi University for Women, Mississippi Valley State University, University of Mississippi, and University of Southern Mississippi.

www.upress.state.ms.us

The University Press of Mississippi is a member of the Association of University Presses.

Copyright © 2025 by Con Chapman
All rights reserved
Manufactured in the United States of America
∞

Publisher: University Press of Mississippi, Jackson, USA
Authorised GPSR Safety Representative: Easy Access System Europe -
Mustamäe tee 50, 10621 Tallinn, Estonia, gpsr.requests@easproject.com

Library of Congress Control Number: 2025931735

Hardback ISBN: 9781496848666

Trade paperback ISBN: 9781496856074

Epub single ISBN: 9781496856081

Epub institutional ISBN: 9781496856098

PDF single ISBN: 9781496856104

PDF institutional ISBN: 9781496856111

British Library Cataloging-in-Publication Data available

I love beauty.
—*Don Byas*

CONTENTS

Prologue. ix

Chapter 1. In the Beginning 3

Chapter 2. Los Angeles Nights 14

Chapter 3. Women and Children 22

Chapter 4. Influences 26

Chapter 5. Move to New York. 39

Chapter 6. Life after Basie 55

Chapter 7. Sax about Town 65

Chapter 8. To Europe 82

Chapter 9. Don, Sam, Carlos 93

Chapter 10. Spanish (and Portuguese) Tinge 107

Chapter 11. Paris Years 114

Chapter 12. Amsterdam Years. 125

Chapter 13. The Sixties. 136

Chapter 14. With Ben, near the End 151

Chapter 15. The Out Chorus. 160

Epilogue. 180

Acknowledgments 183

Notes 185

Selected Bibliography 219

Index 223

PROLOGUE

The first name by which he is known—"Don"—was not his birth name, nor does it appear on his death certificate. He was born in 1913, but at a time when it was expedient—during World War II, when he was subject to conscription—he declared that he was born in 1912.

As an adult, he would be known as "Sam" by some bandmates, but the name "Don" would stick with him until his death. It exemplified, in a way, his desire to create his own identity, in equal parts romantic and noble. By calling himself "Don," he arrogated unto himself a title originally reserved for royalty, just as Edward Kennedy "Duke" Ellington and William James "Count" Basie had before him. When he found himself caught between two jazz dynasties—the rightful claimant to the tenor sax throne still occupied by Coleman Hawkins and the advancing rebels of bebop—he left the American scene in the manner of a second-born son cut off from the family estate by primogeniture to seek his fortune in a distant land. In Europe, he found peace but was often dissatisfied with the quality of the musicians who accompanied him; they were not jazzmen to the manner born.

He came back to the States late in life and found neither the acclaim nor the riches he expected to receive as an early innovator turned elder statesman. He returned to Europe, where he died, professing to be content but—a notoriously fierce competitor in jam sessions from Kansas City to 52nd Street in New York—he wondered what might have been had he never left America.

This is Don Byas's story.

SAX EXPAT

CHAPTER 1

In the Beginning

On October 21, 1913, a boy named "Carlos Wesley" was born in Muskogee, Oklahoma, to Walter Wesley Byas and Dottie Mae (Weaver) Byas.[1] As an adult, the boy would claim that his father was "half Spanish, half Negro" and his mother was a "Cherokee Indian,"[2] but his birth certificate states in the blanks for "Color" that both parents and the child were "Negro." In later years, census officials would categorize the three as simply "Black," perhaps from bureaucratic sloth when faced with mixed-race parents and a limited number of categories to put them in. One final wild card in Byas's genetic makeup: his father was said to have read the Bible in Hebrew, and Byas's second wife said his youngest brother Walter Jackson Byas spoke of the family's Jewish forebears, although the subject "was never talked about in Muskogee."[3]

Walter Wesley Byas was born in Springfield, Missouri, in 1884 (although the boy's birth certificate gives the state of his father's birthplace as Texas). He could read and write and, according to census records, was a high school graduate; Walter's father, Michael, the boy's paternal grandfather (who spelled his name "Bias"), was born in Kentucky in 1838, and his mother, Polly (sometimes spelled "Pollie"), the boy's paternal grandmother, was born in Missouri in 1845; both could read and write and were listed in the 1870 federal census when they lived in Clark's Fork Township, Cooper County, Missouri, as "Mulatto." They married in 1865 when he was twenty-seven years old and she was twenty. The family moved to Muskogee, Oklahoma, in 1905.

Walter's father had been a blacksmith and, perhaps because he was exposed to his father's work in a smithing trade as a youth, Walter became an engraver for a jewelry company; his son Carlos would refer to him as a goldsmith, and the Muskogee *City Directory* for 1936 identifies him as a "jeweler."[4] On Carlos's birth certificate, his father's occupation is listed as "Engraver (temporary)," perhaps an indication that he considered this job classification inadequate to describe his talents and ambitions. A "Muskogee News Note" in the *Tulsa Star* on October 24, 1914, a year later, described Walter Byas as a "young Negro" man who held a responsible place with a "reputable and large white" firm. Many years later, he would open up his own jewelry shop.[5] As evidence of his skills in the trade, at one point, Walter Byas fashioned a striking ring made of four different types of gold and platinum with a cameo set in jade that his son would wear for the rest of his life. "My father used to keep it in the store window to attract attention," Carlos Byas would say. "When people found out how much it cost [around $22,500 in today's dollars], he'd tell them he could make a cheaper ring."[6] The only other mention of Walter Byas found by the author is a notice in the *Tulsa World* on October 15, 1907, in which he was said to have tried to save the life of a friend who was killed in a railroad accident.[7]

Carlos Byas's mother was born in Texas in 1892; she attended Central Texas College and taught school in addition to her tasks as a housewife for a family of three boys. Her father, Elijah B. Weaver, was born in Arkansas in 1860, and her mother, Mary Jane Sedberry, was born in Texas in 1862; they married in 1878 when she was sixteen years old and he was eighteen. She was the youngest of twelve children, but the family was prosperous; her father, a minister, also invested in real estate.[8] Carlos's birth certificate lists the age of his mother at the time of his birth as twenty-three years, but this is incorrect; she was only twenty-one at the time, and her husband's age is similarly misstated as thirty-one when he was, in fact, twenty-nine. The Certificate of Attending Physician or Midwife on the boy's birth certificate is signed by a physician, suggesting that the boy's parents were sufficiently well-established that they could afford to pay for a doctor rather than a midwife. Dottie Mae Byas would outlive her husband, who died in 1950, and marry a man named Lightner; she died in April 1962.[9]

When a census enumerator visited the family's home on January 7, 1920, he determined that they rented the dwelling at 455 North 19th Street. By the fall of the following year, the boy's parents appear to have purchased a home in the Patterson Heights neighborhood but, perhaps reflecting that the transition from renting to ownership was a financial stretch for them, the *Muskogee County Democrat* for November 3, 1921, lists Walter W. Byas as owing $76.44 in tax penalties and costs.

Carlos was his parents' firstborn son, as indicated on the boy's birth certificate, which indicated he was the couple's only child at the time. He would be followed by two brothers: first, Vincent (known as "Vint") Weaver Byas, born September 2, 1915, then Walter Jackson (known as "Jack"), born August 10, 1918. Aaron Bell, who played bass with Duke Ellington and grew up a few houses down from the Byas family, recalled that the three Byas boys were nicknamed "The Professors" for their youthful smarts; Vint and Jack Byas fulfilled that youthful mockery and "went into teaching." Perhaps reflecting the rigors of the musical profession that he chose, Carlos's brothers both outlived him; he died at the age of fifty-eight, while Vint lived to be seventy-four and Jack seventy-nine. As Don's second wife put it, the eldest son "was sort of the black sheep of the family."[10] According to Aaron Bell, both Vincent and Jack "played clarinet, but . . . didn't stay in music." Bell said that Don and a guitar player named Oliver Green would sometimes "get together for little sessions" that enticed him to "go over and listen." He also said that Byas "saved [his] life once, when he pulled me out of an old gravel pit where we used to swim."[11]

The family's last name on the boy's birth certificate is clearly spelled "Byas," although census records reflect a number of alternative spellings: "Bias," "Bogas," "Begas"—even "Bear."[12] Despite this wide orthographic variety, "Byas" is the conventional spelling; the surname is most common among Black Americans, followed by whites and Hispanics.[13] Carlos Wesley Byas (after he became known as "Don") was pleased one night in Barcelona to discover "an excellent Spanish brandy sold by Gonzalez Byass." "It's my cousin's brandy," Byas exclaimed after he'd drunk a bit too much of it—"I love my cousin!"[14] Byas was referred to as "Carlos Byars" in his 1930 graduation picture from Muskogee's Manual Training High School and as "Carlis Byers" in a commemorative publication about the school produced for its Sixth Mammoth Reunion in 2008; the school ceased to exist in 1970. The "manual training" movement was the precursor to vocational training in American high schools; it emphasized "the practical training of the hand and the eye" and taught students "the power of doing things instead of merely thinking about them, talking about them, and writing about them."[15] As Byas's senior class appears to be all-Black, it may also have been a means of informally segregating African American students. The school's motto—"NOT AT THE TOP BUT CLIMBING"—seems faint praise that reflects the limited hopes that the world offered to its graduates at the time.

At the time of the 1930 census, the Byas family had moved to a 610-square-foot house on Fondulac Street in Muskogee that was listed in census records as having a value of $4,000, around $72,000 adjusted for inflation. By the time of the 1940 census (when Byas would have left home), the remaining family members lived at 719 North 24th Street in a 1,222-square-foot house valued at $3,000, around $65,000 today.[16] Byas's mother still resided at this house at the time of her death in 1962. The 1920 census gives Byas's age (as recorded by the "enumerator" on January 7, 1920) as six; the 1930 census gives his age (as recorded on April 22, 1930) as sixteen. These dates and ages are consistent with the year of his birth certificate, 1913, not 1912 as he would claim at an important point later in his life.[17]

Both of Carlos Byas's parents were musical. He said that his father "played almost every instrument, but mainly clarinet and violin," as well as guitar. His mother "played organ in church"[18] and "played many instruments, piano and violin, and gave piano lessons." Carlos learned to play piano from her but said he didn't like it very much.[19] He was trained in a classical repertoire and "played clarinet and viola" from the age of two or three (his accounts differed), and he said he was a "child prodigy," giving concerts from the time he was seven or eight years old. He said he "liked the new sound of jazz," and "whenever he had ten minutes," he "tried some sounds out on his clarinet"—which didn't please his parents. His parents referred to the music that appealed to him as that "terrible ragtime," but he "became obsessed with it."[20] "[M]y father wouldn't have any of it and I got a lot of slaps on my head for it,"[21] he said, and his second wife confirmed that his mother also didn't want him to play jazz.[22] As an adult, Byas would tell a reporter that he became a "jazz prodigy at three"; when he began to play, he wasn't strong enough to hold a clarinet, so his father would rest the bell of the instrument on a stool.[23] Eventually, he abandoned the violin and the clarinet because he "didn't like them for jazz instruments. Of course, clarinet has always been a jazz instrument—but there wasn't enough sound in it for me," he recalled, "so I bought me a second-hand alto saxophone and began to study it"[24] at around the age of thirteen. Byas probably attended either the Douglas Elementary School, which opened in 1906, or the Langston Elementary School, which opened in 1912.[25] His copy of a group picture with his class from an unknown year is inscribed "Carlos Byas" on the back.

As a youngster, Carlos would have had opportunities to hear the developing style of African American music that came to be known as jazz despite Muskogee's relative isolation; the town was founded as a railroad depot for the Missouri, Kansas and Texas Railway (commonly referred to in speech and song as "The Katy," from the last two initials of "MKT"), which carried hundreds of thousands of people through the region.[26] (It is likely that Carlos's grandparents would have ridden the Katy when they moved to Oklahoma from Missouri, as the line ran directly from Sedalia, Missouri, near their home in Cooper County, to Muskogee.) At the time of the 1910 Federal Census, Muskogee was the second-most populous city in the territory, with 25,278 residents compared to 64,205 in Oklahoma City.[27] In 1912, Ferdinand "Jelly Roll" Morton, the first genuine jazz composer, hooked up with McCabe's Troubadours, a minstrel troupe, and performed at an "open-air fun spot" in Muskogee known as The Pastime Theatre. Morton was a failure as a minstrel comedian, but he "played piano before the show, to considerable public approval,"[28] and soon took over from the incumbent pianist.

Morton frequently said that he invented jazz, a claim disputed by some but one that indisputably contained a kernel of truth; Albert Nicholas, a New Orleans clarinetist who was a friend of Morton's, explained that by this assertion he meant that "he created a style of jazz, and he did."[29] While the time Morton spent in Muskogee may not have been the sole or even the principal spark for the development of jazz there, it is nonetheless the case that a number of musicians who would make their mark in the genre were born there. There was trumpeter Terrence "T" Holder, born in Muskogee in 1897, who went on to lead the Alphonso Trent Orchestra and then bands of his own; Walter "Foots" Thomas and his brother Joe, born in 1907 and 1908, respectively, both tenor saxmen;[30] Clarence Love, bandleader, pianist, and violinist, born in 1908, who operated a "territory" band that toured the rural West before settling in Kansas City; and Claude "Fiddler" Williams, born in Muskogee in 1908, who played with Terrence Holder, Andy Kirk, and Count Basie.[31] Later additions to the Muskogee scene include trombonist Druie Bess, who moved to Muskogee in 1929 to play with Bill Lewis's Dixie Ramblers;[32] Barney Kessel, a white guitarist born in Muskogee in 1923, whose childhood home and father's shoe store were located in "the heart of the African-American commercial and entertainment district" among buildings that maps of the town referred to only as "Negro joints";[33] and as noted above, bassist Aaron Bell, born in Muskogee in 1922, who, in addition to his work with Duke Ellington, backed a number of jazz recording artists including Billie Holiday, Miles Davis, Count Basie, Coleman Hawkins, and Ella Fitzgerald.[34]

As for why jazz should have taken root in Oklahoma, the state has a unique history that explains why Blacks have had, since the mid-nineteenth century, a disproportionate impact on its culture by comparison to other Plains states. Beginning in 1830 with the passage of the Indian Removal Act, the federal government began a program of displacing Native Americans from their ancestral homes in the Southeast to free up land desired by white cotton farmers. Members of the major Native American nations in the region—Cherokee, Chickasaw, Choctaw, Muskogee Creek, and Seminole, referred to as the "Five Civilized Tribes"—were uprooted and moved to land set aside for them in what is now Oklahoma; the name of the state "is of Indian origin and signifies 'Home or land of the red men.'"[35] The Native American nations who were thus re-settled were referred to as "civilized" because they had adopted some aspects of the culture of Anglo-Americans who had outnumbered them in the Southeast, including Christianity, literacy, a market economy—and slavery.

As a result, thousands of African Americans were forcibly transplanted along with their Native American owners to the Southwest, where they would gain their freedom with the Emancipation Proclamation.[36] In addition, the Five Civilized Tribes, in some cases, brought with them freed Blacks and runaway slaves who had used the sovereignty of the Native American tribes in the Southeast as a sanctuary to which they fled to escape their masters.[37] Some have suggested that enslavement of Blacks by Native Americans "hardly resembled the institution established in the Deep South," likening it more to indentured servitude found in colonial America whereby a servant gained freedom after serving an agreed-upon term of years, but slaves owned by Native Americans "attempted to escape their bondage by running away" and "revolted against their Indian masters in other ways," confirming the more straightforward view that slavery is slavery, regardless of the race of the master.[38] Ellis Ezell, a reedman who led a band that Byas played with in Muskogee, said that "the Indians had slaves, and they intermarried with their slaves." Ezell's mother was a Cherokee "freedman," meaning she was an African American, not a Cherokee.[39]

After the Civil War ended, the Five Civilized Tribes granted former slaves "citizenship, autonomy, and a level of respect unheard of in the post-Reconstruction South." Blacks farmed alongside their former Native American owners, served as officials in tribal governments, and acted as interpreters with white settlers, and some fifty all-Black towns were formed.[40] The number of Blacks in the state increased further with the Land Rush of 1889, and consequently, a critical mass of potential creators and consumers of African American music was attracted to what would have been, not long before, inhospitable soil for its development. The presence of four racial or ethnic groups—Hispanic, white, African American and Native American—in the Oklahoma territory (and the possibility that he was an admixture of three of them) meant that Byas was exposed to a variety of cultural influences in his youth that may explain his open-mindedness on issues of race as an adult and his embrace of a variety of music styles, from blues to Portuguese *fado* to sentimental pop tunes, over the course of his career.

The age at which Byas began to play professionally is uncertain; in one interview, he said he began to play with the Bennie Moten band when he was fifteen;[41] in another, he said he had played with "well-known bands since" he "was 11."[42] We can perhaps harmonize this discrepancy by making a distinction between Moten's band, which was a highly professional "territory" band that operated throughout the Midwest from a base in Kansas City, and gigs close to home that he and fellow Manual Training High School student James Columbus "Jay" McShann would play with local musicians who, while not as accomplished as the members of Moten's band, were still noteworthy within a smaller geographical area. Today, McShann is best known as the bandleader who hired alto saxophonist Charlie Parker for his first significant professional engagement, but he was much more than that; he developed from an untutored beginner on the piano who couldn't read music into an important transitional figure whose style blended blues and boogie-woogie and served as a bridge between the swing and bop eras. Byas recalled playing with a version of the Moten band that included alto sax Theodore "Doc" Ross,[43] who later played with the Blue Devils at a time when Lester Young was a member of that band.[44]

In their teens, Byas and McShann began to play gigs in Muskogee and surrounding towns, such as Wagoner, Taft, and Haskell, Oklahoma, what McShann called "little ten-cent social dances,"[45] with small combos put together by Kyle Collins, their high school music director. Later, they would join Ellis Ezell's band, "The Rhythm Kings of Muskogee," which was said to "have the reputation of being all that their name implies" in a column that appeared in the national edition of the *Chicago Defender* on January 23, 1932, although this may have just been press agent puffery. The article listed ten band members, but neither Byas nor McShann was included among them at that time.[46] (Barney Kessel was at one time the only white member of Ezell's band.) According to McShann, the two teenagers also played with a man named "Lawyer" Kimble,[47] with "a guy named Weaver," and with a family group called "Professor Gray's Band" that performed in what McShann referred to as "dance towns": little villages, such as Shawnee, Wewoka, and Okmulgee, Oklahoma, that were so small that when a dance band came through it was a cause for widespread excitement.[48] "[W]hen the bands would come into town it was something," McShann said. "Everybody that could would try to get to the dance. That's just like bringing a new culture to you, and everybody wants to see what they're doing."[49] Ezell would recall that when Byas played with Lawyer Kimble's band, he "was a little bitty guy, but all that big tone . . . he has such a fat tone for such a little guy."[50]

Byas was older than McShann by three years, and so introduced him to the life of a teenage professional musician. The two came to be in such demand that they would play multiple gigs without a break:

> [Don] had played with different groups around Muskogee, with the older guys, guys like John Maddox and Funk Wiley. . . . And then, he had a job one Fourth of July. The job was the night before the Fourth of July from nine to one, then the early morning of the Fourth we had another job at about three or four in the morning, for a breakfast dance, from three to seven or four to eight. Then, we played another date at noon in another town called Wagoner. We had three dates right there.

On another occasion, they played four jobs in quick succession: "Don and I made a gig in Wagoner," McShann recalled. "We played the Winter Garden one night, and then left there and played at Wagoner for a breakfast dance. Then we played an afternoon dance back in Muskogee, and then played a night dance out on Stem's Beach at Honor Heights."[51] When their parents would wake up to find that their sons were not yet home, they were alarmed at first, but their concern was overcome by the money the boys made in the lean years of the Great Depression: only 80 cents to

$1.50 cents per job (not including tips), but that amounted to around $14 to $25 a night adjusted for inflation.[52]

Several sources say that, in addition to Moten's group, Byas played with Terrence Holder and Walter Page's Blue Devils,[53] but his name does not appear in various lists of their personnel; jazz writer Gary Giddins refers to Byas's time with these groups as "subbing,"[54] so it may have been that his work with them was too sporadic for him to take part in recording sessions. One source says that in 1929, Byas played alto sax and clarinet with the Blue Devils at the biggest dance hall in Oklahoma City, Oklahoma, in a version of the band that included Jack Washington on bass, T. B. "Turk" Thomas on piano, and Karl George on trumpet, among others, and this tale was also told by Byas's widow.[55] A 1980 article states that Holder heard Byas playing in 1930 at a high school concert in Muskogee and persuaded Byas's parents to let him join the band that Holder had formed after leaving Alphonso Trent's orchestra; Byas would have been seventeen at the time.[56] Various sources that cover the Blue Devils extensively make no mention of Byas,[57] but Count Basie said that Byas joined the group shortly after Basie left them, which would have probably been in 1930 when Byas was sixteen or seventeen.[58] In a 1965 interview, Byas said that when he began to play, he "had to get my parents' permission" to do so.[59] This is consistent with the experience of other musicians who hit the road while still minors, so no negative inference should be drawn from his omission from written and aural records of these groups.[60] According to one source, Byas's parents made Moten promise that he would take good care of their son and bring him back a few days later[61] and that their son would "never be [given] a drop of liquor. But as soon as we were a few miles out of town," Byas said, "I'd be as drunk as a coot."[62] In 1930, the year he graduated from high school, Byas played with Andy Kirk's Clouds of Joy, the band formed by Terrence Holder that Kirk took over when Holder was deposed by band members in 1929[63] for misappropriating their pay on more than one occasion; he would stay with Kirk until 1931.[64] John Williams (future husband of Mary Lou Williams) and John Harrington play alto sax and Lawrence Freeman plays tenor sax on the Kirk band's recordings during this period, so again, Byas may have been hired as a substitute for jobs when these musicians weren't available.[65]

After high school, Byas attended Langston College (since 1941, Langston University), a historically Black institution of higher learning. The school was located in Langston, Oklahoma, an all-Black town founded by Edward

McCabe, an African American lawyer and politician who envisioned it as a haven where "the colored man has the same protection as his white brother."[66] The response by Byas's parents to the 1940 US Federal Census indicates that Byas attended the school for four years, but this is not certain; another source says that Byas was a student there only during 1931 and 1932, leaving Oklahoma for California in 1933.[67] It was in college that Byas acquired—or bestowed on himself—the name "Don." He called the group he formed there "Don Carlos and His Collegiate Ramblers," perhaps in a nod to the Spanish heritage of his father; in Spanish, "Don" is an honorific term that carries with it a bit more cachet than its near-equivalent "Mister" in English, and Byas may have thought it lent an air of romance to an undersized freshman (he was only 5' 6" tall and 135 pounds nine years later when he registered for the draft).[68] Byas may have heard the name as the title of the 1867 Giuseppe Verdi opera *Don Carlos,* based on the 1787 Friedrich Schiller play *Don Karlos, Infant von Spanien* (Don Carlos, Infant of Spain). While this connection may seem far-fetched, remember that Byas's parents were trained in and devotees of classical music, and it is thus not unlikely that he would have heard the opera spoken of or played in his home.

A poster for a dance on April 14, 1932, in Watonga, Oklahoma, declared that Don Carlos and His Collegiate Ramblers was a "13-piece colored orchestra" that "has played to record breaking crowds here at Watonga."[69] French jazz critic Alain Tomas says that this college band was "made up of his high-school comrades," but this is doubtful; Langston, Oklahoma, is 125 miles from Muskogee, and it is unlikely that a college freshman would arrive on campus with enough bookings to keep a band together.[70] It is certainly not true in the case of Jay McShann, who played with Byas in high school but attended Fisk University in Nashville, Tennessee, not Langston College.[71] In a 1961 interview, Byas identified two members of his college band, neither of whom was from Muskogee: Karl George, a trumpeter, and Otto Lee Gaines, whom Byas identified as the "bass singer with the Delta Rhythm Boys."[72] George was born in St. Louis in 1913 and began his career with McKinney's Cotton Pickers. and would later play with Lionel Hampton, Teddy Wilson, Count Basie, and many others.[73] Gaines was from Buena Vista, Mississippi; he formed a vocal quartet at Langston College and went on to write the lyrics to two Billy Strayhorn compositions, "Take the A Train" and "Just A-Sittin' and A-Rockin'."[74]

Not much is known of Byas's time in college, but Frank Wess, a tenor sax a decade younger than Byas, remembered hearing him there. "I'd known Don

Byas from the time I was ten years old in Oklahoma. I went out [to Langston College] during the summer, studying saxophone. He had a band there," Wess recalled, adding that Byas's sound was by then already fully formed. "[H]e always played the same way."[75] According to Byas's widow, Don told her that the Collegiate Ramblers "set out for New York . . . walking from village to village, playing every day, really for a slice of bread. They made banners that said they would perform in the evening and went through the streets playing." This was a promotional practice known as the "ballyhoo" that was a common method of advertising used by early twentieth-century bands, but it was apparently not successful in the Collegiate Ramblers' case. "Every now and then one or two people came," Byas's widow said, and so they traveled "really a nomad life in the beginning on the way to New York."[76]

One source says that Byas decided to switch from alto to tenor after hearing Coleman Hawkins solo on "It's the Talk of the Town" while Hawkins was with the Fletcher Henderson Orchestra;[77] that version of the song was recorded on September 22, 1933.[78] Byas said he was "forced" to switch from alto to tenor in the late 1920s one night in Oklahoma City when he was a member of Bert Johnson's Sharps and Flats. "I was playing first alto, but one day [Johnson] was listening while we were rehearsing, and he said, 'Don, have you ever tried to play tenor?'" Byas said no, and Johnson told him he had "such a big sound" on alto that he would love to hear him on tenor. Byas borrowed the tenor player's sax, played a few choruses, and Johnson told him, "Well, then that is your instrument, man. That's what you should be playing, man, with the sound you get out of that. Your alto sound is bigger than the one he gets out of his tenor."[79] When Byas told Johnson, "I have no money to buy an instrument," the incumbent tenor said, "Well, if you want to play tenor, let's switch. I'll take your alto—you take my tenor." Byas said, "Crazy—okay," and from that day on, he played tenor (although Eddie Barefield tells a slightly different story). Byas said in 1965 that he gave the former tenor player his alto and that he didn't know, "to this day, whatever happened to him." When bandleader Johnson left Dust Bowl Oklahoma sometime in the early to mid-1930s[80] for what he believed would be greener pastures in California, Byas went with him.[81]

CHAPTER 2

Los Angeles Nights

The date on which Don Byas arrived in Los Angeles as a member of Bert Johnson's Sharps and Flats is unknown, but a Behind the Scenes With Harry column in the *California Eagle* on October 12, 1934, said that "Bert Johnson's 'Sharps and Flats'" had "just arrived from the middlewest" and had "made a big hit in their initial presentation at the Orpheum Theatre" the previous Monday night, October 8. The lineup of the group was given as "C. B. Johnson [*sic:* should be "Cee Pee"] director [and drummer][1]; Bert W. Johnson [who played trombone], manager; Victor Mars, Pat Shelton, Don Carles, [*sic*] Byas, O. R. Burley, Leonard Reals, Al Scott, M. Wallace, Eddie Garland and Raybon Tarrant."[2] Byas's Dutch second wife suggested that the personnel was drawn from the group he formed at Langston College, Don Carlos and His Collegiate Ramblers, but this appears to be incorrect, as the personnel named above do not include trumpeter Karl George or Otto Lee Gaines, whom Byas identified as members of his college band and whom he had played with as a member of Walter Page's Blue Devils.[3] One source says that the Sharps and Flats numbered seventeen during the Oklahoma days but had been reduced to six members by the time they reached California; the additional musicians added to increase their size to the eleven named above were presumably picked up in Los Angeles.[4]

Byas told an interviewer in 1952 that he came to Los Angeles and joined Hampton's band in 1933, skipping over his time with Bert (sometimes spelled "Burt") Johnson, who had played trombone on recordings by Texas pianist Sammy Price in 1929 and 1930 before forming his own band[5] presumably because Johnson didn't achieve fame on the level of Hampton's. In the same interview, Byas said that it was "around this time" that he started "blowing a tenor sax" because "everyone told [him] that he sounded better" on it than he did on alto, contradicting his claim that he made the switch before he left Oklahoma when he was still a member of Johnson's band. Byas said that Hampton "had a terrible orchestra at the time" but that Hampton himself "was burning down the stage. He was here, there, in front, behind, everywhere at the same time." Hampton's group was a band that played for dancing, but Hampton himself didn't let that restrain his urge to entertain: "[H]e was doing a lot of numbers without a break, without interrupting the dancing," Byas said. "He sang, he danced, he played the drums, the piano, the vibraphone. He was madly dynamic."[6] One source (Alain Tomas) says that Herschel Evans was in this band before departing to play with Count Basie in 1936, and Tomas finds traces of Evans's influence on Byas's sound several years later, when he was a member of Andy Kirk's band for the second time.[7] "I was in good company with Hampton," Byas said. "Herschel Evans was in the band, before joining Count Basie. Really, for my debut in a large orchestra, it was successful. I stayed with Lionel until 1935."[8]

Hampton said that he hired Byas to replace Paul Howard, whom Jelly Roll Morton called "the first great tenor sax in the USA."[9] Hampton said Howard left to go "back to ballroom music," but this seems to get things backward; Hampton had been a "then-unknown young drummer" (who sometimes sang scat vocals) with Howard's Quality Serenaders, a band led by Howard based in Los Angeles that included future Duke Ellington trombonist Lawrence Brown.[10] Two sources state that Howard was the leader and Hampton a member of the band in 1929,[11] so it seems more accurate to say that Byas was one of the component parts whom Hampton added to Teddy Buckner on trumpet, Tyree Glenn on trombone and vibraphone (and, according to Hampton, "any instrument I put in front of him"), and others to get his group up to big band size. One source says that Hampton made his debut as a conductor/band leader in 1935 and that the band's composition at the time included Byas; Hampton on drums and vibraphone; Herman Grimes, Paul King, and Alton Grant on trumpets; "Country" Allen on trombone; Bob Barefield on alto sax and clarinet; Paul Howard on tenor sax and clarinet;

David Brooks on baritone sax; Buster Wilson on piano; Charlie Rousseau on guitar; and Johnny Miller on bass.[12]

Byas said that he also played in a band led by Les Hite, a Los Angeles alto sax player and bandleader who took over Howard's Quality Serenaders in 1930, but he is not listed in any of Hite's personnel on recordings.[13] Hampton's recollection is that he hired Byas in 1936, a year cited by Panassié and Gautier,[14] but other sources date Byas's tenure with Hampton to June 1935.[15] Hampton formed his big band in 1934 at Sebastian's Cotton Club in Los Angeles,[16] and one source says that when Byas joined the band, Hampton was "little known,"[17] which favors an earlier date; by 1936, Hampton had been in a Bing Crosby movie (*Pennies From Heaven*) with Louis Armstrong and had been hired by Benny Goodman to play in his small groups, so he was one of the more readily recognizable jazz musicians of the day.

Hampton's band played a residency at the Red Car Club located at the corner of Sixth and Main streets in downtown Los Angeles, at the end of a trolley line. The place wasn't fancy; it was frequented by motormen and conductors from the trolley company and sailors on shore leave. "The club was a big beer garden," Hampton recalled. "[I]t seated about four hundred—with sawdust on the floor. The chicks who worked there wore blue-jean overalls—didn't care how they looked"—but it was a steady gig, and so it offered stability to the musicians. Hampton, a serious student of music who took courses in harmony and music theory at the University of Southern California on the side, said that "[t]he guys who went there were interested in beer and girls, not music," so the band "could try out a lot of new stuff. A lot of guys came to me looking for work because I had that kind of freedom." Byas may thus have been attracted to Hampton both by the regular paycheck and the opportunity to play with a group that was innovative. He does not appear on any of Hampton's records, the earliest of which dates from 1937,[18] but they apparently parted on good terms: "The next surprise is my telephone ringing and a voice speaking beautiful French and welcoming me to Paris," Hampton wrote in a show business column in 1953; it was Byas, whom Hampton said "used to be one of the members of my band."[19]

In May 1936, Byas received a passing notice in the *California Eagle*'s "With the Orchestras and Musicians" column by Freddy Doyle, who noted that "Don (ten. sax) Byas plays a lot of horn and I don't mean maybe."[20] Doyle kept up the drumbeat, noting in the November 6, 1936, *Eagle* that "Don Byas on the tenor saxophone has really gained national rating as ace high as a tenor man."[21] Doyle does not identify whom Byas was playing with when these reports were published, but he was for a time a member of a band formed by reedman Eddie Barefield after the latter left Cab Calloway during a West Coast tour, and it is likely that this was the band reviewed by Doyle.[22] One source places Byas's hiring by Barefield in late 1934,[23] but Barefield himself said the date was later, after Calloway's band had finished filming *The Singing Kid* with Al Jolson in November 1935.[24] "I left Cab in California in 1936," Barefield recalled, "not that I was dissatisfied, but I was always a bit of a vagabond and this was the first time I'd been in such a beautiful climate. Also, I was sick with ulcers and I decided I'd settle there."[25] The size of Barefield's band is said to have been as large as fifteen; in addition to Byas on tenor and Barefield and his brother Bob on altos, by one report, it included Paul Howard on tenor; Tyree Glenn, "Country" Allen, and George "Happy" Johnson on trombone; Dudley Brooks on piano; Jack McVea on alto and baritone saxes; Buddy Harper on guitar; Al Morgan on bass; Lester Young's brother Lee on drums; and Morris McClure ("Red Mack"), Pee Wee Brice, and Leroy "Snake" White on trumpets.[26] (In a 1978 interview, Barefield said his pianist was Hugo Dandridge, and he did not list his brother or Happy Johnson as band members.[27])

Leroy White was an old friend of Barefield's from Minneapolis, with whom he had formed a band called "The Do Dads from Diddy Wah Diddy" in the late 1920s.[28] The local musicians' union "raised the customary objections" to White's employment in Barefield's band as an out-of-town musician, so Barefield offered their part-time secretary a full-time job, which persuaded them to relax the formerly strict interpretation of union rules. The band "rehearsed at the union and got a chance to audition for a job at Sebastian's Cotton Club, where Lionel Hampton was playing," Barefield recalled. The owner liked Barefield's band but suggested that he take on Hampton as his drummer; Barefield stood his ground:

> I was stubborn and suggested that both Lee Young and Lionel should play in the show, but we couldn't agree. I told the fellows in the band . . . and Lee said he didn't want to hold everybody from getting the job, but I . . . insisted that either Sebastian took us complete or not at all. Two or three weeks later I got a telephone call from Sebastian and he agreed to take the complete band. I stayed at the Cotton Club about nine months with my band.[29]

Barefield said that Byas still played alto when he joined this band despite the latter's tale of being "forced" to switch to tenor by Bert Johnson. "Don Byas was with us, playing alto," Barefield said. "Me, I needed a tenor and asked him to do that. It didn't come easy. At first he wouldn't hear of it. Finally, the guy who played baritone, Paul Howard, and I, we shook him up good. And he became one of the best tenors in the world."[30] Barefield's band was said by jazz writer Stanley Dance to be "a success" that "played up and down the West Coast"; they appeared in a 1937 movie called *Every Day's a Holiday* with Louis Armstrong, but they apparently did not record. Barefield eventually tired of Los Angeles and decided his ulcers could stand a return to New York when he received an offer to join Fletcher Henderson's band;[31] he appeared on Henderson's recording sessions beginning in May 1938.[32]

Another source—tenor Albert "Budd" Johnson—confirms that Byas continued to play alto as he transitioned to tenor. "Don Byas used to learn Art Tatum's solos and play them on his alto," Johnson said. "That was the way he became anything—he was living in California at that time. This developed a terrific technique for him because trying to copy some of Art Tatum's solos is truly difficult—especially for a horn."[33] On December 4, 1936, Freddy Doyle reported that Art Tatum had "just arrived . . . from the East" and that he was "'swinging' out in Hollywood at the Mellony Grill and really packing" the club "with outstanding celebrities of the movie world." Tatum was said to be "contracted for many motion pictures and broadcasts that will keep him" in Los Angeles for many months, and that "in the next few weeks" he "will make many recordings for Brunswick or Decca." Doyle speculated that in "these recordings he will probably use these 'Cats' 'to 'swing' with him, Eddie Barefield (sax), Al (bass) Morgan, and Don (tenor) Byas."[34] Tatum did go into the Decca studio in Hollywood on February 26, 1937, to record four numbers—"Body and Soul," "What Will I Tell My Heart," "With Plenty of Money and You," and "I've Got My Love to Keep Me Warm"—with five sidemen, but Byas was not among them, and there was no saxophone on the date.[35] Perhaps as a warning after a mediocre night in December 1936 (or maybe he was just kidding), Doyle praised Andy Anderson, a tenor from Cleveland, Ohio, who was in town: "I hear that this new 'Cat' blows a 'fine' horn," Doyle wrote, then went on to say, "Don Byas please take notice?"[36]

Byas is said to have played in a band led by Lorenzo Flennoy, a pianist whose group played at the Trouville Club and the Casablanca Breakfast Club in Los Angeles, and which at one point included Charles Mingus.

Marv Goldberg, who has done extensive research on Flennoy, has found no evidence that Byas played with Flennoy's band but also no reason to doubt the claim,[37] and Byas has been linked with Flennoy during its stay at the Club Alabam located on the thriving Central Avenue nightlife district.[38] A trio led by Flennoy that included guitarist Gene Phillips was recorded in 1944 and 1945, and the group made four "soundies" with singer Mabel Scott, but Flennoy has largely disappeared from jazz history.[39] Byas played in a band with Wilbur "Buck" Clayton during his years in Los Angeles,[40] but Clayton makes no mention of Byas in his autobiography until the two were members of Count Basie's band; again, this may simply be a case of Byas not having a seat in the game of musical chairs that bands played with itinerant sidemen such as him.[41] Flennoy's band was eventually taken over by trumpeter Charlie Echols, who is known to have played at Chez Popkis, a Greek restaurant in Los Angeles.[42] Byas was a member of this band in 1935, along with Buck Clayton, trombonist Tyree Glenn, and tenor sax Herschel Evans; none of Echols's bands were recorded, but "many of the musicians who played in bands led by [him] recalled it with great affection and admiration."[43]

As was Byas's practice throughout his life, during his time in California, he participated in extracurricular jam sessions, a busman's holiday that sharpened his skills and (one suspects) made up for the less-interesting music he had to play as a junior tenor sax in an ensemble. Lee Young recalled that he, Nat "King" Cole, and Ellington bassist Jimmie Blanton became "running buddies" in Los Angeles in the mid-1930s. "[W]e used to jam all the time. Upstairs at the union. That's when Charlie Christian was here. And Don Byas. The people downstairs are trying to work, and we're just tearing the place up. We'd get in there at noon, and when they'd come back from lunch, the building would be shaking."[44]

These faint tracks are all we have to go on in tracing Byas's early West Coast years; he is mentioned only in passing in Ted Gioia's *West Coast Jazz: Modern Jazz in California, 1945–1960*[45] and not at all in "From the Three Deuces to Billy Berg's," a long subchapter on the development of bebop in Los Angeles in Alyn Shipton's *A New History of Jazz*.[46] Nor is Byas identified as a sideman in the biggest compilation of West Coast jazz, *Central Avenue Sounds: Jazz in Los Angeles (1921–1956)*.[47] It may be that he didn't stand out when he was just one of many saxophones in a big band ensemble or couldn't get the solo time he needed when he had to compete with older, more established reedmen; thus, apart from the rave reviews he drew when he played in smaller groups in his early years in California, he passed unnoticed.

It was in California that Byas met Eddie Mallory, a trumpeter and saxophonist who was a member of the band that backed singer-actress Ethel Waters, and it was with Mallory that Byas left California and came to New York. As Eddie Barefield put it, "[M]y band broke up, and Tyree Glenn and Don Byas joined Ethel Waters."[48] Byas took the place of Francis "Doc" Whitby, the incumbent tenor, who decided to leave the Waters troupe when they were in Oklahoma City, his hometown, after the band's car broke down in ice and slush and his "feet became frost-bitten." Waters was on her way to an engagement "at the Trocadero in Los Angeles"; Byas "took Whitby's place in the Mallory band when they reached California," and it was with this entourage that Byas would come to New York.[49] Lee Young dates his employment with Mallory from 1937, when

> Ethel Waters came through [Los Angeles] with . . . Eddie Mallory. And they wanted a drummer. So they heard me play and they wanted me to go with them. And Tyree Glenn. Tyree Glenn and I left together. I'll never forget on the front porch my dad told Tyree, "I want you to really look out for my son because he's never been away from home before." So he said, "Yes, Mr. Young . . . I'll really take care of him." . . . I'm saying to myself, "Whoa," because I already knew him. I was a teetotaler. I didn't drink. I didn't smoke. They couldn't get me to smoke a joint or nothing. I wouldn't do it. I just never did. But these guys were wild, and he's turning me over to the wildest bunch of young musicians from New York.[50]

Byas would return to California and spend a good deal of time there in the early forties after he'd joined Count Basie and become an established figure on the jazz scene. He participated in recording sessions in July 1942 with the Count Basie band before the union ban on studio recordings was imposed on July 31, and then is heard in radio broadcasts from the Trianon Ballroom in Southgate, California, in August and September. While in Hollywood from the summer of 1942 to late 1943, the Basie band played on the soundtracks of *Reveille With Beverly, Hit Parade of 1943, Stagedoor Canteen, Top Man, Choo Choo Swing, Band Parade,* and *Crazy House* (also released as *Funzapoppin*).[51] In April 1942, Billy Berg, a former vaudevillian who owned some of Los Angeles's more notable clubs, lost his entertainment license at a club known as the Capri when a woman attending a film at a nearby theater complained to the mayor that she found a musician with a woman in the back seat of her car when she returned to it one night. Berg opened up a new venue, the Trouville Club, where Sunday jam sessions sponsored by jazz producer Norman Granz featuring Lester Young became popular. As Lee Young described them,

> We used to have jam sessions all the time at Billy Berg's. We had them at the Trouville, some great jam sessions. In all these sessions, Nat [Cole] was the pianist, I was the drummer, and I think by then it was Johnny Miller who was playing bass. Les Paul was playing guitar most of the time. Sometimes Oscar Moore would play. One Sunday I remember we had four tenors: Prez [Lester Young], Ben Webster, Don Byas, and Bumps Myers. And it went on for like three or four hours.[52]

Byas was a frequent participant in these sessions, which were "ferocious," according to Jimmy Rowles, whom Berg later invited to become the house pianist. A "lot of guys didn't care too much for" [Lester] Young "because he didn't play from the Coleman Hawkins school," Rowles said. "They used to come to the club with blood in their eyes to wipe Lester out. Anytime anybody used to come out and try, he'd end up wiping them out. He was always ten miles ahead of Don Byas and all those guys." Young was drafted into the US Army in September 1944 and spent a traumatic year in the service, unable to play his saxophone and confined to detention after he was found in possession of marijuana and liquor. He was dishonorably discharged in late 1945 after serving a year in detention (memorialized in his composition "D.B. Blues," with "D.B." standing for "detention barracks"), and when he returned to the Los Angeles scene, Norman Granz—hoping to become Young's manager—took steps to cheer him up, which included frequent trips to local record shops.

There, he found Young taking a particular interest in buying records of music released since he'd been gone that he'd heard on the radio—by Don Byas.[53]

CHAPTER 3

Women and Children

Don Byas's second wife is known to the world because she has spoken publicly of their relationship and taken steps to preserve his legacy, but before he left America, he was previously married to a woman named Marjorie Bush, who has passed unnoticed in previous accounts of his life. She was born on November 28, 1921, and was twenty years old when they were wed on February 10, 1942. At the time, Don listed his age as twenty-eight, which would mean he was counting 1913 as his birth year.[1] A squib in an entertainment reporter's column described Bush as a schoolteacher.[2]

Marjorie Bush was a resident of Little Rock, Arkansas, and Don's residence is shown as 1524 Ringo, Kings County, New York, on their marriage certificate. This appears to have been a mash-up of two far-apart places on the part of someone, perhaps the Deputy Clerk of Pulaski County, Arkansas, who completed the Affidavit and Marriage License. Kings County is Brooklyn, New York, but there is no Ringo Street there; there *is* a 1524 South Ringo Street in Little Rock, Arkansas. The marriage license form, perhaps reflective of the unequal status of the sexes at the time, called for the street address of the groom but not that of the bride. The Little Rock address is located in the Dunbar Junior High School District, a historically Black neighborhood. The house at 1524 South Ringo Street was built around 1917 for Chester E. Bush, eldest son of John E. Bush, cofounder of the Mosaic Templars of America, a fraternal society formed to provide services—insurance, loans, and medical care—that African Americans may not have been able to obtain from white businesses.

Chester Bush attended public schools in Little Rock and Fisk University in Nashville, Tennessee. Upon graduation from college, he started out as the editor and manager of the group's official publication, the *Mosaic Guide*, and assumed its highest position upon his father's death. Shortly thereafter, he had a new home at 1524 South Ringo Street built for his family. He suffered a stroke in 1924 and died at the age of thirty-eight; he was survived by his wife and three children. His widow remained in the house until her death in 1950, leaving it to her son, John E. Bush III, and daughter, Clothilde, but not to Marjorie, who was still alive at the time. The foregoing information is taken from Historically Black Properties in Little Rock's Dunbar School Neighborhood,[3] which makes no mention of Marjorie Bush, perhaps because her upwardly striving family took a dim view of her marriage to an itinerant jazz musician who lived in New York. Marjorie moved east with Byas after their marriage, and then the two apparently drifted apart.[4] The author has found no record of her divorce from Byas or of any children by this marriage. According to one account, Don didn't speak of his first wife after he moved to Europe and told others that she died young.[5] She did die young, at the age of thirty, on December 13, 1951; an official document on file in Amsterdam states that the marriage was dissolved in December 12, 1951, lending support to the view that the two were not divorced.

Byas was romantically involved with pianist Mary Lou Williams, as were other musicians with whom she played, including reedman John "Bearcat" Williams, her first husband; tenor sax player Ben Webster; and trumpeter Harold "Shorty" Baker, her second husband. While Mary Lou was a confident musician, she was a diffident person once she got up from the piano; as jazz journalist Dave Dexter put it, "At set's end Mary Lou quickly retreats to backstage. She's too shy, too modest, to rap with the dancers jammed around the bandstand."[6] John Williams beat her and collected her pay from the bandleaders they worked for, giving her just enough money to pay for her meals. Webster and Baker were both said to have physically abused her. Mary Lou developed a stutter as a child, the product of abuse by a babysitter, and had a nervous, guilt-ridden personality, the result of her decision to go on the road at a young age (when she was still known as the "Little Piano Girl of East Liberty," the neighborhood where she grew up in Pittsburgh), leaving younger brothers and sisters behind.[7]

Mary Lou and Byas were members of Andy Kirk's Clouds of Joy when they became involved in "a turbulent, at times physically abusive affair," and Mary Lou went to live with her elder sister Mamie. One night, when Byas had been drinking, he "got rough with Mary," and Mamie "threw him not just out of the house, but *down* the stairs."[8] Byas's personality as a lover matched the spectrum of his styles on the saxophone; he would veer from rough to gentle, writing Mary Lou "tenderly lyrical love notes." A photograph that he gave her is inscribed "To Mary—The sweetest girl I've ever known. Here's hoping such a beautiful love as ours can never die. I'll think of you always. Yours forever, Don"—but he couldn't keep his aggressive side under control.[9] Despite their stormy history, Mary Lou was willing to work with Byas after their affair ended. She recorded with him in 1944 and in 1953; the music from the former session can be heard on *Mary Lou Williams: The Chronological Classics, 1944*[10] and from the latter on *The Mary Lou Williams Quartet, featuring Don Byas*.[11] She even composed a song with him, "Man o' Mine," also known as "My Last Affair."[12]

It is likely that Byas had many flings along the way that were not formalized legally or recorded by observers of the jazz scene as his stormy affair with Mary Lou Williams was; as Byas would say later in life, "I don't play the saxophone, I play the *sexophone*."[13] It is believed that Byas fathered a son to a Belgian woman, whom he presumably met while touring the country in the spring of 1947. The boy was born on January 20, 1949, in Brussels, Belgium, and named Carlos.[14] A notice in the February 1949 issue of *L'Actualité Musical et Artistique* congratulated Byas on the birth of his son, called him a "graaf pey" (Brussels slang for "cool guy" or "fine fellow") and said, "La maman n'est soulagée et le papa n'en joue pas moins bien" ("The mother is relieved and the dad does not play less well.") In 1950, Byas would tour Europe with the Duke Ellington Orchestra, and Arthur Goepfert wrote an article for the July issue of *Jazz Journal* in which he said that he "noticed Don Byas at the [railroad] station, complete with big horn, wife and baby" when the band arrived in Switzerland in May, so this was presumably the son that was born a year earlier.[15] Byas would write a song titled "Janine (I Can't Explain)" that he recorded on October 11, 1947, after he'd left Belgium for Spain and was working in Barcelona. Those lyrics express his longing for Janine, a woman whom he says walks in his sleep and fills his day with dreams, and conclude by saying:

All day long I'm dreamin'
all night long I'm schemin'
how to get you Janine.[16]

The album on which this song is heard includes a dedication "to his Belgian lady friend." Byas sold his rights in "Janine" to Ritmo y Melodia for a 10 percent royalty.[17]

Boris Vian included Byas in the personalities profiled in his book, *Manual of Saint Germain-des-Prés*, about a neighborhood in Paris known for its bohemian character and at the end of World War II, its jazz scene. Vian said Byas was "an unrepentant skirt-chaser" who "easily falls prey to the weaker sex, for which he himself has much too great a weakness."[18] In the end, Byas found domestic tranquility with Johanna "Jopie" Eksteen.

CHAPTER 4

Influences

Don Byas was candid about those whom he consciously counted as his influences: "In the beginning," he told Arthur Taylor, a drummer who was also a jazz writer, "Hawk [Coleman Hawkins]. That sound always stayed with me and never got away. In fact, I think I have a bigger sound now [November 11, 1969, when he was fifty-six] than he had," Byas said. "Apart from that, I dug what he was playing."[1]

Coleman Randolph Hawkins, born in 1901 and thus approximately a decade older than Byas, was a native of St. Joseph, Missouri, who started out playing cello and piano, subsequently learned to play saxophone at the age of nine, and was playing professionally by the time he was sixteen. He switched to tenor sax full-time after joining Jesse Stone's Blues Serenaders. "We tried to get him to join the group but he thought it was not a good idea to try to play dance music with a cello," Stone recalled, "so he got a saxophone and he was playing that sax in four or five months. Yeah, he could play it." At the time, the saxophone was still considered a novelty instrument, that is, one that called for the musician who played it to incorporate an element of spectacle in addition to pure musicality. This usage reflected the realities of the entertainment industry of the time, in which "it was necessary to have a novel effect" for a musician "to stand any chance of being noticed" or advance out of the orchestra pit or ensemble.[2] As Stone put it, Hawkins and future Basie tenor Herschel Evans (a cousin of Stone's) "both used to have the same style . . . they used to 'slap tongue' . . . popped a note, make it have a hard attack . . . and they used to have a feature thing . . . where they would be doing this at each other like they were shooting pistols. It was a novelty."[3] When Hawkins started out on the saxophone, it was thus used more for striking effect than musicality, but Hawkins demonstrated that it could stand on its own without the addition of comic touches. As Duke Ellington put it, Hawkins "was the greatest influence and stimulated the greatest change in saxophone style very abruptly."[4] He created the river that the fish who came after him would swim in.

Hawkins left Stone's band to join Mamie Smith and Her Jazz Hounds in the summer of 1921 when she offered him, as Stone put it, "more money than I could ever give him."[5] He toured extensively with Smith until 1923, when he got tired of the road and left her in New York to gig around at first and then to join the band of Wilbur Sweatman, a transitional clarinetist who played both ragtime and jazz, at Connie's Inn in July of that year. During his engagement with Sweatman, Hawkins was heard by Fletcher Henderson, who invited him to play on a record date; Hawkins would join Henderson's band on a full-time basis in 1924.[6]

In 1934, Hawkins left Henderson's band and departed for Europe, playing first as a solo, then hooking up with a succession of bands in England, France, the Netherlands, Switzerland, Belgium, and Scandinavian countries.[7] According to his biographer, John Chilton, Hawkins was rarely "challenged in Europe, as he would have been back home"[8] in America, but when he returned to America, he was in fine form; he recorded "Body and Soul" on October 11, 1939,[9] and thereby changed the course of jazz saxophone. The song was written in 1930 and had been first recorded in a jazz style that year by Louis Armstrong, but Hawkins's rendition was heard as a breakthrough; he opens with two choruses of improvisation over the song's chord progressions, providing only hints of the melody, anticipating bebop. He was criticized, he recalled, for playing "wrong notes" by "a lot of people who didn't know about flatted fifths and augmented changes."[10]

When Hawkins returned to America in the summer of 1939, Byas and other tenors tried to get him to reengage with them, but Hawkins was cagey at first. "We tried to get Hawkins to play but he wouldn't," Byas said, recalling a "tenor conclave" at drummer Nightsy "Puss" Johnson's place at 134th Street and Saint Nicholas Avenue in Harlem, which had become an after-hours hangout for entertainers and musicians. "Nevertheless, there was Chu Berry,

Ben Webster, Herschel Evans, Lester Young—it was a fantastic sight." Jo Jones and Big Sid Catlett were there to play drums, with "Slam Stewart on bass. I'll never forget that night," Byas said.[11] Hawkins was biding his time, however, waiting for the right moment to exact revenge on Young, who had bested him in a December 18, 1933, jam session in Kansas City before he left for Europe. As recounted by Mary Lou Williams, Hawkins was in town with Fletcher Henderson's band,[12] which had finished their gig and were cruising around town looking for action; they stopped at the Cherry Blossom club, where Count Basie was playing, and some of the musicians in the place began to ask Hawkins to play. He demurred at first until finally, Basie said, Hawkins "went across the street" to his hotel and came back with his horn. Basie was sitting with bassist John Kirby, who said, "I ain't never seen that before," and Basie replied, "I ain't either" because "[n]obody had ever seen Hawk bring his horn in somewhere to get in a jam session."[13] Hawkins typically avoided jamming; the pay was lousy or nonexistent, and there was no upside for the top-ranked tenor to engage in title bouts with contenders. When he was asked to participate, he would typically offer an excuse: he was just resting, he had pawned his sax, he had a toothache, and so on.

Hawkins returned to the Cherry Blossom with his saxophone and faced a lineup of challengers who, according to Basie, "were up there calling for their favorite tunes, and then Hawk went up there, and he knew all of the tunes, and he started calling for all of those hard keys, like E-flat and B-natural. That took care of quite a few local characters right away."[14] The semi-finalists included Hawkins, Ben Webster, Herschel Evans, Lester Young and—according to Basie bandmember Eddie Durham—Don Byas.[15] The session went on so long that reinforcements were called in for the rhythm section, and when Mary Lou Williams arrived to replace the piano player, she found Hawkins "in his singlet [a sleeveless garment worn under a shirt; that is, he had stripped down] taking turns with the Kaycee men. It seems he had run into something he didn't expect."[16] While the talents of all three of Hawkins's competitors were formidable, the man who knocked him out was Lester Young, the tenor equivalent of a "sweet science" boxer, not a puncher like Webster or Evans. "Lester's style was light," Williams said, "it took him maybe five choruses to warm up. But then he would really blow; then you couldn't handle him on a cutting session. That was how Hawkins got hung up."[17]

Thus, when Hawkins returned from Europe and became famous on the strength of "Body and Soul," he was nonetheless still smarting over his defeat by Young. He scouted out Puss Johnson's place for several weeks, arriving around three or four in the morning without his horn, just listening while musicians displayed their wares on the assumption that Hawkins might be forming a new band or have an album in the works. "The tension continued to build," wrote Ellington trumpeter Rex Stewart. "Is this the night he will play?" All the leading tenor men "had their innings," according to Stewart: "Illinois Jacquet, Chu Berry, Don Byas, Dick Wilson, and so on."[18] Hawkins had put off requests to jam until he walked in one night with his instrument case when Young was accompanying Billie Holiday. Holiday, like Hawkins, rarely participated in jam sessions; if she accepted an invitation to sing while out at a club, she expected the owner to compensate her in kind with drinks or dinner on the house.[19] As her song came to an end that night, she began to "signify," that is, to make offhand remarks apparently addressed to no one in particular but pointedly intended for the ears of one person present. She said it had been her pleasure to have the world's greatest tenor saxophonist— Lester Young—backing her up. When Hawkins ignored her, she intensified her praise of Young, damning Hawkins by indirection, saying, "[H]er man . . . was the only tenor saxophone in the world . . . and it really wasn't any use for any tired old man to try and blow against her Pres," her nickname for Young—short for "President," as the number one man in the country on his instrument.

According to Ellington trumpeter Rex Stewart, "You could have heard a pin drop after that remark," but still Hawkins said nothing. Instead, he joined the jam session, taking his turn on a fast tune that showed he had lost none of his former fire. He then "sauntered to the bar, had a big drink, and waited to see how the cats would follow his avalanche of virtuosity. For some reason, nobody felt like blowing" to follow him, so Hawkins "picked up where he left off, this time with a ballad" that "he proceeded to" embellish, "finishing up with an incredible cadenza, to thundering applause," then "gallantly started toying with *Honeysuckle Rose*" and motioned "for Chu [Berry] and Don Byas to join him." Dick Wilson, who was in the audience, turned to Elmer Williams, tenor sax player with Fletcher Henderson, and said, "Well, that's that. Coleman is still the boss."[20]

The development of the tenor sax as a jazz instrument begins with Hawkins, not because no one played the instrument before him, but because the music played by those who preceded him was less jazz than ragtime. As Joachim Ernst Berendt put it, "[T]here were some tenor players before

[Hawkins], but the instrument was not an acknowledged jazz horn."[21] Hawkins was aware of his reputation as an original: "Some people say there was no jazz tenor before me," he is widely quoted as saying. "All I know is I just had a way of playing and I didn't think in terms of any other instrument but the tenor." Byas adopted many of the characteristics that one heard in Hawkins's play, such as a rich vibrato, the oblique introductions over chord progressions that seem at first unrelated to a song's melody, and the unremitting improvisations that made him—like Hawkins—a force in jam sessions. Jazz scholar Martin Williams called Byas "the most brilliant . . . of Hawkins's more direct pupils" but still placed him beneath his model: "Byas was never as successful as Hawkins in varying his phrasing: even the staggeringly sophisticated techniques of finger and harmony on Byas's *I Got Rhythm* or *Indiana* are phrased and accented with freight-train regularity."[22]

Unfortunately for Byas, he came to be too closely identified with Hawkins. "Don told me on the [1946 European] tour that he didn't get enough credit at home," said pianist Billy Taylor. "In New York, Hawk was the man. Don loved Hawk, but [he] said, 'I played in his band. I know what he's doing and I know what I'm doing. Why can't everyone hear what I'm doing?'"[23] Byas may have been smarting then—and throughout his career—at a perceived slight by Hawkins in ranking Byas as the seventh-best tenor player (not including Hawkins himself) in an August 1941 ranking he put together for *Music and Rhythm* magazine; Hawkins rated Ben Webster, Chu Berry, Lester Young, Georgie Auld, Charlie Barnet, and Bud Freeman ahead of Byas and faintly praised him by writing "Don Byas's strongest point is execution. Don is young [he was then nearly twenty-eight] and has plenty on the ball."[24] As late as July 4, 1964, at a concert in the Haarlem Rembrandt Theater, patrons called for Byas to play "Body and Soul" and whistled for "it in desperation, relentlessly without success," as he declined to subject himself to a comparison with Hawkins.[25]

Byas and Hawkins can be heard playing together on several recordings, beginning with an April 1941 session when Hawkins appeared as a guest with the Count Basie orchestra, but neither man soloed on any of the songs. In February 1944, Byas joined Hawkins and his orchestra as they recorded six titles on the fledgling Apollo label, including "Rainbow Mist," a cognate of "Body and Soul" that Hawkins recorded under a different title.[26] Frank "Professor Jazz" Vallade, one of the owners of Apollo, came up with the idea of recording a counterfeit of Hawkins's big hit as a means of boosting his new label—Apollo's version sold for $1.05.[27] RCA Victor—whose catalog included

"Body and Soul"—soon became "aware of the marked similarity between" the two and "'found a solution short of the law courts' (as *DownBeat* magazine put it) by reissuing the 1939 original on its thirty-five-cent Bluebird label in an attempt to win sales over" from Apollo.[28] The sessions produced what are now viewed as "the very first bebop on records" as Hawkins—"always an open-minded musician"—invited "promising young players (including trumpeter Dizzy Gillespie, bassist Oscar Pettiford and drummer Max Roach)" for the session, in the words of Scott Yanow.[29] The omission of Byas from this list (from 1998) is curious but understandable, given that he never emerges from the ensemble, with Hawkins taking all the tenor solos.

In May 1944, Hawkins and Byas were again in the studio together, this time for Keynote, recording "On the Sunny Side of the Street," "Three Little Words," "Battle of the Saxes," and "Louise."[30] Byas's stature has increased dramatically in three months; he now takes a share of the solos that is approximately equal to Hawkins, and moreover, there is no longer any "master-disciple relationship" as the older and younger tenors are now "two equals."[31] Hawkins's biographer, John Chilton, said, "This was a golden period for Don Byas and he offers a serious challenge to Hawkins on every track."[32] In Chilton's view, Hawkins's decision to hire Byas, who was "emerging as a leading contender for Hawk's 'king of the tenor saxists' crown . . . was a bold move by Hawkins . . . Byas was by this time a supremely accomplished technician full of bold ideas that utilized his vast harmonic knowledge." Despite Byas's "naturally competitive personality," which contained "a streak of aggressive awkwardness that could surface without warning when he had too much to drink," his "stay with Hawk's sextet was harmonious on and off the bandstand."[33] Nonetheless, while Hawkins would say, "I love to play with Don," he didn't develop a long-term relationship with the younger tenor. "I can't have him in my band," Hawkins said. "He makes me blow too hard!"[34]

Second on Byas's list of acknowledged influences was Art Tatum, the protean pianist who was as much a composer at the keyboard as a performer. "Art Tatum really turned me on," Byas said. "That's where my style came from . . . style . . . I haven't got any style. I just blow, like Art. He didn't have any style, he just played the piano, and that's the way I play."[35] Earle Warren, an alto sax player four years younger than Tatum who—like him—was born and raised in Ohio, recalled Byas working with Tatum when both were still relatively unknown and before Tatum moved to New York in 1932.[36] "Don Byas used to come to play at a little house off Cedar Avenue, around 89th Street, with Art

Tatum in Cleveland," Warren said. "It was among some little shacks, and the man had a bar, a few tables with sawdust on the floor, and an upright piano with a little dim light over it. That became the new after-hours spot. It was one of those old-time upright pianos. It was kept in great condition and it made a beautiful sound. Of course, Art would make *any* piano sound good."[37]

Byas claimed that he and Tatum "were real close, and he loved me,"[38] and Warren seconds this. "If a cat could play, Art loved to hear him," Warren said. "I never saw him show any particular partiality, although I know he loved to play with Don Byas." The attraction between the two was based on mutual inspiration. "Art would come up with chords and changes an ordinary mind wouldn't think of," Warren said. "I think Don Byas was one of the few instrumentalists that really grasped what was happening. He learned those changes, and his knowledge of his instrument was affected. After they had worked together on 52nd Street and Don left, it was hard for anybody else to work with Art. I think that background and Art's influence helped Don blossom and become a stellar saxophone player."[39]

Byas claimed that he and Tatum "hung out together every night" in New York, and he apparently profited both from the pianist's example and his advice. "There was nobody playing what I was playing because I played all that stuff from Tatum," Byas said. "That F-sharp, B-natural, E, A, D, G, C, F, like in rhythm, instead of playing rhythm chords. Everybody was saying what is that? Where did this cat come from? Who is he? There weren't any horn players following piano players at that time, so I was ahead of everybody."[40] As for advice, Byas said Tatum told him

> Don't ever worry about what you're going to play or where the ideas are going to come from. Just remember there is no such thing as a wrong note. What makes a note wrong is when you don't know where to go after that one. As long as you know how to get to the next note, there's no such thing as a wrong note. You hit any note you want and it fits in any chord.[41]

It is fairly certain that this bland statement of principle is inapplicable to the great mass of men who do not have the musical talent of Tatum, but for Byas, it was a revelation. "That's when the doors started opening for me music wise," Byas said. "From that time I started practicing and remembering that and all of a sudden I said, 'That's where it is.' There's no way you can hit a wrong note, as long as you know where to go after. You just keep weaving and there's no way in the world you can get lost . . . As long as you keep going you're all right, but don't stop, because if you stop you're in trouble. Don't ever stop unless you know you're at a station. If you're at a station then you stop, take a breath and make it to the next station. Tatum turned me onto that. He was a genius."[42]

Tatum was an avid football fan,[43] and one does get the sense at times when he abandons the melody of a song to go off on one of his trademark improvisational deviations—a countermelody, a quotation from another song, an ad-lib in a different key—of a downfield runner breaking tackles, faking, and spinning away from defenders. Byas had a more limited range of options as you can only play one note at a time on a saxophone as opposed to ten on a piano, but he achieved much the same effect without the ability to play chords or counterpoint. In his improvisations when not with a band playing an arrangement, such as those from the 1945 Town Hall concert with bassist Slam Stewart, Byas is similarly free and untethered and yet remains within hailing distance of the melody, to which he returns when he has—as he put it—arrives at a station stop.

Tatum's influence on Byas was noted by others, such as Johnny Griffin, a successor-in-style to Byas. Griffin called Byas "the Art Tatum of the tenor saxophone"[44] and tried to use the same approach in his own music. "I use Tatum's things like Don Byas," Griffin said. "Until I spoke to Don recently [1969], I didn't know how close he had been with Tatum. As a kid coming up, I could hear something in it. Now twenty years later I find out that Don was around Tatum and he was using his harmonic solutions."[45] Billy Taylor perceived Tatum's impact on Byas as well. "[Don] was trying to make the tenor saxophone sound like Art Tatum," Taylor said.

> He and Coltrane had the same idea for the same reason. They both had heard Art's seamless runs on the piano. Don was trying to do that on the tenor back then. He was head and shoulders above everyone else. Don was playing bebop and pre-bop. What I mean by pre-bop is he was playing things that led up to bebop. They were long phrases and new ways of using harmonies so they sounded like the dominant melody. This stuff hadn't been done yet until Don started playing them.[46]

Ultimately, no higher commendation can be heard on the issue than from Tatum himself, who allegedly said to Byas at one point, "You play the saxophone like I play the piano."[47]

Byas has another line of forebears that has generally been overlooked: Johnny Hodges was born in 1907, Ben Webster was born in 1909, and Byas in 1913, and the last-born of the three carried on the trade of the other two as "classic" saxophonists "whose personalities are divulged through timbre," in the words of Gary Giddins[48]—or what Count Basie tenor Eric Dixon called "old school."[49] "I think it all comes from Sidney Bechet," Johnny Griffin mused. "I found out later on that Johnny Hodges was kind of a Bechet protégé."[50] What Hodges learned from Bechet was to perfect his tone first, then move on to virtuosity: "[P]ut your whole body into your music. *Lean* into the note. The horn is you," Bechet said. "See how many ways you can play that note—growl it, smear it, flat it, sharp it, do anything you want to it. That's how you express your feelings in this music. It's like talking."[51] Griffin found another ground on which to compare Byas to Hodges: "You know Don, like Johnny Hodges, plays so easily that he gives one the impression that he doesn't care. But it isn't true!" Griffin said. "I've seen that man play—he's tricky like that; I've watched them both and they've played so well for so long, they've just got it."[52]

Two years younger than Hodges, Webster said after Hodges died that "[h]e showed me the way to play my horn. That's what I tried to do—play Johnny on tenor."[53] There was an emotional as well as a musical bond between the two; they spent three years together in the Duke Ellington Orchestra, sitting side by side—a tear can be seen rolling down Webster's cheek as he played "Old Folks" on a Danish television show shortly after learning of Hodges's death.[54] Hodges "brought out the tenderness in Ben," fellow Ellington tenor sax Al Sears said. "Johnny rubbed the edges off him."[55] As he aged and his improvisational skills declined, Webster mellowed as a soloist so that, in the words of British saxophonist and jazz critic Benny Green, "he could create authentic jazz just by playing the tune, for his tone was so redolent of the jazz spirit, and his sense of time and rhythm and harmony so profound, that he could take a ballad . . . and merely by rocking it gently in the arms of his style, squeeze more jazz out of it than a great many young men."[56] Byas drew a similar reaction from French critic Pierre Voran: "Don Byas gave pride of place to one thing over all else: sound. He would blow a note and then hold it, making it swell into something ample and magnificent. Each note had the beauty of a cathedral."[57]

Hodges, Webster, and Byas have been linked together on record only once, on the album *Sax in Satin: Don Byas, Ben Webster, Johnny Hodges*, a compilation with separate selections by each of them.[58] Hodges and Webster played together many times when both were members of Duke Ellington's Orchestra and made an album on which both were featured in 1960.[59] Byas cited Webster as an influence at least once, in a 1958 interview by Kurt Mohr;[60] Webster and Byas played together many times and, in 1968, made an album on which both were featured, *Ben Webster Meets Don Byas*, released in 1973 after Byas's death.[61] Hodges and Byas played together in January 1946 as members of the Esquire All-American 1946 Award Winners. Four numbers resulted from that session—"Long Long Journey," "Snafu," "The One That Got Away," and "Gone with the Wind"; on the last-named, both Byas and Hodges solo. Byas and Hodges played together for a time during Duke Ellington's tour of Europe in 1950 and can be heard in that version of the Ellington orchestra on May 2, 1950, in Zurich, Switzerland, with Byas featured on "How High the Moon" but otherwise not soloing.[62] Byas was also a sideman on two Hodges recording sessions: on April 14, 1950, he played on four numbers recorded in Paris for the Swing label that were issued under the name of Johnny Hodges All Stars with the song "Only Wish I Knew" credited as a joint composition by the two. On April 15, 1950, Byas joined Johnny Hodges and His Orchestra in Paris to record four songs: "Jump That's All," "Last Legs Blues," "Nix It, Mix It," and "Time on My Hands" for the Vogue label.[63] Finally, on November 1, 1969, Byas and Hodges played together on "Diminuendo and Crescendo in Blue" at the Salle Pleyel when Ellington asked Byas to sit in, using Paul Gonsalves's tenor.[64] In addition to the two men's similar warm tone, there is at least one identifiable trace of Hodges's influence on Byas: his practice of scooping up to "longer notes from a quarter of a tone or so below their actual pitch,"[65] which Byas regularly used to pleasing (if precarious) effect in the opening bars of "Laura."

There are no recordings known, to this writer at least, on which Hodges, Webster, and Byas play together, but tenor Johnny Griffin linked the three. When asked who his influences were on the saxophone, he said, "I have to say two musicians, because they are so much alike, except that they play two different saxophones: Johnny Hodges and Ben Webster. I was playing alto and with a little tempo I'd try to get that big sound like Ben had and play rough. If we played a ballad, I'd try to emulate Johnny Hodges's sweetness." Then he went on to say, "Don Byas also had a definite influence on me. I liked the way he mastered his instrument."[66]

While more than one person has identified Leon Brown "Chu" Berry,[67] born in 1908, as the link between Hawkins and Byas, Byas himself never made the connection. Teddy Reig, one of Byas's producers, expressed it thusly: Byas "was a fantastic player—in my opinion, he was the heir to that Chu Berry running thing."[68] Like Byas, Berry started out playing alto sax in local groups but switched to tenor while a member of Sammy Stewart's band once he heard Coleman Hawkins. After playing with Cecil Scott, Benny Carter, and Teddy Hill, Berry achieved greater prominence with Fletcher Henderson's orchestra during the years 1935 to 1936, when he was a featured soloist and composed the jazz standard "Christopher Columbus" with Andy Razaf. From there, Berry went on to play for Cab Calloway from 1937 to 1941, when he died in a car accident. Berry is credited with helping transform Calloway's group from a novelty band into a legitimate jazz ensemble during his four-year tenure.[69] He was noted for a paradoxical combination of speed with a lush, mellow tone, and in that sense, he is a natural bridge from Hawkins to Byas. At least one critic detected Berry's influence on Byas's early work and didn't think it was salutary; Gary Giddins praised a live album Byas made from a 1963 performance in Denmark by noting that "he swings harder than ever, plays with vigor and ideas that belie his Swing-Era credentials, and there is not a whit of the sentimentality he was heir to when Chu Berry was a more decisive influence" on him.[70] Perhaps Byas's failure to acknowledge Berry is a case of the narcissism of small differences; they were only five years apart in age and thus were sometimes grouped together as members of the coming generation of competing pretenders to Hawkins's big-bodied tenor title. In addition to the pair's participation in the jam session at Puss Johnson's bar with Coleman Hawkins noted above, Berry and Byas both jammed at Minton's Playhouse during the incubation years of bebop, and Berry—like Byas—impressed Dizzy Gillespie and Charlie Parker as an old hand who could more than hold his own among the younger musicians pushing against the boundaries of swing. Parker even named his first son "Leon" to honor Berry.

Another tenor close in age to Byas (four years older, born in 1909) whom he cited as an influence was Herschel Evans, with whom he played in the bands of Lionel Hampton and Charlie Echols and possibly those of Buck Clayton and Bennie Moten as well. Evans was a cousin of territory bandleader Jesse Stone, who at one time employed both him and Coleman Hawkins as dueling tenors in a model that was subsequently imitated by Count Basie. Evans took his first recorded solo on "Shadowland Blues" as a member of Troy Floyd's band, which was in residence at a San Antonio hotel and from which it was broadcast over a local radio station. Floyd was said by his trumpeter Don Albert (né Albert Dominique) to have "held Herschel Evans back. Maybe it's a blessing he did because Herschel would have outshone everything that we had in the band."[71] Evans, like Byas, would trade places with Lester Young at one point in his career, choosing to join the combined band of George E. Lee and Bennie Moten in 1934, while Young left the former group and became a member of Count Basie's band for an ill-fated engagement in Little Rock, Arkansas.[72] "Considered one of the finest soloists of the warm-toned Coleman Hawkins school," as Leonard Feather put it, Evans influenced Buddy Tate, Illinois Jacquet, and Arnett Cobb, among other Southwestern tenors.[73]

Finally, it should be noted that Byas told French pianist Henri Renaud at a 1947 concert in Toulouse that "the foremost of his inspirations was Benny Carter,"[74] who was born in 1907 and was thus a half decade older than Byas. While this comment undercuts the musical genealogy by which Byas is an heir to Hodges and Webster, the two views are consistent in that Byas combined Carter's advanced harmonic skills—which both Hodges and Webster lacked—with the sumptuous tone of Hodges and Webster. "Don was very proud of his tone," said Dutch tenor player Hans Dulfer,[75] which he achieved while using a Berg Larsen 150 mouthpiece, described by one saxman as "made for someone with lips of steel" with "a big tip opening."[76] The adjective used most often to describe Byas's sound was "big," and to him, this was a matter of customer satisfaction: "It sort of goes with what I have to say on my instrument," he said. "[T]o me there are, shall we say, two extremes—music and noise. There is the dividing line in the middle. Well, in order to play jazz music—in order for it to remain music—it should have as big and beautiful a sound as possible . . . because the masses are not jazz-lovers. So I try to give it to them dressed up as prettily as possible."[77]

Benny Carter's tone was instantly recognizable but it was not his strong suit, so Byas's attraction to the elder saxman must have been based on Carter's seemingly inexhaustible capacity for melodic invention; he was, like Byas, an assiduous student of harmony and a calm but fierce competitor in jam sessions, having once been called upon to join a jam session in Harlem as a late-inning reliever for Johnny Hodges, who had been cut by Jimmy Dorsey on alto. According to fellow saxophonist Benny Waters, "[S]omebody said, 'Call up Benny Carter.' So Benny came around there with his own piano player. . . . Benny started playing 'Georgia Brown'. . . . And here's what Benny was doing: Benny played along with Jimmy, and every four bars he'd move into a different key." Waters said Dorsey "got all red in the face and practically hauled up and walked out—looked like a drowned rat," leaving Carter—whose nickname was "The King"—the winner.[78] Byas and Carter would play together on five recording sessions in 1945 and 1946, all in New York City. The first, on February 26, 1945, was with Timmie Rogers and His Orchestra and produced four songs: "Daddy-O," "A Good Deal," "Capacity," and "If You Can't Smile and Say Yes Don't Cry and Say No." The first two were released on the Regis label; the last two were not released. On February 27, 1945, the two performed as members of Savannah Churchill and Her All Star Orchestra on two songs recorded for the Manor label, "All Alone" and "Daddy Daddy," with Byas soloing on the latter.[79] The next two sessions took place on January 7 and 8, 1946, with Carter as leader of his own orchestra recording for De Luxe Records.

Byas and Carter would play together for the last time during the 1960 Jazz at the Philharmonic tour of Europe. Their November 21 session was as part of an all-star group comprised of them and Roy Eldridge on trumpet, Coleman Hawkins on tenor, Lalo Schifrin on piano, Art Davis on bass, and Jo Jones on drums. It was recorded and released on Norman Granz's Verve label and includes the standards "Indiana," "Take the 'A' Train," and "The Nearness of You," plus "A Jazz Portrait of Brigitte Bardot."[80] Carter seems to be trying to catch up to his younger admirer on these selections, his tone more strident than the smooth approach for which he was known, his lines less symmetrical than his norm. In jazz, a half decade's difference in age can seem like a light year, and Byas had put some distance between himself and a man he had grown up admiring.

CHAPTER 5

Move to New York

In a 1970 interview, Don Byas said that he first came to New York in 1937,[1] but Timme Rosenkrantz claimed that he "discovered" Byas and his trombone-playing sidekick Tyree Glenn in 1936, when they were members of a band led by trumpeter and saxophonist Eddie Mallory. According to multiple sources, including trumpeter Buck Clayton, this group "was really Ethel Waters's band under the direction of" Mallory.[2]

Mallory was a trumpeter and saxophonist who had parlayed his job backing Waters, a ground-breaking African American singer and actress, into a band of his own. "One hell of a good trumpet player named Eddie Mallory had accompanied me in some of my numbers in *At Home Abroad*," a musical revue that opened on Broadway in September 1935, Waters said.[3] The two met when they were playing at the Cotton Club; at the time, he was with the Mills Blue Rhythm Band and she was performing as a headliner, singing her hits such as "Stormy Weather."[4] When *At Home Abroad* closed on March 7, 1936, Mallory told Waters, "[H]e was ambitious to build up a band of his own." Waters said they had grown "very fond of each other," so she assisted him and acquired a band to back her in the bargain. Byas would say that he came to New York "accompanying Ethel Waters who had just married Mallory in California,"[5] which places the date of his arrival in 1935.[6] (Mallory is often referred to as one of Waters's husbands, but it is doubtful that they ever married.) Waters and the Mallory band were booked at the

Cotton Club, alternating with Duke Ellington, when they first arrived in New York, and Byas recalled his first in-person exposure to the Ellington orchestra as "the greatest musical thrill of my life."[7] Waters and Mallory played week-long engagements at the Apollo Theater during July and October, then headed south for shows in Philadelphia in November and Spartanburg, South Carolina, in December 1937. In 1938, the troupe was back in New York in February, where an article in the *New York Amsterdam News* said Eddie Mallory's orchestra (sans Waters) was "going places."[8] The troupe traveled to New Orleans in April, then returned to New York, where Timme Rosenkrantz heard Byas and Glenn, and through his initiative and intervention, they escaped from the comparative anonymity of the Mallory ensemble.[9]

The assertion by Rosenkrantz or his biographers that he "found" or "discovered" Don Byas should be put in perspective. By the time Rosenkrantz heard him for the first time, Byas had already played with a long list of noteworthy bands, so the claim should be limited to the fact that he was the first to record Byas. It is patronizing to imply that a talent such as Byas would have remained in obscurity without one's involvement, but the lordly tone may have come naturally to Rosenkrantz; he was a member of the Danish nobility with the rank of baron whose family could trace their lineage back to the thirteenth century[10] (there is a character named "Rosenkrantz" in Shakespeare's *Hamlet*). His father had been a novelist, and Timme continued this dilettante's line of business by "writing humorous stories and books, which were genuinely funny but perhaps a bit too Danish in the humor to translate well," said his fellow Dane and jazz enthusiast Dan Morgenstern.[11] His enthusiasm for jazz was genuine, as demonstrated by his willingness to devote his resources to the promotion of the music. According to pianist Billy Taylor, Rosenkrantz was "the black sheep of that family. They had paid him to stay out of Denmark. They said, 'You like nothing but black women and you like to hang out with jazz musicians so why don't you stay in America or somewhere. Just don't disgrace the family.'"[12] Whether this is true or a story Rosenkrantz told in order to distance himself from his royal lineage is unclear; Morgenstern says Rosenkrantz "spent the war years in New York" because he was "conveniently trapped there by the German invasion of his homeland."[13]

At the age of twenty-two, Rosenkrantz founded *JazzRevy* (*Jazz Review*), one of the first jazz magazines published in Europe; like many of his business endeavors, it didn't last long, folding after two years. Beginning in 1934, he lived half of the year in Harlem despite warnings from some (including Milt

Gabler of the Commodore Records shop) that it was a dangerous neighborhood for whites, but he ignored the advice and operated a short-lived jazz record store there. Rosenkrantz became friends with fellow jazz enthusiast John Hammond, who would play a central role in the promotion of Count Basie's Kansas City-based band to national stature. With introductions from Hammond, Rosenkrantz came to be known in New York jazz circles and began to write on the subject for publications that included *DownBeat*, *Metronome*, *Esquire*, and *Melody Maker*.[14]

Rosenkrantz was the model of the parsimonious patrician who stretches a dwindling fortune to pursue an avocation—in his case, jazz. He lived in an apartment at 7 West 46th Street in New York, owned by a wealthy philanthropist who charged him below-market rent. He set up a recording studio there with two professional-quality recording machines, and musicians would call him when they were going to play on the radio and ask him to record their broadcast music as "air checks," which he did for a modest fee. He held jam sessions in his apartment that he recorded, and Byas participated in at least twelve of these.[15] Rosenkrantz said that the proceeds of these sidelines paid his rent "and three meals a day with suitable beverages."[16]

Rosenkrantz saw Mallory's band on the night of its first performance at the Savoy Ballroom in New York and was "totally captivated" by what he called "one wailing ensemble." He was particularly impressed by "two youngsters who generated all the excitement": trombonist William Tyree Glenn and Byas, noting that "[u]ntil skinny little Don arrived from California with that big, fat tone, Coleman Hawkins and Chu Berry were the 'head' tenor men in the east." Rosenkrantz preferred Byas over the reigning tenors of the day (assuming he could have afforded them) for a recording date he had lined up for the Victor label because Byas "played just as well and . . . was new in town, with a fresher sound."[17]

Rosenkrantz made offers to the two tyros, and they accepted. "[T]hey were tickled, since neither of them had made a record before," Rosenkrantz recalled.[18] (They remained employees of Mallory's band for the time being, however.[19]) He then persuaded producer Eli Oberstein, producer for the Victor record label, to let him hire Byas and Glenn for his group, which was to be known as "Timme Rosenkrantz and His Barrelhouse Barons" even though Rosenkrantz would not play in it. In addition to Byas and Glenn, the ensemble included Duke Ellington band member Rex Stewart on trumpet; future Ellingtonian Russell Procope on alto sax; two members of Count

Basie's rhythm section, Walter Page on bass and Jo Jones on drums; Rudy Williams on alto; Billy Hicks on trumpet; Billy Kyle on piano; and Brick Fleagle on guitar.[20] Studio time was booked for May 27, 1938, but when the day arrived, Jo Jones was two hours late for the session because he got lost on the subway, and, as a result, all four songs had to be recorded in a single take.[21] Byas is heard on two numbers from the session, "A Wee Bit of Swing" and a vocal for Inez Cavanaugh, who would become Rosenkrantz's lifelong companion. The song was written by Danish pianist/composer Leo Mathisen and offered first to W. C. Handy, who turned it down after six months' consideration. Rosenkrantz and Cavanaugh wrote new lyrics for the piece, which was retitled "Is This to Be My Souvenir?" and recorded it with Byas, who takes an introductory solo of four bars, another later for sixteen bars, and then six more on the bridge. Throughout, Byas sounds mature for a twenty-four-year-old making his first recording and successfully swims against the song's sentimental undertow.

Late in life, Byas would describe the difficulties he faced as a young freelance sax player in New York. "It was very difficult to get accepted there," he recalled.

> When I arrived you had a few tenor players who were famous. Coleman Hawkins, Lester Young, [Leonard] "Chu" Berry, they were the three biggest and you had to get past them. In the beginning I went where I heard there was going to be a jam session. I took my instrument of course, but I didn't dare play. I sat and listened. That went on for a few weeks, and Hawkins and Berry just looked at me and said "Hey, that boy comes here every night with his saxophone," and they asked me "Can you play that thing?" And I said, "Yes, a little." They asked if I wanted to play a song. Then I played a few songs, and from then on I was in it.[22]

After Don Byas's first session under the auspices of Rosenkrantz in May 1938, he disappears from view for a while. He is said to have played with Don Redman for a time in 1938 through 1940, although he does not appear on any recordings by that band until January 1946.[23] He became a member of Lucky Millinder's Orchestra[24] and is heard with that group on the soundtrack of *Readin' Ritin' and Rhythm* made in late 1938, but Millinder's band did not begin to record regularly in studios until June 1941, by which time Byas was gone.[25] The film was released in February 1939, and Byas can be heard soloing on two numbers: "Ride, Red, Ride" and an untitled song.[26] The film is a "variety short," ten minutes in length—a precursor to the music videos of today—and Millinder's band provides the music for a "snappy routine put on by some youthful jitterbugs." Byas "enters with a defiant vibrato and continues with a strong solo with tempo shifts." At the time, he was twenty-five years old and, by his own account, had been playing professionally for a decade; reflecting his journeyman status, his playing is confident and displays "sure execution and flawless technique."[27] Despite the lack of recorded evidence, contemporaries said Millinder's band during this period was a high-quality unit. "Lucky had a good band," said trumpeter Harry "Sweets" Edison, who was with the group for a period he recalled as approximately six months. "He had Charlie Shavers, Carl Warwick, Billy Kyle, Tab Smith, Don Byas and Andy Gibson."[28]

Byas's future employer, Count Basie, attested to the strength of Millinder's group after a February 1938 "battle of music" against them in Baltimore. "We went on first," Basie said,

> and I guess we must have been playing for about fifteen or twenty minutes before Lucky and his band showed up. I thought we were playing very well, so we just went on; and when we finished that first set, I moved on back into one of the corners and started talking with somebody while [Millinder's musicians] were getting set up. Then the next thing I knew, Lucky had come in and jumped up on that little box he used to stand on, and when the band hit, everybody stopped talking, and I looked up and saw the whole crowd moving across the dance floor toward the bandstand. Lucky and those guys turned it on! Boy, did they turn it on.

Basie summed the evening's competition up by saying it "was a rough night. Lucky had a lot of top-notch musicians in that band. He had Billy Kyle on piano. He had Tab Smith on alto and Don Byas on tenor." Even though "*The Pittsburgh Courier* and a few other papers gave" Basie's men "a little edge," he wasn't confident that they were the better band that night, saying, "It was very close."[29]

On March 16, 1939, Byas would record as a member of Andy Kirk's orchestra, with whom he would continue to play until at least May 6, 1940. Byas replaced John Williams, who had separated from his wife, the band's pianist/ arranger Mary Lou Williams; Williams left Kirk to play first with Cootie Williams, then Earl Hines's band.[30] An item in the July 23, 1939, Oklahoma City Black Dispatch reported that "Muskogee's Don Carlos Byas, who began with the Langston Collegians," was "tooting the sax with Kirk's aggregation" at a July 10 appearance at the Trianon Ballroom and "was featured on several of his own arrangements." Byas got solo time with Kirk's band from the start; he is heard for eight bars on "You Set Me on Fire" and "I'll Never Fail You," recorded in March 1939, and on "I'm Getting Nowhere with You" and "Please Don't Talk about Me When I'm Gone," recorded in November 1939. At times, he has to yield to fellow tenor Dick Wilson, much admired by Mary Lou Williams. "Don Byas came into the band, and now we had two great tenormen—Don and Dick Wilson," she said. "[I]t was these two who kept me in the band" at a time when she "was really feeling dragged" about her role with Kirk. "I got real kicks out of jamming with them. I began to feel better," she said.[31]

Richard "Dick" Wilson was a highly regarded tenor who is little remembered today because he died young (age thirty) and didn't have the opportunity to realize the potential that Mary Lou Williams heard in him. Born in Mt. Vernon, Illinois, in 1911,[32] he was an early lab partner with her when she began to experiment with what she called "Zombie music," sounds that reminded her and *simpatico* musicians "of music from *Frankenstein* or any horror film." "I was one of the first with these frozen sounds," she said, "and after a night's jamming would sit and play weird harmonies (just chord progressions) with Dick Wilson, a very advanced tenor player."[33] Wilson was Kirk's featured tenor soloist when Byas was hired, having been with the band since 1935 when he replaced Buddy Tate.[34] Byas and Wilson would sometimes play in unison (as on "Big Jim Blues"),[35] but they would mainly compete for solo time, with Wilson getting the lion's share; on a December night in 1939, for example, Wilson took all the solos on four titles broadcast over radio station WJZ at a time when Byas was present. Byas can be heard on a January 2, 1940, date for Decca, soloing for thirty-two bars on two takes of "Wham" and then on a four-bar passage on "It Always Will Be You." Several airchecks of the band survive from the spring of 1940, but Byas emerges from the ensemble on only one, soloing on "Marcheta" on May 5, 1940, in a broadcast from the Cotton Club. On this number, Wilson and Byas are both featured.[36]

Byas failed to capitalize on an opportunity born of unfortunate circumstances when Wilson's health began to fail in 1939. Wilson was hospitalized once, and (according to Williams) when he returned to the band, he "started disappearing upstairs during intermission."[37] He would die while the Clouds of Joy were on a tour of the South without him in November 1941, but Byas wasn't around to replace him, having left the Kirk band involuntarily before Wilson's death. The end of Byas's tenure with Kirk may have been the product of his drinking or the emotional strain of a tempestuous affair he was involved in with Mary Lou Williams. When Byas "slapped her around publicly at a gig," it was "the last straw" for Kirk, who fired Byas, at the same time warning Mary Lou not to get involved with musicians in the band again.[38] Kirk's success (as the case with most successful bandleaders) was the product of his even-tempered professionalism; he disliked disruptions, either musical or personal, in the smooth operation of his orchestra, and Byas had to go. Again, like many a bandleader of the time—both Count Basie and Duke Ellington come to mind—Kirk was circumspect about Byas's departure and did not mention it in his autobiography.[39] Despite the friction between her and Byas, Mary Lou Williams made only a brief, bland comment about his departure: "Don Byas . . . left and was replaced by Edward Inge."[40]

After his dismissal by Kirk in May 1940,[41] Byas may have scuffled a bit, although one curious item suggests he may have been planning to leave Kirk anyway; in February 1940, his name is listed on a record cut at Melodisk Studios in Boston with Hillary Rose (a man) on piano, John Brown on drums, and Bert Frosberg on bass, but it is not clear that this was ever released.[42] While Brown and Frosberg have disappeared from jazz history, Rose was a keyboard player born in 1913 in Barbados. He organized his first band, Hillary Rose and His Rhythm Boys, in 1935 and later studied at the Boston Conservatory and Berklee College of Music.[43] For a time, he replaced Robert Carroll in Edgar Hayes's orchestra and is said to have toured with Benny Carter in September of that year,[44] but the leading source on Carter's work does not support this claim.[45] His next recording date was September 12, 1940, with Billie Holiday and a band assembled for an Okeh session that included Roy Eldridge on trumpet; Georgie Auld and Don Redman on alto saxes; Byas and Jimmy Hamilton on tenor saxes; Teddy Wilson on piano; John Collins on guitar; Al Hall on bass; and Kenny Clarke on drums. Holiday would recognize Byas for the creative force that he was or was becoming: "With artists like Lester [Young], Don Byas, Benny Carter and Coleman Hawkins," she said, "something was always happening,"[46] by contrast with what she considered to be the over-rehearsed recording sessions she participated in during the 1950s.[47] On October 16, 1940, Byas registered for the draft; he listed his employer as the Edgar Hayes Orchestra and gave his place of employment as the West End Theatre, 125th Street and St. Nicholas Avenue, New York.

Byas listed his birth year as 1912, contrary to the 1913 date that appears on his birth certificate and in census records for 1920, 1930, and 1940. His age as recorded by a US Census enumerator on May 10, 1940—just five months earlier—was twenty-six; since he was born on October 21, this would mean that the last official record of his birth date prior to his registration for the draft used 1913 as the year of his birth.

As to why someone would use an earlier birthdate to register for the military draft than in other public records, otherwise eligible men were classified as 1-H—deferred but still available for military service—once they reached the age of twenty-eight on July 1 of each year from 1941 onward; by using the earlier date, Byas would thus have been deferred from conscription on July 1, 1941, just nine months later, rather than July 1, 1942.[48] While there is no evidence that it was Byas's intent to thus reduce the likelihood that he would be called to serve, the possibility cannot be entirely ruled out. He would not have been the only jazz musician who tried to avoid the draft during World War II; his high school bandmate Jay McShann succeeded in delaying military service by telling his local draft board to send induction notices to him where he was currently playing, not disclosing that he was booked a year in advance to play as many as ninety straight one-night stands[49] and thus would be gone by the time any notice arrived. When draft officials finally caught up with McShann one night in Kansas City, he was taken off the bandstand mid-gig for "immediate induction,"[50] meaning no opportunity for the physical exam that would have revealed he had the condition known as "flat feet"—which would have exempted him from military service altogether. On February 25, 1954, after World War II had ended and he was living in France (and thus beyond the reach of the US Selective Service System), Byas would revert to listing his birthday as "21.10.1913" on his French *carte d'identité*.

Edgar Junius Hayes, the bandleader and pianist Byas gave as his employer, was born in 1902 in Lexington, Kentucky. He attended Wilberforce University and graduated with a music degree in the early 1920s. In 1922, he toured with clarinetist Fess Williams, then formed and led several groups—the Blue Grass Buddies, Eight Black Pirates, and the Symphonic Harmonists—before he was hired to play piano and write arrangements for the Mills Blue Rhythm Band in 1931. He would leave that group and form his own orchestra in 1937, and it was this group that Byas was a member of, along with drummer Kenny Clarke. The group's most popular recording was a version of "Stardust," music by Hoagy Carmichael with lyrics by Mitchell Parish. According to Leonard

Feather, Hayes's band "scored national success with . . . a flashy, florid version of *Star Dust* [*sic*]."[51] According to trumpeter Harvey Davis, "Edgar Hayes was known for his playing on *Stardust*, but he started to relinquish some of it to Don Byas, who would come out on stage and play so much *Stardust* that Edgar Hayes had to give it to him."[52] In 1938, the Hayes orchestra was the first to record "In the Mood" by Wingy Manone, Joe Garland, and Andy Razaf, later covered by Glenn Miller, to great success.[53] Byas replaced Robert Carroll in the Hayes orchestra, which at the time included reedman Garvin Bushell, like Byas, a former member of the Mallory band.[54] Both drummer Kenny "Klook" Clarke and trumpeter Dizzy Gillespie passed through the Hayes orchestra, and it is possible that this is when Byas first met these pioneers of bebop; Clarke is heard on several recordings by Hayes's orchestra and quintet, but not Gillespie or Byas.[55]

In November 1940, Byas was a member of an all-star cast of musicians assembled for a tribute to the jazz style that developed in Kansas City during the period from January 16, 1920, when the sale of alcohol was made illegal by the Eighteenth Amendment to the US Constitution, to May 29, 1939, when the city's mayor, Thomas Pendergast, was sent to federal prison for failure to pay taxes on income from his various illegal enterprises.[56] The session was conceived by Dave E. Dexter Jr., a writer who had done much to promote the jazz of Kansas City. Byas played on three of the album's twelve numbers: "Lafayette," an Eddie Durham composition first recorded by Bennie Moten's Kansas City Orchestra; "South," a composition by Moten and Thamon Hayes, with Byas listed as a member of Oran "Hot Lips" Page's Orchestra; and "627 Stomp" ("627" refers to the number of the Kansas City Colored Musicians Union local), for which he was included in the ensemble backing pianist Pete Johnson.[57]

In 1941, Byas would get the break he needed to join a top band again. The January 1, 1941, issue of *DownBeat* magazine reported that Count Basie and Lester Young, "friends and co-workers for the past five years, parted two weeks ago." The next issue of the magazine on January 15 said that "Don Byas will probably inherit Lester Young's tenor chair. Basie has been using several subs since Young was fired," sparking an angry rejoinder from Young's wife: "May I correct Mr. Ed Flynn, who wrote in the January 15 'Down Beat' that Lester Young (formerly of Count Basie's orchestra) was fired. My husband was not fired. He quit for reasons of his own." The conflict between these accounts may be a matter of interpretation. On Friday, December 13, 1940,

Young failed to show up for a recording session. "The whole band waited in the studio about three hours," said one account, "but no Lester." A band representative came to the Woodside Hotel where Young lived, but Young turned him away, saying, "Go 'way and lemme sleep—a man's got no business makin' music on Friday the 13th."[58] Finally, Basie called Young, "and Lester says 'Daddy, I'm sorry. I don't work on no Friday the 13th,' to which Basie replied, 'Well, if you don't work on Friday the 13th, then you don't work at *all* with Basie.'"

It is possible that both parties used this incident as a pretext: the Basie band's arrangements had become more formal and elaborate, with reduced opportunities for creative section work and "head" arrangements that had been part of the original appeal of the band to Young; other top instrumentalists had recently demonstrated that they could do fine without a big band behind them, such as Lionel Hampton, who had left Benny Goodman, and Coleman Hawkins, who had great success with "Body and Soul" without a name backing band. Finally, Young had recently asked for a raise, which Basie turned down after consulting with John Hammond, so Byas may have seemed to be the low-cost alternative to a tenor who was getting a big head. After a short-lived (one-month) transitional experiment with Paul Bascomb, best known before and after his time with Basie as a member of Erskine Hawkins's band,[59] in January 1941, Byas was hired as Young's replacement. Though largely forgotten today, Bascombe was no slouch; in a December 1946 poll ranking tenors, he took fourth place, ahead of Byas but behind Lester Young, Arnett Cobb, and Illinois Jacquet.[60]

Whatever the reason for Basie's decision to let Young go, it opened a door for Byas to perform on a bigger stage and become known to a wider audience. "He had played with several good bands" before, wrote Dan Morgenstern, "but was known only among musicians" when he accepted Basie's offer.[61] As Byas recounted his hiring, Basie called him and said, "Don, would you like to make a record date?" and Byas replied, "Beautiful," and claimed that he "stayed four years in the band."[62] Actually, two and a half years; perhaps Byas rounded up because he was embarrassed at his firing the same way that John Coltrane told Leonard Feather that he played with Johnny Hodges's combo for a year and a half when he was fired after a tenure of about six months.[63] Things did not go smoothly for Byas at first, as Basie wanted him to reproduce Young's solos "note by note." Efforts to force a new saxophonist to duplicate the sound of his predecessor had failed before; witness what happened when Young took

Coleman Hawkins's place in Fletcher Henderson's orchestra in 1934. "They couldn't stand him," producer John Hammond said of Henderson's men. Hawkins had a large, heavy tone, and Young's tone was lighter. Band members said Young "sounds like another alto, the section doesn't have any body."[64] Byas tried to be the new Lester Young for a few weeks but said, "[I]t didn't work. It wasn't my style. Finally I said to Basie, 'Look, I can't take another one,' and Basie said, 'You know what we do, you're going to try to play your own style. Let's just forget about Lester's solos.' So I did and Basie liked it."[65]

Consistent with the upgrade in status that membership in the Basie band conferred on Byas, in 1942, he appears for the first time in the directory of Local No. 802, American Federation of Musicians, the New York musicians' union, and he lists an address in Harlem where he can be reached—2139 7th Avenue—and a telephone number, UN4-6027. He would remain at this address until 1945, when he moved to 2040 7th Avenue and got a new phone number, UN4-9073. Byas had apparently survived without becoming a member of the musicians' union since he first arrived in New York as he does not appear in the union's membership directories for the years 1936 through 1941, but a large, established band such as Count Basie's could not risk union sanctions for hiring a nonunion employee.

Byas recorded three titles with the Basie band for the Okeh label on January 20 and 22, 1941, on one of which ("You Lied to Me") he solos for eight bars. After getting his legs under him, a week later he returned to the studio to record five titles: "Music Makers," "Deep in the Blues," "Jitters," "Tuesday at Ten," and "Jump the Blues Away." On each, Byas is allowed to stretch out as a soloist; on "Jump the Blues Away," a composition by trumpeter Ed Lewis who Byas would have known from Bennie Moten's band, he establishes himself with a warm tone at the beginning of a sixteen-bar solo marked by concise figures that the big band setting limited him to. He wasn't Prez, a listener new to his sound could easily deduce, but his style was just as unique and appealing in its own way.

Over the next ten months, Byas would play with Basie on six recording sessions, plus radio broadcasts and two short musical films: *Air Mail Special*, on which he solos for eight bars, and *Take Me Back, Baby* (he appears on camera in both).[66] An April 10, 1941, session for Okeh Records in Chicago provided the occasion for Byas and his first model to play together when Coleman Hawkins appeared as a guest with the Basie orchestra; in hindsight, the session was a missed opportunity, as five numbers were recorded, but none of them include solos by either tenor. Over the course of the year, Basie frequently gave Byas the opportunity to solo, but these were, for the most part, short in duration, with little opportunity for him to do more than state the melody and embellish it a bit. He nonetheless found the Basie band a comfortable fit because of its rhythm section, which the band's publicists touted as the "Great American Rhythm Section." "What a rhythm section," Byas would say in 1961. "Old [guitarist] Freddie Green sitting there like a sheep dog, looking around to see that nothing is going astray. Fine drummer Jo Jones."[67] For much of his time with Basie, Green and Jones were joined in the rhythm section by Walter "Big 'Un" Page, whom Byas would have encountered as a member of the Blue Devils and Bennie Moten's band.

Byas would record a solo for the ages on November 17, 1941, with the introduction he plays on "Harvard Blues," a song whose lyrics were written by George Frazier, an acerbic Boston journalist and the first writer with a regular jazz column to appear in a big city daily (the *Boston Herald*). The song recalls Frazier's undergraduate days at Harvard; Frazier had told Basie about a socially inept student named "Rinehart" who stood under his own dormitory window and called out to himself at night in order to create the illusion that he was popular. His ruse was ultimately discovered, and his name entered Harvard folklore: "[O]n the eve or the morning of the Harvard-Yale game," wrote Frazier's biographer Charles Fountain, "part of the atmosphere . . . was the faithful and incessant paging of 'Mr. Rinehart—Call for Mr. Rinehart! Call for Mr. Rinehart!'—with never a Mr. Rinehart to answer."[68]

It is hard for us today—our ears worn down by pyrotechnic electric guitars blasted at us in every public space—to appreciate Byas's quiet and deliberate solo, at the same time bluesy and even-tempered. "'Harvard Blues,'" wrote Basie scholar Loren Schoenberg, "is perfectly sculpted. Don Byas plays one of his best recorded solos: two svelte blues choruses that are a tune in and of themselves."[69] Gunther Schuller described Byas's intro as "Perfectly constructed, it is simple and affecting, poignant and languorous. Playing softly with a sense of intimacy not often encountered in jazz, Byas places each of his notes as if they were a series of incontrovertible truths."[70]

The song would be understood by most Harvard men at the time, but by now, the lyrics are as indecipherable as hieroglyphics to the average undergrad in Cambridge, Massachusetts; the ironic contrast between the earthy tones of Byas's tenor and Jimmy Rushing's vocal on the one hand and the arcane folkways of Boston Brahmins alluded to in the words of the song surely account for some of its enduring appeal. Novelist Anton Myrer, an undergraduate at Harvard when the song was released, said it "was always eerily amusing to hear Jimmy Rushing belt out those raffiné Ivy League verses in his gravelly tenor."[71]

Throughout his time with Basie, Byas continued to jam prolifically, sometimes with Basie band members but also with a cast of characters who were expanding the boundaries of jazz, including Charlie Christian on guitar, Kenny Clarke on drums, Dizzy Gillespie on trumpet, and Thelonious Monk on piano. These sessions were, contrary to the image of jamming as a case of spontaneous musical combustion, orchestrated affairs sponsored by nightclub managers. As Gillespie put it,

> On Monday nights, we used to have a ball. Everybody from the Apollo ... was a guest at Minton's [Playhouse], the whole band. We had a big jam session. Monday night was the big night, the musician's night off. There was always some food there for you. Oh, that part was beautiful. Teddy Hill treated the guys well. He didn't pay them much money—I never did get paid—but he treated the guys nicely.[72]

Teddy Hill was an ex-bandleader and tenor sax who was hired by club owner Henry Minton, the first African American delegate to New York Musician's Union Local 802, to handle bookings at his new club in the Hotel Cecil in Harlem. Hill assembled a house band that could back featured performers and serve as the rhythm section in residence for jam sessions. His first hire was Kenny Clarke, who had played drums in Hill's big band, followed by Nick Fenton on bass and Monk—then an unknown quantity—as pianist. Some of the music performed on those nights was recorded by jazz fans and thus was not lost to the obscurity that is the typical fate of a jam session. "Jerry Newman, among many others, recorded us in Minton's with Charlie Christian. He had a wire recorder,"[73] Dizzy Gillespie said. Newman was a Columbia University student who used an early portable device called a disc recorder to capture the jam sessions for posterity; the apparatus produced "finished metal discs ... twelve or ten inches in diameter with a lacquer finish ... called acetates."[74] The informality of the sessions carried over into legal matters. "[Newman] just brought [his recording equipment] down there and went home and put out a record," Gillespie rightfully griped. "He never gave any of us a dime, not me, Joe Guy, Don Byas, Chu Berry, Charlie Christian, Nick Fenton, Ken Kersey, nor Kenny Clarke."[75]

In addition to lost revenues from bootleg releases, jam sessions exposed musicians to another form of financial risk: the musician's union frowned upon these dates because they got no cut of the noncash compensation (free food and liquor) that was the only remuneration that most club owners paid for their members' services. "There were big fines for playing jam sessions, and the union had 'walking' delegates who would check on all the places that were frequented by jazz musicians," Gillespie said. These union snoops would "follow you around just waiting to see you pick up your horn without a contract, and fine you a hundred to five hundred dollars."[76] Byas's output in jam sessions was recorded a number of times, beginning with a formal date at Carnegie Hall on April 23, 1941, playing with Buck Clayton and Charlie Shavers on trumpets, J. C. Higginbotham and Will Bradley on trombones, Buster Bailey on clarinet, Tab Smith on alto and Buddy Tate on tenor saxes, Count Basie and Pete Johnson on piano, Freddie Green on guitar, Walter Page on bass, and Jo Jones on drums. That concert was sponsored by Café Society, a New York venue that was the first racially integrated nightclub in America, and recorded on discs, which were later used in the Voice of America's "Notes on Jazz" series.[77] There are from seven to ten other sessions taped at Clark Monroe's Uptown House or Minton's Playhouse,[78] some of which were commercially released.[79]

But Byas's day job at the time was with Count Basie.

As for the circumstances under which Byas left Basie in November 1943, there are several versions of the story. Basie, typical of name bandleaders, was diplomatically forgetful. "That's when Earl [alto sax Earle Warren] came back off leave," Basie recalled, "and it was also when Don Byas cut out, and Lester came back and took over his old chair again. I don't remember why Don cut out at that time, and I've also forgotten how we happened to get back in touch with Lester."[80] In a brief note, entertainment reporter Billy Rowe cryptically said that Byas was dismissed because he "spoke out of turn,"[81] but the conflict leading to his dismissal went beyond mere words. At the time, the Basie band was playing in the Blue Room at the Hotel Lincoln in New York, a choice venue; it was, Basie said, "one of our three top midtown Manhattan showcases during the rest of the war years," noting that each time they were booked there, "it was for four weeks or more with an option to extend,"[82] a welcome respite for a frequently road-weary group. As such, a premium was placed on good behavior, and standards of conduct were raised. According to Buddy Tate, on the fateful night, "Basie asked Don to get up and let Ben [Webster] play." The Hotel Lincoln was connected by an underground passage "to a bar called Martin's that had three-for-ones—three drinks for the price of one," and according to Tate, Byas—his pride perhaps hurt—"went across the street and got stoned." [83] Byas "had about nine or 12 of those drinks," Tate said, "And he couldn't drink much—he got crazy when he'd drink."[84]

Webster sat down in Byas's chair and began to play using the latter's tenor sax, impressing the Basie musicians. "I never heard anyone sound like that in my life, and the cats flipped over Ben," Tate said. The band's reaction was all the more remarkable since, in Tate's view "nobody in the world could touch Don Byas at the time. Nobody. Not nobody I know. He had everything—speed, sound—you couldn't play too fast for him. He was ahead of everybody." When Byas returned from the bar, he heard "the guys in the band ... bragging on Ben. He just sat in the back and listened, and the guys were going, 'Ohhh, we never heard anything like this' and so-and-so talking about Ben." Byas "couldn't handle it," said Tate, and when "Basie said something to him ... they got to arguing. Then [Byas] pulled out this little .22, the size of your palm, and said, 'All of you, up against the wall.'" Tate and Basie both complied, but "the house dick [slang for a detective] and the valet [of the Basie band] eased up behind [Byas] and they pinned him, and we brought him uptown [to his hotel]. The next day, Basie sent him his salary—two weeks [severance pay]." Still hung over, Byas "raised out of the bed, looked at it, and said 'It's about time Basie gave me a raise.' He didn't remember the night before. The valet said, 'He raised you all right, he raised you right out of the band.'"[85]

According to one account, there was a backstory to this incident that explains, if not excuses, Byas's short fuse that night. Lester Young had returned to New York at the end of September 1943 after playing with a band sponsored by the United Services Organization, a government-funded body that provided entertainment for American servicemen. The Basie band was in residence at the Apollo Club at the time, and Basie asked Young to "cover for an ailing Don Byas," according to Young biographer Dave Gelly. The audience at the Apollo greeted the news of Young's return with enthusiasm, but when Byas learned that he was being replaced, he recovered from whatever ailed him, retook his spot in the band, and Young left. Byas's supposed ailment may have been excessive consumption of alcohol, however.

"Don Byas was drinking heavily," notes Gelly. "He was a man of notoriously uncertain moods and dangerous temper, and alcohol made him quarrelsome."[86] Entertainment reporter Billy Rowe had alluded discreetly to the problem earlier in the year: "Don Byas," Billy Rowe wrote, "is about to lush himself out of a good sax-blowing job."[87]

Having terminated Byas, Basie then dispatched Jo Jones to fetch Lester Young at the White Rose, a "musicians' 52nd Street watering-hole," where he expected Young would be at the end of his night's work at the Onyx Club.[88] Jones gave a detailed account of how he recruited Young to return, leading one to doubt Basie's amnesia on the point:

> I went round to the White Rose and got Lester . . . I bought him a beer and told him, "You're due at work tomorrow night at seven o'clock. You come to the Hotel Lincoln . . . . And there he was! Nobody said nothing. He just sat down and started playing . . . . They didn't say, "Hello, Lester, where have you been?" or nothing. He came back to the band just like he'd just left 15 minutes ago.[89]

There is a minority viewpoint, promulgated most actively by Byas himself, under which he quit rather than being fired, a not uncommon discrepancy in accounts when a musician is dismissed from a band. According to this version of the breakup, Byas said to the bandleader, "Basie, in four weeks I will have been gone two."[90] After he left America for Europe, Byas claimed, Basie asked him to come back. According to Byas, Basie was in Paris playing the Salle Pleyel in 1949 and approached him backstage during intermission, asking him, "Don, why don't you come home and rejoin my band? I'll pay you $400 a week," adding "after three years, aren't you homesick yet?" To which Byas supposedly replied, "No, man, I'm just sick of home."[91]

Whatever the exact circumstances of Byas's departure from the Basie band and however defensive he may have felt at the time, in later years, he looked back on the rupture with regret. "I really enjoyed my time with Basie's band," he would say. "It was so necessary for the fulfillment of my career. I needed that whole experience, in order to grow as a player and, as you might say, to find myself."

Perhaps allowing nostalgia to airbrush the image he held in his mind, he added, "Those were the happiest years of my life, I think. Because I *really* enjoyed that time I spent with Basie's band."[92]

CHAPTER 6

Life after Basie

When he was fired by Count Basie (and he would maintain that he quit the band against the evidence[1]), Don Byas was in his early thirties and at the top of his game. Pianist Erroll Garner was new to New York, and according to Byas, his first step after parting ways with Basie was to form a group that included Garner, bassist Slam Stewart, and drummer Harold "Doc" West. "I really like the tenor sax-piano-bass-drums formula," he said, "and we teamed up in a cabaret."[2]

All the musicians were grounded in swing, but West was "adapting very nicely" to the new rhythms of bop (in the words of jazz critic Ira Gitler [3]), and he would go on to become a sometime member of the house band at Minton's.[4] This group's music is lost to history because a recording ban imposed by the American Federation of Musicians beginning August 1, 1942, barred union musicians from making studio recordings. Timme Rosenkrantz claimed to have discovered both Garner and Byas, and while this may overstate the case, he knew both from their early days in New York, was the first to record both, and thus might have been the go-between who connected them. Byas claimed that he formed this band in 1943, but this is open to question: Rosenkrantz recalls in great detail that Erroll Garner spent his first Christmas in New York in 1944 at the apartment Rosenkrantz shared with singer Inez Cavanaugh; Rosenkrantz recalled that Garner brought the couple a poinsettia when he discovered that they didn't have a Christmas tree. When Garner first arrived in New York, he was the intermission pianist at a nightclub operated by Tondaleyo, a dancer and singer, on 52nd Street near Fifth Avenue. Louis Prima, an Italian singer and trumpeter from New Orleans, led a five-piece band there, and according to Rosenkrantz, "no one paid any attention to" Garner, who had moved to New York from Pittsburgh "in late 1944 to try his luck in New York." Garner was discouraged by his prospects and talked of returning to Pittsburgh, but Rosenkrantz persuaded him to stay and brought him to the attention of jazz critics, which led to recording dates and a concert.[5]

The union recording ban was gradually eroded by various means,[6] and on February 12, 1944, Byas recorded four titles as a member of Albert Ammons and His Rhythm Kings for the Commodore label: "Blues in the Groove," "The Breaks," "Jammin' the Boogie," and "Bottom Blues." He then found work with Coleman Hawkins, recording six titles for Apollo in two sessions during February 1944 as a member of Hawkins's full orchestra. The first, on February 16, 1944, produced "Woody 'n' You," written by Dizzy Gillespie for Woody Herman (although never recorded by the latter, who used it only as backing music for tap dancers[7]), which has become a jazz standard. The folklore on the song is that Gillespie wrote it "fooling around at the piano, during the break between takes,"[8] and that Johnson, musical director in Hawkins's orchestra with an ear attuned to the changes that Gillespie and others were working out, persuaded Hawkins to use it (with Johnson playing baritone rather than his customary tenor sax). The February 16 session is frequently cited as the first recording of the bop movement[9] and included Johnson's "Bu-Dee-Daht." The second session produced "a blues head arrangement, *Disorder at the Border*," and these three numbers "constitute the first bebop ensembles put on commercial recordings," according to *DownBeat* writer George Hoefer. Byas does not solo on any song recorded in these two seminal sessions.[10]

Byas would perform as a member of Hawkins's sextet during this period, with Thelonious Monk on piano, Benny Harris on trumpet, Denzil Best on drums, and either Selwyn Warner or Eddie Robertson on bass. After a tour of Canada and New England (they played at the Savoy Ballroom in Boston in March and April 1944), this configuration opened at the Yacht Club on 52nd Street beginning on April 28, 1944, and among the luminaries in the audience on opening night were Duke Ellington, Count Basie, and Ethel Waters. Hawkins was referred to in a newspaper article the next day as "the world's greatest saxophonist," while Byas was described as the "fine jump tenor [who] sparked the Basie band for some time."[11] The Yacht Club engagement was brief, as the club closed due to a new wartime cabaret tax—at first 30 percent, later reduced to a still-steep 20 percent—which hastened the transition from swing to bebop. "Clubs that provided strictly instrumental music to which no one danced were exempt from the cabaret tax," wrote Eric Felten, and it was "no coincidence that in the back half of the 1940s a new and undance-able jazz performed primarily by instrumental groups—bebop—emerged as the music of the moment."[12] The club was sold to new owners in May who reopened it as the Downbeat Club, where the group was in residence from mid-May until July, when the later iteration of the venue also folded and the group disbanded.[13]

In May 1944, Byas would play a one-off session with the orchestra of Eddie Heywood Jr. Heywood first achieved notoriety on the New York jazz scene in 1939 with Benny Carter's band, but he tends to be overlooked in jazz history because his career was interrupted for four years when he suffered partial paralysis in his hands in 1947.[14] Byas's solos on the four recorded titles— "How High the Moon," "Sarcastic Lady," "Them There Eyes," and "Penthouse Serenade (When We're Alone)"—show Byas to advantage in both his up-tempo and ballad modes.[15] That same month, newspapers in New York and Hollywood, California, would report that Byas had followed a trend among jazz musicians inspired by US sailors in the Pacific Theater of World War II; he grew a beard, as did Ray Nance of Duke Ellington's orchestra. The traces of a single press agent in these two news items can be deduced from the fact that both stories referred to Nance as "Roy" rather than "Ray."[16]

Coleman Hawkins was intrigued by the new sounds he'd been hearing up and down 52nd Street and told Budd Johnson, "I'm gonna surround myself with some of the cats that are playin' it, and we're gonna make a record date."[17] His desire to experiment with bop came to fruition on May 24, 1944, with a seven-member group that he dubbed his "Sax Ensemble," assembled for a recording on the Keynote label, which included himself and Byas on tenors, Ellingtonians Harry Carney on baritone sax and Sid Catlett on drums, Tab Smith on alto, Johnny Guarnieri on piano, and Al Lucas on bass. Byas soloes at length on "Three Little Words," "Louise," "Battle of the Saxes," and "On the Sunny Side of the Street."[18]

In June 1944, Byas would reunite with Mary Lou Williams for a session under the auspices of Asch Recordings, an independent label founded by Moe

Asch that focused initially on blues and folk music, particularly Jewish. At the urging of jazz writer Charles Edward Smith, Asch began to sign jazz artists in the 1940s, and Williams was his first exclusive artist. Asch gave Williams free rein, perhaps in part because of her stature as one of the few female instrumentalists in jazz but also because that was his preferred approach: "He never told a performer how to record or what to do," Williams said. "If you only burped, Moe recorded it. It was different because Moe Asch had more love and he had more respect for jazz artists. . . . He'd turn the tape on and go away, let you record anything you wanted to record, and it always worked out great."[19] Asch's laissez-faire approach produced mixed results on her session with Byas and Dick Vance on trumpet, Vic Dickenson on trombone, Claude Green on clarinet, Al Lucas on bass, and Jack "The Bear" Parker on drums. A joint Williams–Byas composition, "Man o' Mine," never gets untracked; at the time, Williams was experimenting by adding dissonant tones to conventional harmonic progressions, and what might have been a comfortable byplay between her and Byas had it been delivered as a straight-ahead blues gets bogged down with attempted innovation. A week later, Byas would join the Benny Goodman orchestra in the recording studio for Capitol, soloing with assertiveness for eight bars on "All the Cats Join In."[20]

That same month, Byas began to play with trumpeter Oran "Hot Lips" Page, an association that would result in fifteen recorded titles from the summer through the fall of 1944. Page and Byas had played together before, most recently in November 1940, for the album produced by *DownBeat* writer Dave Dexter as a tribute to Kansas City jazz of the twenties and thirties. It is likely that their acquaintance went back further as Page was a boyhood friend of trombonist Tyree Glenn growing up in Dallas, Texas, and he had played with Walter Page's Blue Devils and Bennie Moten's band, two territory bands that Byas played in.[21] The sessions are, understandably, designed to highlight Page, playing either with a full orchestra or his Swing Seven small unit, but on a June 14 session, Byas is given twenty-four bars with the latter group on "Paging Mr. Page" and cools down what is otherwise a proto-rock 'n' roll number.

It was not until July 28, 1944, that Byas would make his first record under his own name, leading a group dubbed Don Byas and His Swing Shifters for the Savoy label. The other personnel were Charlie Shavers on trumpet, Clyde Hart on piano (sometimes doubling on celeste), Slam Stewart on bass, and Jack "The Bear" Parker on drums.[22] The session continued on August 17 with alto sax player Rudy Williams joining the group for "Just Can't Make Up My Mind (1944 Stomp)," "Savoy Jam Party" parts I and II, "What Do You Want with My Heart?" and the punning "Bass C Jam" (a nod to Count Basie). Hart was a swing veteran who had played with McKinney's Cotton Pickers and one of Jasper "Jap" Allen's territory bands, and an arranger as well. Shavers and Hart were veterans of the sextet that bassist John Kirby formed in 1937, which came to be known as the Biggest Little Band in the Land for their tight virtuosic arrangements. Kirby's group anticipated later developments in the chamber jazz mode by "swinging the classics"—for example, their "Mr. Haydn Gets Hip"[23]—and echoes of that group can be heard in "Riffin' and Jivin," on which Byas solos for thirty-two bars. Byas was next recorded with Kirby's group, including Shavers, Hart, and Kirby with Buster Bailey on clarinet, George Johnson on alto sax, and Bill Beason on drums, by "electrical transcription," that is, by recording the program on acetate-based discs. This method, developed for radio before the invention of tape recording, avoided the cost of paying musicians and support staff for broadcasts to different time zones while producing a sound quality that was better than the shellac records sold to consumers, which were also more expensive to produce.[24] Byas soloes on five of the eleven titles he recorded in this session.[25]

Byas would next record with The Emmett Berry Five in August 1944. Berry, a trumpeter, was another veteran of John Kirby's band, who, on this rare occasion as a leader for National Records, allowed Byas to record two of his own compositions, thus increasing the tenor sax's return from the session. Byas's contributions are a tribute to his favorite New York bar—"White Rose Kick"—and a play on his name, "Byas'd Opinion," on both of which he soloes at length.[26] Byas would next be a member of an all-star session put together by songwriter/producer Samuel "Buck" Ram in September 1944 for Savoy Records. While forgotten today, Ram was one of BMI's top five songwriters in its first fifty years measured by airplay of his compositions, writing under both his own name and three pseudonyms, presumably to avoid contractual restrictions on his songwriting output. The lineup included, in addition to Byas, trumpeters Frankie Newton and Shad Collins; Tyree Glenn on trombone; Earl Bostic on alto sax; Ernie Caceres on baritone sax; Red Norvo on vibraphone; Teddy Wilson on piano; Remo Palmieri on guitar; Slam Stewart on bass; and Cozy Cole on drums.[27] There would be more of these one-day sessions at which Byas played the role of tenor sax-for-hire with groups put together to record with different leaders, such as clarinetist Hank D'Amico, pianist Cyril Haynes, trombonist James "Trummy" (a corruption of "trombone") Young, and drummer Cozy Cole. The last-named allowed Byas to add another one of his punning titles to the set list, "Comes the Don,"[28] and Cole added him to a regular Sunday afternoon jam session at Lincoln Square Center in November as well.[29]

In December 1944, Byas would share a bill with singer Pearl Bailey, Erroll Garner, violinist Hezekiah Leroy Gordon "Stuff" Smith, and clarinetist Barney Bigard at Times Hall in New York, with unknown accompanists.[30] In that month, he would also participate in the first of three recording sessions for V-Disc, a record label formed in 1943 to provide records for US military personnel during the 1942–44 musicians' strike and thereby (it was said) boost servicemen's morale. The American Federation of Musicians agreed to allow its members to record for the label, which was supervised by Captain George Robert Vincent of the Special Services, the entertainment branch of the US military, subject to certain conditions; the Special Services agreed to limitations on the use of the recordings, including prohibitions on their sale, and an agreement that the master recordings would be destroyed. These restrictions were taken seriously by the musicians' union; the FBI and military police confiscated and destroyed many V-Discs that servicemen smuggled home, and an employee of a Los Angeles company served a prison sentence for illegal possession of the records.[31] In the first such session, on December 6, 1944, Byas solos for thirty-two bars on "Rosetta" as part of a V-Disc All Star Jam Session. On January 24, 1945, Byas recorded the Johnny Hodges's signature piece "The Jeep is Jumpin'" and "Stompin' at the Savoy" as a member of Nat Jaffe and His V-Disc Jumpers, and on July 18, 1945, he would record five songs with Trummy Young and the Guys from V-Disc."[32]

During this period, Byas would sometimes accompany up-and-coming female singers, such as Sarah Vaughan and Dinah Washington.[33] Vaughan, born in 1924, was a singer who came of age just as bop was taking off; in late 1943, she transitioned out of the Earl Hines big band to the breakaway group led by singer Billy Eckstine that included Charlie Parker, Dizzy Gillespie, and trombonist Benny Green. One source says that Byas was a member of "an incredibly talented stream of musicians and singers" who "passed through" Eckstine's band between the years 1944 and '47,[34] but if so, his tenure was so brief as to go unnoticed in standard jazz reference works. (Byas played on a January 7, 1946, date with Benny Carter and His Orchestra that was erroneously attributed to Eckstine and included on the Eckstine album *Mr. B*,[35] and as will be noted in a later chapter, he is heard on the 1957 Eckstine album *Mr. B in Paris*, sitting in with Eddie Barclay et son Grand Orchestre.) In 1944, Byas was a member of the Teddy Wilson Octet when they backed Vaughan on "Penthouse Serenade," "Don't Worry 'bout Me," "I Want to Be Happy," and "Just One of Those Things" on the Musicraft label.[36] Dinah Washington (née Ruth Lee Jones) was born the same year as Vaughan but began her career as a blues singer; her first hit was "Evil Gal Blues," written by jazz critic Leonard Feather, which she followed with a similar title, "Salty Papa Blues." She is seen in a photograph dated "Spring of 1946" singing with the Don Byas Orchestra comprised of Sylvester "Sonny" Payne on drums, Bud Powell on piano, Leonard Gaskin on bass, Scoville Brown on clarinet, and Leonard Hawkins on trumpet at the Brooklyn Academy of Music.

On January 4, 1945, Byas was part of recording sessions under the leadership of pianist Clyde Hart that included Charlie Parker, Dizzy Gillespie, Oscar Pettiford, and Trummy Young (among others)[37] that, while they were "pre-bop," as pianist Billy Taylor would put it, contained intimations of what was to come and that were a revelation to other musicians straining against the limitations of swing. As pianist Hampton Hawes put it, "I was in junior high school with Eric Dolphy, and one day he asked me to come to his house to hear some new stuff. Then I heard Dizzy Gillespie, and that did it. I said, 'This is what I want to play!' It was the hippest music I had ever heard in my life. Dizzy, Don Byas . . . playing be-bop. I knew that was the way I wanted to go."[38] It would be the last time Byas would play with Hart, with whom he had collaborated eleven times since a February 16, 1944, session as component parts of Coleman Hawkins and His Orchestra. Born in 1910, Hart was a contemporary of Byas and the two spanned the swing and bop eras. Hart recorded with Billie Holiday and Charlie Parker, was a member of groups led by Stuff Smith and John Kirby, and led his own band at the Tondelayo Club in New York in the fall of 1944.[39] He would die of tuberculosis on March 19, 1945, at the age of thirty-five, and jazz critic Whitney Balliett speculated that his death was one factor in Byas's decision to remain in Europe after his 1946 tour of the continent with Don Redman.[40]

On January 9, 1945, Byas would join bassist Oscar Pettiford—a fellow "Okie," born September 30, 1922, in Okmulgee, Oklahoma—as one of Pettiford's "18 All Stars" assembled for a recording session on the Manor label. Like Byas, he was part African American and part Native American; his mother was Choctaw, and his father was half Cherokee. Pettiford "started on piano in 1933, picked up bass three years later and toured until 1941 with" a family band comprised of his parents and ten other children. After getting his start with Charlie Barnet, he began to frequent Minton's and played at the Onyx Club with Roy Eldridge. Bass players toil in obscurity and are the butt of many a jazz joke,[41] but Pettiford was a musician who transcended the then-perceived limits of his instrument, "virtually unique in jazz . . . melodically inventive and technically agile . . . unequaled since Jimmy Blanton" in the view of Leonard Feather.[42] Pettiford's group grew out of a combo that was playing at the Onyx late in 1943, which included Gillespie, Pettiford, George Wallington or Thelonious Monk on piano, Harold "Doc" West on drums, and Lester Young on tenor. When Byas was fired by Count Basie, Young took his place, and Byas would join the proto-bop group.[43]

The group, which included Dizzy Gillespie on trumpet and Clyde Hart on piano, would record three numbers, then scale down its personnel to six musicians (Pettiford, Gillespie, Byas, Hart, and Shelly Manne or Irv Kluger on drums) to record four songs as the Dizzy Gillespie Sextet. These included the standard "I Can't Get Started" but also three tunes with recognizable bop touches: Tadd Dameron's "Good Bait" and Gillespie's "Be-Bop (Dizzy's Fingers)" and "Salt Peanuts,"[44] mistitled by the record company as "Salted Peanuts."[45] (The label on "Good Bait" credits Gillespie as cowriter, perhaps as an inducement by Dameron to get him to record it.) Byas still thought of himself as a swing sax player or at least preferred to characterize himself as such for marketing purposes: the group he formed in 1944 for his first recording session was called The Swing Shifters, and the one that recorded under his name in 1945 was called The Swing Seven. It wasn't until 1947 that he added a dash of bop lingo to the name of a combo (Don Byas' Ree-Boppers).[46] On these early bebop recordings, in the words of Martin Williams, what "is not so expected . . . is the ease and the verge [*sic*; probably "verve"] with which [Byas] plays the unison ensembles in the accents of bop."[47] The group split up in March 1944, presumably because Gillespie and Pettiford could each make more as a leader than as part of a two-headed band with the leader's share of $150 divided in half. By then, Byas had already left the group "when a possibility came up for him to join Duke Ellington's band," which never materialized; he was replaced by Budd Johnson.[48] "The night Byas left the band I came down to the club with my horn," Johnson said. "The place had closed, and we stayed and rehearsed until early morning. Nothing was written down; every night they'd teach me some of the tunes, all by ear."[49]

Byas would continue to record as leader of the musicians he assembled as "All Star" groups, using Johnny Guarnieri and Kenny Watts on piano; Cozy Cole or Slick Jones on drums; Billy Taylor or John Levy on bass; and on one January 1945 date, Joe Thomas on trumpet. He would record with groups that have faded from jazz history (Timmie Rogers and His Orchestra, Savannah Churchill and Her All Star Orchestra, the Cyril Haynes Sextet) and others that sailed under a false flag. "Little Sam & Orchestra," with whom Byas recorded four songs in March 1945, is actually a Big Bill Broonzy vehicle. Broonzy was also known as "Little Sam" and "Sammy Sampson," and the record company (Hub) decided to use the former name on the label.[50] There was more subterfuge of this sort on another Byas session from this period; on April 14, 1945, Dizzy Gillespie was listed as "John Kildare" on four songs sung by Albinia Jones backed by Don Byas's Swing Seven. Byas is not known to have used a pseudonym in his career, perhaps because he was never signed to a long-term recording contract and generally worked independently, but Gillespie used nine different *nom de jazz*: In addition to Kildare (probably a riff on "Dr. Kildare," a popular radio show of the time), he played under three variations of his first and middle name (John Berks, John Birks, and John Burk), B. Bopstein (a pun on the genre that he and others created), Gabriel, and Izzie (or Izzy) Goldberg.[51]

Among the better-known groups that Byas played with during this period were Woody Herman and the Woodchoppers, with whom he played on what appears to be a vanity number for a member of the wealthy Vanderbilt family. The session was recorded at the Vanderbilt Theatre on West 48th Street in New York on January 25, 1945, and the lone title is "J. P. Vanderbilt IV." Despite its overtones of affluence, the piece is a hot one, with Byas and trumpeter Charlie Shavers given ample solo time. Byas would do three sessions in February, March, and April 1945 with drummer Cozy Cole's orchestra on the Keynote and Guild labels. Cole's jazz pedigree extended back to the dawn of the jazz age as he played with both clarinetist Wilbur Sweatman in the late 1920s and pianist/composer Jelly Roll Morton as a member of the latter's Red Hot Peppers in 1930. Cole had a #1 R&B hit with the instrumental "Topsy II" in 1958, and he was still working into the 1960s.[52] Byas was reunited with pianist Pete Johnson and singer Joe Turner on February 2, 1945, in a reprise of the November 1940 tribute to Kansas City jazz that he played on. Turner covered the two-part "S. K. Blues," which had been a minor hit for Saunders King (hence, "S. K."), a rhythm and blues singer, and sang "Johnson and Turner Blues" and "Watch That Jive."[53]

Byas played live dates in February 1945, both on 52nd Street (at the Spotlite Club with Nat Jaffe and his band to which trumpeter Charlie Shavers and Byas were added) and off; he played a dance and jam session at Lincoln Square Center on West 66th Street as a member of the "52nd St. Jam Stars"— as if the musicians were exotic imports from fourteen blocks south.[54] As he came to be better known, Byas would increasingly play dates as headliner with pickup rhythm sections. Clarinetist Albert Nicholas tells the story of one such engagement, a three-week gig in Chicago. The first night was a success, and as Byas left the club through the back door, he was met by a shadowy figure with slicked-back hair, a cigarette in his mouth, and gaudy striped pants in the style favored by local gangsters. "It's you, Don Byas, isn't it?" the man asked.

"Yes," Byas replied.

"I can see it from your saxophone—you just played there."

"Yes."

"And it went well—didn't it?"

"Yes, it went fine," Byas said, "and I'm very happy about it."

"My boss would like you to play for him," the man said.

"Thanks a lot," Byas replied. "I'd like to do it. Please tell him it's okay with me."

"That's fine," the man said. "You start tomorrow."

"I can't," Byas replied. "I just made a contract for three weeks at this place here, but after that I really would like to come and play for your boss."

"You start tomorrow," the man said and walked away.

When Byas arrived at work the next night, the club where he had been playing was gone; it had been blown up, and the mysterious man from the night before was there, leaning against a wall, smoking a cigarette.

"What do you say—would you like to play for my boss now?" And Byas followed him to his new engagement.[55]

CHAPTER 7

Sax about Town

The first man to record Don Byas, Timme Rosenkrantz, would provide him with another platform six years later when he began to produce concerts of music that he considered to be representative of the swing style of jazz. Rosenkrantz's choice of programming put him in a no man's land between jazz's past and the advancing forces of the bop avant-garde. Beginning in the mid-1940s, guitarist Eddie Condon, a vocal critic of bebop, began to stage weekly "Dixieland" concerts at Town Hall, and an organization called the New Jazz Foundation, which supported the newer sounds, retaliated with a concert series of its own. Rosenkrantz produced his first concert on December 20, 1944, under the auspices of *View* magazine, the house organ of the Museum of Modern Art. The audience was comprised of museum supporters and arts aficionados and included surrealist painter Salvador Dali, wearing a single diamond earring—at the time, a novelty in New York. According to Rosenkrantz, the crowd applauded every solo by a group of musicians that included violinist Stuff Smith, pianist Billy Taylor, bassist Ted Sturgis, Bill Coleman on trumpet, and the duo of Don Byas and bassist Slam Stewart, whom Rosenkrantz said "were the showstoppers."[1] Encouraged by the enthusiastic reception of his program, Rosenkrantz rented Town Hall on his own for the afternoon of Saturday, June 9, 1945; the charge to rent the facility was seventy-five dollars, which he characterized as "all the money I had."[2]

The New Jazz Foundation took this booking—which fell between two concerts of theirs scheduled for May 16 and June 22—as a pledge of Rosenkrantz's allegiance to their enemies and began to take steps to sabotage him. Led by disc jockey Sidney Tarnopol—a.k.a. Sid Torin, the "Symphony Sid" referred to in the bop anthem "Jumpin' with Symphony Sid"—the group began to picket Town Hall, claiming that the musicians advertised as performers wouldn't appear at the concert because Rosenkrantz couldn't pay them (a real possibility). When agents for Billie Holiday, Erroll Garner, and Mary Lou Williams heard about the pickets, they canceled their clients' commitments, leaving Rosenkrantz scrambling. Gene Krupa agreed to play with his trio for free and the show went on, but the pickets hurt ticket sales.

The concert was an artistic (if not financial) success. In a notice headed "Season's Best Jazz Bash Financial Flop!" *DownBeat* magazine reported that "few fans showed" up because "[a]pparently a lot of people have tired of the recklessly exaggerated statements of jazz promoters, whose advance publicity lists every 'hot name' in town on the program but rarely lives up to its promises."[3] The program included performances by vibraphonist Red Norvo, trumpeter Shorty Rogers, tenorman Flip Phillips, and pianist Teddy Wilson. Byas and Stewart played two duets, "Indiana" and "I Got Rhythm," which have since become the subject of much speculative admiration. Jazz scholar Martin Williams included the latter number in The Smithsonian Collection of Classic Jazz and claimed that the "duo was spontaneously formed when Byas and Stewart were the only performers who had arrived when a Town Hall audience was assembled and ready for a concert;[4] the other musicians were supposedly held up in traffic. This assertion has given the pieces an enhanced aura of spontaneity that they don't need in order to justify their place in jazz history.

As Art Tatum, one of Byas's heroes and models, put it, "You have to practice improvisation, let no one kid you about it," and Byas himself said he tried to make the listener think he was hearing improvised music even when he wasn't.[5] Byas and Stewart had, in fact, performed the two numbers before, in Rosenkrantz's apartment at 7 West 46th Street in New York, "one night" in the autumn of 1944 "when everyone else took off" for their gigs," according to Rosenkrantz. They had been expecting a pianist—according to one account, Jimmy Jones[6]—to join them for a rehearsal, but "[h]e had broken his arm in a bar." After waiting an hour for him to arrive, Inez Cavanaugh said, "What do you need with a piano . . . play on!"—so they began, and

Rosenkrantz said, "[T]he result was exhilarating, so we put them on" the program "doing the same tunes, 'Indiana' and 'I Got Rhythm.'" The suggestion that Byas and Stewart went on first because other musicians were stuck in traffic also appears to be more folklore than fact. A contemporaneous review by Leonard Feather referred to the duets as an "interlude,"[7] and *DownBeat* reported that Red Norvo's group played first for "nearly an hour, playing a mixture of long jam session-length tunes and standard ballads," followed by "Vocalist Fran Warren," then "a duet by tenorman Don Byas and Slam [Stewart]."[8] Whatever the order of their appearance on the bill and regardless of whether they had prepared for their apparently impromptu performance, the results remain astounding to the ear nearly eight decades later. "They blew out the lights," Rosenkrantz said. When Byas and Stewart listened to the acetate discs of the concert, they both said they had "never played better."[9] (A third number with Byas and Stewart was recorded at the concert: "Candy," with pianist Teddy Wilson.[10])

Born a year after Byas in 1914, Leroy "Slam" Stewart was an innovator on the double bass, developing a style in which he hummed along an octave above the notes he played with his hands. This mystified some; one writer referred to him as "the humming 'dog-house' demon,"[11] but his antic approach masked serious musicianship; he had studied at the Boston Conservatory of Music, which is where he picked up the technique from listening to violinist Ray Perry sing along with his instrument. He formed a team with guitarist Slim Gaillard, and in 1938, the two had a national hit with "Flat Foot Floogee," a song whose lyrics were taken from the hipster jive of the time.[12] He had even played in a musical, *Glad to See You*, with music and lyrics by Jule Styne and Sammy Cahn, but it closed after out-of-town tryouts.[13] Despite his comic persona, Stewart could keep up with a virtuoso such as Art Tatum, with whom he served several tenures as a sideman, and he played with Benny Goodman, a known stickler for high standards. Byas and Stewart had played together on six recording sessions before the Town Hall concerts and would do so on four more occasions before Byas left for Europe. Byas would include three of Stewart's eponymous compositions—"Slammin' Around," "Slamboree," and "Slam, Don't Shake like That"—on sessions where he was leader.[14]

Rosenkrantz would say that the duets were historic for an additional reason: "Bass and saxophone alone had never been heard before, at least [not] on record." While it would be difficult to verify this claim, the combination has proven fruitful for other pairs, such as (saxes listed first): Houston

Person and Ron Carter; Archie Shepp and Niels-Henning Ørsted Pedersen; Warne Marsh and Red Mitchell; and Sam Rivers and Dave Holland. Byas and Stewart would collaborate profitably on other material after the Town Hall concert as members of the Don Byas Quartet; on August 30, 1945, they recorded, along with Erroll Garner on piano and Doc West on drums on, four numbers: "Three O'Clock in the Morning," "One O'Clock Jump," "Harvard Blues" (without a vocal), and "Slam-In' Around." On September 12, 1945, along with Johnny Guarnieri on piano and J. C. Heard on drums, they recorded "Dark Eyes," "Laura," "Stardust," and "Slam, Don't Shake like That." While the last-named is marred by a forgettable novelty introduction, all remain fresh nearly eight decades later, particularly "Three O'Clock in the Morning."[15]

The supposed conflict between the old guard and the avant-garde leading up to the Town Hall concert makes for good drama in retrospect (if bad box office at the time), but this appears to have been, like the Battle of New Orleans, a skirmish fought after the larger war was over. Audience members would have heard more than a little bop-flavored music at Town Hall that night, including Red Norvo's opening piece "1-2-3-4," a variation on the "mop, mop" phrase heard in Tiny Grimes's "Red Cross," Sir Charles Thompson's "The Street Beat," and "Popity Pop" by Slim Galliard; all of these include Charlie Parker as a sideman, and Dizzy Gillespie plays on the last-named as well, so Norvo's piece had legitimate bop bona fides. Byas would appear at a subsequent Town Hall concert on June 22, 1945, subbing for a late-arriving Charlie Parker on "Bebop" and playing with the Erroll Garner Quartet and Quintet on "Indiana," "Royal Garden Blues," and "You Call It Madness (But I Call It Love)." The first is available on various Parker–Gillespie records, but Garner's estate would not permit the release of the last three.[16]

On September 6, 1945, Don Byas recorded "Laura" with Slam Stewart on bass, Johnny Guarnieri on piano, and J. C. Heard on drums, and for the rest of his career, he would be associated with the song. While only a modest hit commercially, Byas's interpretation heightened his profile among jazz audiences and critics; in February 1946, he received an Esquire magazine silver "Esky" Award (a statuette in the caricatured likeness of Arnold Gingrich, the magazine's publisher) but still had to be resigned to placing behind Coleman Hawkins, who won the magazine's gold award on the tenor sax.[17] "Laura" was the song of choice for romantically inclined girls: "When Don Byas' 'Laura' was placed on that contraption, we call a recording machine, all the girls began wondering what boy they could imagine they were with," wrote a columnist in the *Philadelphia Tribune* in July 1946.[18] There are thirteen surviving recordings of Byas playing the David Raskin–Johnny Mercer number ranging from jam sessions (1946, Restaurant München, Copenhagen), to airchecks (a jam session, 1951), to radio recordings (Don Redman and His Orchestra, 1946), to private recordings (with Bill Coleman and The Edwards Jazz Band, 1949), to groups under his name (Don Byas et Ses Rythmes, 1952), to all-star sessions on the 1960 Jazz at the Philharmonic tour. It became his calling card, and one can only assume that the number of times he played it in person for the rest of his life was exponentially larger.

The music for "Laura" was composed by David Raskin, known as the "Grandfather of Film Music" because of his long and prolific output as a film and television composer—approximately one hundred film scores and three hundred television scores. Written for the 1944 film of the same name starring Gene Tierney and Dana Andrews, the melody is heard frequently throughout the movie. Director Otto Preminger wanted to use Duke Ellington's "Sophisticated Lady" as the theme, but Raskin disagreed, saying it didn't suitably convey the emotionally fraught mood of the film. Unhappy with his subordinate's resistance, Preminger gave Raskin just one weekend to come up with an alternative. As it happened, Raskin's wife sent him a "Dear John" letter breaking up with him while he was thus under the gun, and on the Sunday before his new composition was due "the haunting theme seemed to write itself."[19] (Preminger would subsequently hire Ellington to write the score for his *Anatomy of a Murder* and would cast Ellington as "Pie-Eye," the leader of a roadhouse band, in the film.)

Shortly after the film was released in October 1944, Abe Olman of Robbins Music, the publisher, asked Johnny Mercer to write lyrics for the melody. Mercer had seen the film but admitted that he didn't remember the tune. Olman provided Mercer with the music, told him the title had to be "Laura," and Mercer got to work. The melody grew on him, and he wrote lyrics to match the romantic, somewhat haunting story of the film. In 1945, five different recordings of the song made it into the top ten records on popular music charts, with Woody Herman's climbing the highest, to number 4. Dizzy Gillespie quotes the first ten notes of the melody in his solo on Juan Tizol's "Perdido" at the May 15, 1953, concert at Massey Hall, Toronto, featuring five of the leading modern players of the day (Gillespie, Charlie Parker, Bud Powell, Charles Mingus, and Max Roach), and the crowd claps and laughs in recognition. According to pianist Billy Taylor, Byas "went to see the picture

Laura and fell in love with the melody" of the theme song. At the time, Byas was playing in his combo with Erroll Garner and he "taught it to" Garner "because Errol didn't read music and Don only had the sheet music to go by." So Byas "sat down and played it through on the piano and Erroll said, 'Oh, yeah, okay.' After he heard it he could play it, and added his own harmony and his own dimension to it."[20] Byas began to play the song in club dates, and by the time he recorded it a year after the film was released, he had put a distinctive stamp on the ballad.

The dilemma of a hit for a jazz artist was that while it would generate fan interest beyond a small circle of enthusiasts, it could also be a burden as audiences demanded to hear it at every one-night stand in the way that the most popular Duke Ellington songs came to be referred to by musicians in his orchestra as the "dreaded medley," the routine that would be required of them every night as long as they worked for him. Coleman Hawkins was ambivalent about performing "Body and Soul," the record that had made him famous, because "he disliked a situation in which he felt forced to play any tune, whatever its merits." In order to avoid boredom, Hawkins began to "change key every eight bars" when he played the song, according to bandleader Eddie Johnson. "He might start off in F, go to D, and then to A," Johnson said. "You could hear the piano player modulating from one key to another and Hawkins was gone."[21] Byas didn't let the popularity of the song hold him back at first, but he eventually settled on a standard version. As pianist Frans Elsen put it, "From that month with Don [at the Sheherazade club in the mid-1950s], I remember that he played the same choruses on 'Laura' every night. He had recorded that solo long ago and liked it so much that he repeated it every night."[22] He would continue to play it but with resignation: in Lionel Pailler's graphic comic-strip style biography of Byas, he is depicted sitting in a bar, having had one-too-many cognacs, complaining that "Everyone wants to hear my 'Laura'!"[23]

In addition to this link to the movies, Byas had a cameo of sorts in a Broadway play, *The Seven Lively Arts*,[24] based on the 1923 book by Gilbert Seldes that attempted to treat popular culture—including jazz—with the same sort of seriousness used to examine highbrow art.[25] Pianist Billy Taylor said the opportunity came about because he was playing at the time with multi-reedman Walter "Foots" Thomas, who shared a studio on West 48th Street with Cozy Cole, where they taught music. Thomas introduced Taylor to Cole, who hired him, Don Byas, Billy Taylor Sr. (the former Duke Ellington bassist), and Tiny Grimes on guitar to form a combo that replaced the Benny Goodman Sextet in the show. "It was a wonderful chance," Taylor, the pianist said. "All we had to do in the whole time was play seven minutes but it was at the end of the first half of the show and we were surrounded by six foot gorgeous ladies with no clothes on hardly . . . [I]t was very difficult to look at anything other than the six ladies that were surrounding the piano, but it was a very exciting part of the show." The show ran for 183 performances from December 7, 1944, through May 12, 1945. Taylor said that the group "recorded that material that we played with Cozy Cole . . . I don't remember what the label was."[26] While Taylor and Byas played on three different sessions led by Cole in February, March, and April 1945,[27] none contain any of the Cole Porter songs from the show, the most enduring of which is "Ev'ry Time We Say Goodbye," so the seven minutes in question must have been purely a jazz interlude.[28]

When Byas was off the clock for his full-time employer, he would regularly check out the competition on tenor. "There was a club before the time of Minton's, where all the musicians came every night. It was called the Yeah Man on 7th Avenue in Harlem," Byas recalled. Jamming would last through the night and "sometimes up to 12 o'clock the next day. We never slept, we didn't have time for that."[29] Minton's Playhouse was a club at the Hotel Cecil on West 188th Street in Harlem started in 1938 by Henry Minton, an ex-saxophonist and the first Black delegate to the New York musicians' union. Minton converted a "run-down dining room" in the hotel to a jazz club and hired Teddy Hill, a former saxophone player and bandleader, to manage it. At first, the music was limited to "a little band in the back room" led by Albert "Happy" Cauldwell, a veteran reedman then in his late thirties.[30] Hill assembled a house band that included Kenny Clarke on drums and Thelonious Monk on piano, and, with frequent guests, such as Dizzy Gillespie on trumpet and Charlie Christian on guitar (and the prospect of free food and drinks provided by the owners of the nearby Apollo Theater), jam sessions held at the club on Monday nights (musicians' night off) became an incubator for bebop. Because of Minton's ties to the union, musicians could participate without fear of being fined for participating in an unpaid jam session.[31] Byas was recorded by Jerry Newman at Minton's sessions in May 1941.[32]

The jam sessions frequently escalated into "cutting contests" between musicians who played the same instrument. Roy Eldridge, born in 1911, and Gillespie, born in 1917, often tangled on the trumpet, with the younger man eventually surpassing the elder in much the same manner that Gillespie's bop had displaced Eldridge's swing. On tenor, Byas had to contend with four more experienced players: Coleman Hawkins (born in 1904), Leonard "Chu" Berry (1908), and Lester Young and Ben Webster (both born 1909). Sonny Stitt (*né* Edward Hammond Boatner Jr.) witnessed a session at Minton's in which all five participated and gave the following postgame account: "Can you imagine Lester Young, Coleman Hawkins, Chu Berry, Don Byas and Ben Webster on the same little jam session? . . . And these guys, man, nothing like it. And guess who won the fight? Don Byas walked off with everything."[33] According to Byas, Hill never exerted any influence over his house band and guests in their choice of repertoire, a turnabout in his musical tastes since he had fired Clarke from his band just a few years earlier for being too modern. "Everything was accepted," Byas said, "we were left completely free. . . . The people who came there to listen were always people who loved what we did. The others didn't come and that was nice for us too—I was glad they didn't."[34]

While the birth of bebop is often explained in nonmusical terms as a "revolt by African-American musicians" who developed new and more complex musical ideas in after-hours sessions at Minton's and Clark Monroe's Uptown House in order to keep "less adept musicians (predominantly, by implication, white swing players)" from being able to keep up with them,[35] Byas disclaimed any such intention. "In Minton's we experimented every night . . . not to play the white swing guys out, but just because we wanted to go as far as possible," he told a Dutch newspaper in 1964.[36] To the extent that this sentiment was not universal among musicians of the era, Byas's lack of racially motivated spite may perhaps be chalked up to the fact that he himself was triracial, with Mexican, Cherokee, and Black ancestors. Byas was not alone in his desire to subordinate extraneous sociological elements associated with bebop to its musical character, however; Charlie Parker objected to "articles about modern jazz that ignored him or treated his music as a by-product of hipster jive and frantic hype."[37]

Over time, New York nightlife began to move south from Harlem to midtown Manhattan, abetted by the efforts of club owners in the latter area to portray Harlem as dangerous. "Be careful going to Harlem," guitarist Danny Barker recalled the newspapers saying. "You risk being mugged, beaten and robbed."[38] With tongue planted deeply in his cheek, English composer/musician and jazz writer Spike Hughes asked in *Melody Maker*, "Why they do not move the Cotton Club down to the Forties I cannot imagine. It would save many an expensive taxi-fare. On the other hand, the unimaginative American business man and his peroxide stenographer might not feel that they were being 'wicked' if it were located in the mid-town section."[39] The Cotton Club, where Duke Ellington first came to prominence, followed the trend by moving from 142nd Street to 48th Street in 1936.

As Prohibition came to an end, some clubs in the area made a seamless transition from speakeasy to legitimate nightspot, one being The Onyx Club at 35 West 52nd Street. Opened by Joseph Jerome "Joe" Helbock in 1927, seven years into the Prohibition era (January 1920 to December 1933), in its outlaw days The Onyx Club had specialized in what its owner called "polite" bootlegging. "We made our deliveries in brief cases instead of paper bags," Helbock said. From the start of its new life as a legal bar after Prohibition ended, The Onyx Club provided musical entertainment for customers, and Helbock became a "self-appointed patron of jazz."[40] In early 1934, Helbock moved across the street "to number 72 and reopened as a full-scale nightclub."[41] The club was honored by musicians who wrote songs about it: "Onyx Club Spree" and "Onyx Club Stomp" by violinist Stuff Smith; "Onyx Club Revue" by violinist Joe Venuti; and "Onyx Bringdown" by pianist Joe Sullivan.[42] It served as a sort of home-away-from-home for musicians: "This was a place where musicians could pick up phone messages or have their mail delivered, or even leave their horns for safekeeping," noted trumpeter Jim Cullum.[43]

The Onyx "set the standard for the new type of jazz club that would dominate 52nd Street," jazz writer Alyn Shipton noted. In its early days, "patrons might be entertained by a pianist, such as Joe Sullivan, or a singing string band, such as the Spirits of Rhythm," but the format for musical entertainment that evolved in the midtown clubs was "a small band—often just a quartet—with a famous leader, such as trumpeter Henry 'Red' Allen or saxophonist Pete Brown" or pianist Art Tatum. "The band would play sets of about 50 minutes, and alternate with an intermission act . . . the stylistic divisions among the groups playing on the street gradually began to erode, and an informal swing approach started to coalesce. More and more African-American players were employed, and many of these musicians made their living by flitting from one club to another or from one band to another."[44]

This appears to be an accurate description of how Byas came to play the role of an elder statesman to the first generation of bebop musicians. He was older than boppers Charlie Parker (born in 1920), Dizzy Gillespie and Thelonious Monk (both born in 1917), and Oscar Pettiford (1922). As jazz critic Martin Williams noted, the age difference was apparent when Byas first began to jam with the boppers at Monroe's in May 1941. "[T]he sober, introspective half-chorus at [Gillespie's] second entrance on 'Star Dust II' might stand with Gillespie's great ballad improvisations," Williams wrote. "Yet compare him with Don Byas here. Byas is already a master player in command of his own probing, Coleman Hawkins-based style. Gillespie is only at the beginning of his musical self-knowledge."[45] On February 10, 1945, Byas played the first of a series of dates at The Three Deuces, located between 5th and 6th Avenues on the south side of 52nd Street. He would play there again in March and from April 26 to August 4, 1945, with a rotating rhythm section that included (among others) Clyde Hart, Deryck Sampson, and Erroll Garner on piano, Ted Sturgis and Al Lucas on bass, and Cliff Leeman and Harold West on drums.[46] As Pettiford described the sequence of events leading to the collaboration, "Dizzy Gillespie and I went looking up and down 52nd Street for work in [late] 1943. We turned down $75 a week apiece at Kelly's Stables. I had worked at the Onyx Club before, and I was good friends with the owner, Mike Westerman, so I asked if I could be re-engaged. I was welcomed back gladly. . . . [W]e made it the Gillespie–Pettiford group."[47]

Gillespie picks up the tale from there:

> After I left Billy Eckstine, I went to Fifty-second Street. Oscar Pettiford and I opened at the Onyx Club with Billie Holiday and Al Casey, and we decided to get Yard (Charlie "Yardbird" Parker). We sent him a telegram to Kansas City and we didn't get any answer. The telegram just laid there. So the club hired Don Byas as a soloist, not with our group.[48]

Byas was playing at the Onyx with the trio of guitarist Al Casey backing him, evidence of his status as a virtuoso, part of a trend noted by a Philadelphia jazz writer: "An added queer quirk of the artistic aspects of jazz and swing music," he wrote, "is the development of solo artists akin to virtuosos who . . . have moved into position where they can give concerts or make public appearances with skeleton groups who act strictly as background only."[49] Byas wasn't at that stage yet, but he was getting there; pianist Billy Taylor said Byas had "worked with just about everybody. Erroll Garner and others up and down the Street. But, Don wasn't a big enough name to draw the crowds on his own. In fact, Budd Johnson, who eventually replaced him, was far better known to the general public because he'd been with some high-profile big bands like Earl Hines, which had put him in the public eye more than Don."[50]

Byas would listen to the Gillespie–Pettiford band rehearse and eventually came to view them as a more challenging opportunity than the straight-ahead group he was fronting: "We used to rehearse all the time," Gillespie said, "and Don Byas would come to the rehearsals."[51] "We were cooking so much that [he] . . . said, 'Unh, unh,' and he came to our rehearsals and joined our group."[52] Byas, the eldest musician in the group by a period of years that may seem brief in retrospect, but which, given the rapid expansion of the jazz universe at the time, was a quantum leap, "fell right in the group," Gillespie said. "He learned all the arrangements and everything. We were cookin' so much, oh man, that was bad! The people couldn't believe it. That was really bad. All the musicians from everywhere used to come, the soldiers, when the ships docked: Onyx Club!"[53] Byas was paid $60 a week, which brought the take for Gillespie and Pettiford down to $75 a week, the figure they had turned down before to play at Kelly's Stables.[54] Drummer Max Roach confirmed that "the first [bop] quintet did include Don Byas, Oscar Pettiford, Dizzy, George Wallington on piano, and me; and we played the Onyx Club."[55]

When Parker arrived, the group would be five in number—him on alto, Gillespie on trumpet, Max Roach on drums, Pettiford on bass, Byas on tenor—but no piano at first. "Bud Powell was supposed to make it on piano," Billy Taylor said, but he "was in Cootie Williams' band and was under age [Powell would have been nineteen in 1943]. Cootie was his guardian and wouldn't let him go. So the band opened without a piano."[56] (Thelonious Monk, George Wallington, and Taylor would all play piano with the group at various times.) Max Roach, who was probably in a better position to know, said, "[T]he reason they couldn't get Bud Powell was not so much that Cootie Williams refused to let him go as that Powell's mother 'didn't want Bud to play with Diz, because she thought Diz was crazy.'"[57] Despite his initial provisional status within the group, Byas would be included on the Gillespie–Pettiford recordings for the Manor label on January 9, 1945.[58]

Byas said that he and Parker were friends from Kansas City and that "[e]ven after Bird got to New York with Jay McShann, we were still real tight, and he used to always come and get me when he wanted to go and jam, which was damn near every night."[59] One night, Parker got Byas out of bed to jam because he "was the only guy around who could play fast enough" to satisfy Parker's appetite for speed and improvisational innovation.[60] These claims appear to be more than mere boasting on Byas's part. Parker left McShann's band in 1942 to join Earl Hines, who fired him in exasperation after a year, begging McShann to take him back. What was the problem, McShann asked. "He owes everybody in the band," Hines said. "He owes every loan shark. He owes everybody in New York! I bought him a brand new horn, and he doesn't know where the horn is. He doesn't know what he did with it."[61] McShann declined to rehire Parker, who, at loose ends, became part of a floating mass of young musicians who played in after-hours clubs in Harlem such as Clark Monroe's Uptown House. Of these sessions, where he cut his bebop teeth, Parker said, "I heard sessions with a pianist named Allen Tinney; I'd listen to trumpet men like Lips Page, Roy [Eldridge], Dizzy and Charlie Shavers outblowing each other all night long." And the saxophonist, who at the time, impressed him the most? "Don Byas was there," Parker said, "playing everything there was to be played."[62]

Their shared history notwithstanding, it is not clear that Parker's arrival in New York to play with the Gillespie–Pettiford group was welcomed by Byas, who may have felt that he was being pushed aside for the younger man to take the spotlight. Parker was an unabashed admirer of Byas's music, but the feeling wasn't mutual—at first. When Byas first heard Parker play, he told him, "You ain't sayin' nothin' on your horn." Parker "gave him a hard look and told him to come outside. Byas walked out" and Parker pulled out a knife. "Byas calmly drew out a blade of his own. Bird looked at him, smiled, and"—according to Byas—"put his weapon away." Perhaps knowing Byas's reputation for having a hot temper, Parker said (according to Byas), "I really think you'd cut me."[63] Byas eventually got over his resentment of the adulation that Parker received from fellow musicians and the jazz press and would refer to him as "that wonder of wonders" when introducing a Parker composition that one of his groups played.

Whatever their differences—Byas may have seen Parker as foreclosing his last, best chance to achieve preeminence on the American jazz scene— Byas and Parker would play together a number of times before the former departed for Europe in 1946. On January 4, 1945, they were both present at a recording session for Continental Records as members of pianist Clyde Hart's All-Stars, and on January 14, they would appear together in support of an "All-Soldier Quartet" (Buck Clayton trumpet, Ken Kersey piano, Hayes Alvis bass, and James Crawford drums) at the Spotlite Club for a jam session that lasted four hours.[64] From March through May 1945, the Dizzy Gillespie/

Charlie Parker Combo opened at the Three Deuces opposite the Don Byas Band and the Erroll Garner Trio,[65] and on March 25, Byas played at Lincoln Square Center for a "Palm Sunday Dance and Jam Session" in which Parker probably participated. On April 19, Byas accompanied Dizzy Gillespie and His Band Featuring Charlie Parker at The Three Deuces, and on May 30, Byas and Parker were part of a Memorial Day Benefit Jam Session and Dance at Lincoln Square Center in support of the Salvation Army's Servicemen's Center in New York. On June 5, Byas and Parker were in Philadelphia for a concert with Dizzy Gillespie and His Quintet at the Academy of Music, followed by a jam session in which Parker insisted Gerry Mulligan, then only seventeen years old, participate.[66]

At the time, Mulligan was arranger for the Elliot Lawrence Radio Orchestra and played tenor that day rather than his usual baritone because Frank Lewis, the incumbent tenor, had (according to Mulligan) "tripped on the stairs at home, his kid left his skate or something, and he broke his wrist." Parker complimented Mulligan on his charts and invited him to a postconcert jam at the Downbeat Club. Mulligan "arrived at the club, checked the tenor in the coat room, and listened to two sets of Bird, Diz, and Don Byas." Mulligan said Byas "had a wonderful sound and great command and he was a fast, really dynamic player." Mulligan started to leave "because he had to get up the next day" and was a bit discouraged. "Can you see me playing with them?" he said. "Don Byas would have cut me five new belly buttons." Parker intervened, retrieved the tenor from the coat room, and insisted that Mulligan join the jam despite the challenging competition.[67]

On June 22, Byas and Parker were part of a concert sponsored by the New Jazz Foundation, Timme Rosenkrantz's rival, that turned out to be a disappointment because in a turnabout from Symphony Sid's claim that artists wouldn't show up for Rosenkrantz's June 9 Town Hall concert, neither Coleman Hawkins nor Slam Stewart appeared as advertised; "Jazz Stars Absence Drag Gillespie Bash," read the headline in *DownBeat*.[68] Byas would be advertised as a full-fledged member of Charlie Parker and His Quintet for performances at the Three Deuces in New York in July 1945 and the Downbeat Club in Philadelphia in August 1945, along with Al Haig on piano, Stan Levey on drums, and Curley Russell on bass. This group was formed by Parker after he participated in a few rehearsals as a member of Dizzy Gillespie's big band.[69] From 1944 to 1945, Byas and Parker participated in Sunday jam sessions at the Heat Wave nightclub located at 266 West 145 Street in New York;[70] the two were both leading bands playing there at the time, as recalled by tenor sax Hal Singer: "I was [at the Heat Wave club] with Don Byas's group" for a Sunday jam session, he said. "It was not [Don's] regular group that played in the Three Deuces. Charlie Parker was the headliner. Don's group played a set, and then Parker played a set. Earl Bostic sat in with us, so it was three Oklahoma boys—Don, Bostic, and me."[71] (Both Bostic and Singer were born in Tulsa, Singer in 1919, Bostic in 1925.) In addition to their home state, Byas and Bostic had several bands on their resumes in common, including Bennie Moten, Edgar Hayes, Don Redman, and Hot Lips Page.

At some point, Byas was dropped from Parker's quintet, and the two would play together thereafter (with one exception) only in staged jam sessions à la Jazz at the Philharmonic. They were both present at a crowded jam session-style concert on September 8, 1945, that included Ben Webster, Dizzy Gillespie, Erroll Garner, Stuff Smith, Eddie Barefield, and Dexter Gordon at Lincoln Square Center; eight days later, they were part of a possibly even larger group crammed into the Spotlite Club, a smaller venue. Participants in the latter session, produced by Mal Braverman and Milt Shaw as "Mad Music," included Gillespie, Parker, Byas, trumpeter Al Killian, drummer Morey Feld, "Al Cohen" (probably tenor sax player Al Cohn), and others, including "Guests from the Dorsey and Barnet bands." There was a jam session at the Fifth Regiment Armory in Baltimore on October 30, 1945, that drew a crowd of 5,000, at which Parker and Byas competed for solo time with a cast of horns that included Coleman Hawkins, Ray Nance, and Harry Carney.[72] There were doubtless more jams that went unrecorded.

Byas's position as a transitional figure between swing and bop is exemplified by his double duty during the summer of 1945 when Coleman Hawkins was playing at the Downbeat and Charlie Parker was at The Three Deuces next door. Byas was in Parker's band at the time—a notice in the *Chicago Defender* said Parker's band was "featuring Don Byas on the tenor sax"[73]—but at intermissions, he would "move into the adjoining club to play duets with Hawkins."[74] He tried his hand at writing in a bop mode: "Byas-A-Drink" is also known as "Bopland," and it has some of the same rhythmic and harmonic touches that one would expect to hear in a Gillespie number; a March 1946 newspaper column described the number as "gone and . . . groovy with some weird riffs."[75] Bop did not immediately displace swing in the minds of jazz fans, however, and there was too big a market for more accessible music for record producers to ignore, so Byas remained in demand for more hummable, danceable music. In September 1945, Byas would record with the Guarnieri Quartet, a foursome led by pianist Johnny Guarneri with J. C. Heard on drums and Leo Guarneri on bass (the Guarneris were descendants of the Guarneri family of violin makers). The four songs the group recorded include Duke Ellington's "Sophisticated Lady" and three dance tunes with no trace of bop rhythms: "Armand the Groove" and "Dot's My Baby" evoke images of box-stepping couples, and "I'd Do Anything for You" is a lightly swinging number with conventional harmony and melody lines. Guarneri had played on Byas's "Laura," and the two would work together in Byas's final months before he left for Europe in quartets that recorded on September 12 and October 3, 1945. While largely forgotten now, from 1943 to 1947, Guarnieri was "one of the most recorded artists in jazz, making hundreds of sessions with every type of group" and composed "more than 3,500 selections of all types short of rock 'n' roll."[76]

Byas would be added to a recording session with Earl Bostic late in 1945 that produced four titles: the George and Ira Gershwin torch song "The Man I Love," "Hurricane Blues" with a vocal by Roger Jones, "The Major and Minor" (a cognate for "Broadway" by Wilbur H. Bird, Teddy McRae, and Henri Woode), and "All On," cowritten by Bostic and Lionel Hampton.[77] There is not a boppish flatted fifth or ninth to be heard in the bunch. Bostic's group offered (according to Gunther Schuller) an alternative for "Black audiences [who] could no longer tolerate the increasingly insipid and tame dance music of the white bands . . . but at the same time . . . could not keep up with the rapid advances in black orchestras . . . and the switch to small be-bop combos playing 'esoteric,' 'intellectual' jazz. . . . Rhythm and blues was the answer for them." Bostic and others like him, such as Bill Doggett, Wynonie Harris, and Louis Jordan, found in "the R&B field . . . a musical haven where they could in fact still function professionally." Although Bostic made a living playing "totally commercial music which permitted no fundamental stylistic deviations or advances,"[78] he was present at the beginning of bebop.

On his next record, Byas backed singer George Williams on "A Woman Gets Tired of One Man All the Time" and "Don't Care Blues," with Eddie Durham playing an amplified guitar.[79] George Williams was a vaudeville performer (sometimes in blackface) who performed comic songs with his wife, Bessie Brown, on the Theatre Owners Booking Association circuit (whose acronym—"TOBA"—was jokingly translated as "Tough on Black Asses" by performers due to its poor pay and working conditions). He had recorded "A Woman Gets Tired of One Man All the Time" in 1923, accompanied by Fletcher Henderson on the piano, so the song was a chestnut two decades later that Byas, Durham, and three unidentified sidemen revived with a rhythm 'n' blues approach.

During his last years in America, Byas was a part of two other concert series. The first was put together by Barry Ulanov, a jazz writer and promoter and an early biographer of Duke Ellington, who rented Times Hall on December 20, 1944, and June 22, 1945, for all-star concerts of "The New Jazz" that included—along with Byas—Coleman Hawkins, Dizzy Gillespie, Buck Clayton, Stuff Smith, and Erroll Garner, among others. The second was put together by Gordon "Specs" Powell, a drummer whom Byas may have met when he played with Edgar Hayes. Powell was the first Black musician hired by the CBS radio network, and he tried his hand at concert promotion under the brand name "Best in American Jazz." Powell's aim was "to appeal to the general public" who hadn't warmed to jazz as normally presented, that is, concerts that "usually started late and were without production, timing or taste." Musicians who performed for him were "all clothed alike and the shows" were "produced with radio-like clockwork," according to a newspaper report.[80] Powell rented Town Hall on September 23 and December 29, 1945, for concerts that included, along with Byas, Charlie Parker, Stuff Smith, Al Haig, and trumpeters Bill Coleman and Frankie Newton.[81]

In January 1946, Byas got the opportunity to record with a boyhood hero, Benny Carter, who hired him to play with his orchestra on two sessions. Carter assembled a unit for the occasion that included Dicky Wells on trombone (he was between stints with Count Basie), Russell Procope on alto (before he joined Duke Ellington), and Flip Phillips twinned with Byas on tenor sax. On January 7, the group recorded "Diga Diga Do,"[82] "Some of These Days," and "Who's Sorry Now"; Byas solos on the first two.[83] At a second session the next day, Byas provided the sensuous introduction to "I'm the Caring Kind" and a solo on "Rose Room" but remained in the ensemble while fellow tenor Dexter Gordon soloed on "Looking for a Boy."[84] On January 10 and 11, Byas recorded four numbers with the Esquire All-American Award Winners, a group that included Louis Armstrong, Duke Ellington, and Johnny Hodges, among others. Byas is given solo space on "Gone with the Wind," where he complements the silky tone of Hodges on alto and on "The One That Got Away." The Esquire honor was recognition that Byas deserved a place among jazz's elite.

In the fall of 1946, Byas would sign on to record with Don Redman, Teddy Wilson, and Dizzy Gillespie, as well as leading sessions under his own name, before making the fateful decision to join a tour of Europe as a member of a band led by Don Redman, put together by his old promoter, Timme Rosenkrantz.[85]

CHAPTER 8

To Europe

Timme Rosenkrantz returned to Denmark with Inez Cavanaugh in 1945 after World War II ended and began efforts to revitalize jazz in the Scandinavian countries. He was unable to persuade a big-name band such as those led by Duke Ellington and Count Basie to commit to a tour and so decided to contact Don Redman, whom he had known for many years.[1] Redman was forty-five years old at the time and had reduced the level of his activities since disbanding his full-scale orchestra in 1940; he had, however, continued to put bands together on a bespoke basis under contract,[2] and he told Rosenkrantz he would be willing to assemble a group for a European tour.[3] Redman recorded with a ten-piece pick-up band in New York in January 1946 that included Don Byas, and it is possible that this unit was formed in anticipation of Rosenkrantz's tour.[4]

Donald Matthew Redman was born in 1900 into a musical family—his father was a music teacher and his mother a vocalist—and he was a precocious instrumentalist, playing trumpet at the age of three and (according to one possibly hyperbolic source) "all wind instruments by the time he was twelve."[5] He had been in the music business since 1922, when he began to play in Pittsburgh with Billy Paige's Broadway Syncopators, for whom he wrote arrangements that caused the band to stand out from their competitors when they moved to New York in 1923. When that group broke up, Redman became a freelance musician/arranger in recording studios where his skills came to the attention of Fletcher Henderson, who would sometimes hire freelance musicians to give form to his ideas. Out of this loose aggregation of talent, a working group coalesced with Henderson as leader and Redman as lead saxophone and musical director.[6]

As Henderson's principal arranger, Redman is credited with taking published "stock" charts and enhancing them with jazz stylings; what might have been a polite society dance tune when played by another band became a hotter number after Redman was through with it. He translated the trumpet innovations of Louis Armstrong—who played with Henderson from 1924 to 1925—into a big band context, pitted brass and reed sections against each other in call-and-response patterns, and provided settings for instrumental solos against ensembles, influencing the sound of many bands that came after him, including Benny Goodman's. He went on to McKinney's Cotton Pickers, a Detroit band that was known for its tight rhythmic unity under his direction; the Cotton Pickers "stepped on" Bennie Moten's orchestra in a battle of the bands that Bill—not yet "Count"—Basie found so painful he "couldn't even stand to stay around and listen" to his opponents once they took the stage.[7] In 1931, Redman returned to New York and led a band at Connie's Inn in Harlem. While swing has many fathers, Redman's DNA is very much in the mix.

Redman's place in jazz history was thus secure, and he could pick and choose arranging jobs for Jimmy Dorsey and Count Basie, among others, and occasional short-term hires of other leaders' bands (such as Jay McShann's[8]) that he would lead under his own name. In short, Redman didn't need to borrow cachet from a Danish baron when he signed on to the project, especially since Rosenkrantz lacked "the economic and organizational powers to set up an extended Europe tour for an American jazz orchestra." Rosenkrantz teamed with Danish impresario Richard Stangerup,[9] whose financial backing and business acumen may have persuaded Redman to come to terms with the Baron, who hadn't been able to pay the musicians for his Town Hall concert until he sold his recording equipment and his "good new clothes"[10] on the following Monday to raise money. (The musicians would later receive some more money when Milt Gabler's Commodore Records issued recordings of the concert.[11]) Byas recorded with Redman's orchestra on January 29, 1946, for the Swan record label in New York, a date that produced four songs: "Dark Glasses," "Mickey Finn," "Carrie Mae Blues," and "Midnite Moods" (Byas soloed on the last two), so Redman would have had recent and direct exposure to Byas as he began to plan the band he would take to Europe.[12]

After the one-day session with Don Redman and His Orchestra on January 29, Byas participated in the historic bop session with Dizzy Gillespie and His Orchestra in New York on February 22, 1946, at which Gillespie's most famous version of "A Night in Tunisia" was recorded. The tune had been previously recorded as a broadcast from the Onyx Club by the Gillespie/Pettiford quintet (with Budd Johnson on tenor, George Wallington on piano, and Max Roach on drums); by Boyd Raeburn's orchestra in several versions; and by Sarah Vaughan under a different title ("Interlude"), but it is this version that has taken a place in history, having been inducted to the Grammy Hall of Fame in 2004. Byas vamps to Dizzy's statement of the theme on this version and soloes as well. This was, in the words of Joop Visser, "the first time a major record company had recorded any modern jazz."[13] The other titles played by the group at this session were Thelonious Monk's "52nd Street Theme" and "Ol' Man Rebop"—Gillespie's playful take-off on "Ol' Man River" by Jerome Kern and Oscar Hammerstein II.

Byas then accompanied the Benny Carter band on a tour of California in March; a notice in the *Chicago Defender* on March 16, 1946, said Byas put "in his farewell appearance before leaving for Hollywood" and "was the guest of honor at" a "swing-fest, along with Trummy Young, Max Roach," and a number of others on March 10.[14] Upon his return from California, Byas would lead several New York recording sessions in the spring. The first was with sidemen who have vanished from jazz history (Teddy Brannon, piano, celeste; Frank Skeete, bass; Fred Radcliffe, drums) on May 17 for the Savoy label in New York that produced interpretations of four standards: "Cherokee," "Old Folks," "London Donnie (Danny Boy)," and "I Don't Know Why (I Just Do)."[15] The last-named is a good example of Byas's ability to take a treacly pop tune and use it as a canvas on which to paint one of his concise and restrained solos along the lines of his introduction to "Harvard Blues" that gained him fame when he was with Count Basie. The second session on August 21, 1946, again for Savoy, included a better-known rhythm section: Max Roach on drums, Leonard Gaskin on bass, and Sanford Gold on piano.[16] In between, there was a date with the Teddy Wilson Octet backing Sarah Vaughan on two numbers ("Penthouse Serenade" and "Don't Worry 'bout Me") and two standards ("I Want to Be Happy" and "Just One of Those Things") without her.[17] In September, Byas participated in a final American session for the

Gotham label backed by Beryl Booker on piano, John Simmons on bass, and Fred Radcliffe on drums before leaving for Europe. The selections were all "slow ballads in a sad mood," including "Gloomy Sunday"—also known as "The Hungarian Suicide Song"—written by Hungarian pianist and composer Rezsö Seress that has become a minor (in both senses) jazz standard, recorded previously by Billie Holiday and later by Johnny Hodges.

In addition to Byas on tenor sax, the group that Redman put together for the European tour consisted of himself on alto sax; Herbert Lee "Peanuts" Holland, Bob Williams, and Alan Jeffreys on trumpets; Tyree Glenn, Quentin Jackson, and Jack Carman on trombones; Pete Clark on clarinet, alto, and baritone saxes; Chauncey "Shorty" Haughton on alto and baritone saxes; Ray Abrams on tenor; Billy Taylor on piano; Ted Sturgis on bass; and Buford Oliver on drums. Singing duties were shared among Peanuts Holland, Tyree Glenn, Quentin Jackson, Redman, and Inez Cavanaugh. Pianist Billy Taylor, who was newly married, was allowed to bring his wife Theodora ("Teddy") along and, as a result, arrived later than the majority of the musicians.[18] Taylor said that Byas acted as one of his wife's "protectors" on the tour. "Most of those musicians had been on the road quite a bit," he said. "Teddy was a newly married young lady and the youngest person on the bus and boy she really caught it because I mean they put her on unbelievably. . . . Don Byas was very chivalrous and several other guys just kind of looked out for her when I wasn't around. But Tyree Glenn and some of the other guys really put her on."[19]

Due to a seamen's strike, band members made the trip by plane, arriving ahead of schedule at Kastrup Airport, Copenhagen, on September 7, 1946; they were met by a contingent of Danish jazz musicians from Leo "The Lion" Mathisen's band playing "St. Louis Blues" in pouring rain—and tears filled Byas's eyes at the sound.[20] The band used the time they had saved by air travel to rehearse. After checking into their hotel, bandmembers went out looking for jam sessions, which they found in abundance: with Leo Mathisen at Restaurant München; with Peter Rasmussen's band at Restaurant Skandia; and with "The Harlem Kiddies" at Restaurant Gold Digger. A recording of the Mathisen session was made that includes Byas playing an up-tempo version of "Sweet Georgia Brown" and his hit "Laura."[21]

Danish jazz enthusiasts were alternately enthused and confused by what they heard at some of the impromptu jam sessions that Redman's band members participated in. Danish pianist Boris Rabinowitch, who later became a jazz critic, said, "[T]he sound that came out of their horns was," in a few cases, "weird." Rabinowitch and trombonist John Darville agreed that several members of the band were "crazy" until they realized that the "odd phrases and figures" the Americans played were intentional. "[F]or the first time in my life I heard the word 'rebop,'" Rabinowitch said, "[a]nd I'm sorry to admit that my feelings for the idols of that time like Sidney Bechet and Johnny Hodges would never be the same again."[22] The bop touches that the Danes heard came from several sources: Redman's band book included "For Europeans Only," a composition by Tadd Dameron, who would go on to become one of the leading arrangers of the bop era, and trumpeter Alan Jeffreys who had played with Boyd Raeburn's band, cited (along with Woody Herman's band) as "one of the two main big-band gathering places for young talent of the nascent bop school."[23] Jeffreys and Jack Carman were participants in what is often cited as the first European bebop recording session in Paris on July 4, 1947, with Robert Mavounzy & His Be-Boppers.[24]

In addition to jazz standards and the new sound of bebop, Redman plugged "his newest symphonic composition, 'Frantic Atlantic,'" which a newspaper notice said, "in the near future will be performed by no less than the Boston Symphonic Orchestra." On hearing the work, Nicolai Andreyevich Malko, an expatriate Russian conductor, pronounced Redman "maybe the greatest musical talent" in America and said he hoped to incorporate "Frantic Atlantic" into his repertoire.[25] (The piece is currently available on the Redman album *For Europeans Only*,[26] but Byas does not solo on it.)

The tour officially began on September 15, 1946, with three performances at K. B. Hallen in Copenhagen, about which a reporter for the newspaper *Berlingske Tidende* wrote, "There was wild enthusiasm in KB-Hallen, many encores and flowers. It is seldom that one here in Denmark has the opportunity to meet the genuine jazz music, as only the Negroes are able to perform it. Yesterday one once again got the proof that jazz is the black man's property, and that white men only are able to perform in it as guests." In *Politiken*, Herbert Steinthal, a jazz writer using the pseudonym "Goofy," wrote that Byas's playing was "strongly sensual," that his recorded version of "Laura" was "America's greatest hit success for the moment," and that Byas might be "the finest tenor-saxophonist in the world." Redman began to include this encomium when he introduced a Byas number, which drew a dissenting opinion from a reviewer who used the name "Pele" writing for *Expressen* in a review of the October 3 concert at Konzerthuset in Stockholm. ("Don

Byas . . . in our opinion, is not the 'world's best tenor player as Don Redman so generously dubbed him."') The change of scenery from the US to Europe was beginning to allow Byas to escape from the long shadow of Coleman Hawkins, however.

The band then played concerts in Odense, Århus, Aalborg, Hjørring, Esbjerg, and Svendborg, Denmark, before returning to Copenhagen for three concerts at K. B. Hallen on September 22, 1946. Jazz critic Dan Morgenstern, then a teenager growing up in Copenhagen, said that "the big hit of" the Redman concerts in Denmark was "Byas doing 'Laura.' He was a wonderful ballad player, beautiful sound. That really hit home."[27] The band then left for Norway, playing two concerts along the way in each of Hälsingborg and Göteborg, Sweden, before arriving in Oslo on September 26; there, they played six concerts in the Colosseum Theater, three in the Sage Theater, plus a "tea dance" (usually referring to a performance at which liquor was not served, except surreptitiously) in the Regnbuen restaurant before leaving at the end of the month to return to Sweden. Their Swedish itinerary for the month of October called for twenty-two concerts, sometimes two in one day; when they arrived in Stockholm on October 3, they recorded several numbers for Swedish Radio and then participated in a jam session with local musicians. Before the tour was a month old, the band had already played more than forty dates as a whole, and various combinations of its musicians had played in a number of extracurricular jam sessions; as a result, the group was starting to show signs of fatigue. "Redman's bandstand manner was charming, refreshing, and natural," wrote "Pele" in *Expressen* on October 4. "He succeeded in lifting the spirits of a travel-weary and exhausted orchestra, which would probably have been able to deliver a much better program if its members had had the opportunity to catch a few hours sleep."[28]

Other critics, while properly recording the enthusiasm of jazz-starved Scandinavian audiences and their own fondness for the idiom, also had misgivings. "[I]t is always amusing to listen to a Negro orchestra, because there is something inexplicable about it, in rhythm as well as in mood," wrote Julius Jacobsen, said to be an expert on Don Redman, in *Orkester Journalen*. Jacobsen went on to say he was disappointed that the band assembled for the tour was a "scrape-together of second-rate musicians with 4–5 absolute top soloists." Harry Nicolausson, the editor of the magazine, was similarly critical, saying Redman "had not succeeded in giving [the orchestra] a personal stamp, what foremost was caused by the weak arrangements." While acknowledging the skills of the soloists, he accused them of "empty audience-pleasing grandstanding and lack of personality."[29]

As November approached, Nils Hällström, the editor of *Estrad* magazine, who had organized the Swedish leg of the tour, found it necessary to make some apologies for the band in print; there had been delayed concerts, caused in part by transportation problems, but attributable in some instances to what he perceived to be lax attitudes on the part of the musicians. "If only the discipline in the band had been in line with the sometimes brilliant jazz music and festive performing enthusiasm . . . we should have been able to call Don Redman's orchestra anno 1946 one of the really great jazz occurrences in Sweden." Instead, he wrote, "I hope never more to have to be confronted with so much grumbling, scolding, and lacking will to work, which characterized about half of the members of this band. The bus was not comfortable, the food was not good, the hotels were bad, the travels too long, two concerts a day and three on Sundays were too much." He called some of the musicians "troublemakers" who had "got their perspectives twisted" after the enthusiastic reception they received in Copenhagen. Timme Rosenkrantz, whose companion Inez Cavanaugh was African American, sought to mollify the promoter-editor by saying that "you cannot expect that" bandmembers "instantly should be first-rate beings, when they have grown up under seventh-rate conditions." Hällström found it in his heart to acknowledge this, perhaps because his artistic assessment of them was so high: "But they could play," he wrote. "They could!"[30] In Zurich, Switzerland, on November 1 through 3, Hällström's problems became visible to paying customers when a few musicians (in particular, drummer Buford Oliver) either failed to show up for the first set of a concert or walked off.[31] Oliver's absence may have been the result of an injury; he had broken his leg in Copenhagen, and when he rejoined the band in Switzerland, his right foot was still in a cast and he could not play bass drum.

On October 21, the band arrived in Belgium for dates in Antwerp, Namur, and Brussels that had been added after the tour began; the next date was originally scheduled for Switzerland. Jackie Tunis, a Belgian who had recorded most recently with Robert De Kers and His Orchestra and Ivon De Bie,[32] filled in for the injured Oliver. The Hot Club of Belgium organized a press conference at a phonograph and record store and featured Redman and the band in the December issue of *Hot Club Magazine*. From there, the band traveled by train to Geneva, Switzerland, for concerts at Victoria Hall on the 27th and

28th. A preview of the concerts in *Hot-Revue* contained extensive background sketches of various band members but included only an entry stating "(tenor sax) Voir Discographie" ("See Discography") for Byas; he was thus not yet considered a headliner. After the concert on October 28, the band went to Palais d'Hiver (Winter Palace) for a jam session with Jerry Thomas and His Swingtette. There, Byas met a fellow expatriate saxman from the American Midwest, Glyn Paque, from Poplar Bluff, Missouri, who played alto. Paque was born in 1906 or 1907[33] and had played with Jelly Roll Morton and King Oliver, among others. Paque went to Europe with Bobby Martin's Orchestra in 1937, took over the band when Martin returned to the US, and remained in Switzerland until his death in August 1953.

Perhaps in response to jazz critics, Redman became a stricter disciplinarian on musical issues as the tour continued. Trumpeter Peanuts Holland was quoted in *Hot-Revue* for December 1946 as saying that the band was "on the edge" at concerts because "no wrong notes were allowed." The band must have responded, for when they reached the German-speaking part of Switzerland, an article by a writer using the nom de plume "Pic-up" in *Schweizer Filmzeitung* asserted that "[o]ne could even argue that" Redman's band "is the best orchestra that ever played on Swiss ground. Louis Armstrong came here with a just average orchestra, and Coleman Hawkins played with Swiss ensembles." A writer reviewing the band's concert in Bern gave them measured praise for playing "matter-of-factly without any pretension" and for their "modest and respectable" appearance and added that if they were to "take part in the degeneration to which jazz has become addicted" since the golden age of "Louis Armstrong, Duke Ellington, Johnny Dodds and their ilk," the blame would rest with audiences and the "rather undiscerning applause of our jazz-mad youth." Like many a jazz writer, his feelings could be expressed in a paraphrase of Professor Henry Higgins in the musical *My Fair Lady:* "Why can't the fans . . . be more like a critic?" The writer found "fine moments, even moments of the best kind . . . when the Negroes awakened to be their own true selves—that is in regard to the accomplishments of the orchestra's three outstanding soloists," Don Byas (whose embellishments on "Laura" he compared to Maurice Ravel), Peanuts Holland, and Tyree Glenn.

This ambivalent sense of simultaneous attraction and repulsion was expressed in an unsigned review of the band's November 8, 1946, Basel, Switzerland, concert that appeared in *Basler Woche*:

No, these were not our guarded Basel people anymore. This was a powerful thunderous eruptive element. . . . For sure the cause for this could not be found in the purely musical area. It was the true American jazz and hot that mostly the younger generation succumbed to.

One could even have a certain prejudice against jazz . . . We try to define the music so that the absolute mastering of the instruments gives sound to the primeval rhythm, the inner feeling. A moan, and at the same time a cheer, a shrill harmonically sounding ripping, a swelling of the sound up to the highest possible volume. Is it race, the feeling of being oppressed that shall be expressed here?

Certainly this presentation must also be assessed as art. An art of its own kind—nearly abstract—as it belongs to primitive peoples.[34]

While these critics couldn't bring themselves to rate the music of Redman's band at the same high level as that produced by Bach and Mozart, once they'd heard it in the flesh, they were unable to resist its allure, even as they were cautious of the disruptive effect it had on them. A review of one of the concerts the band gave at the Corso Palais in Zurich during the first week of November made it clear that more racial diversity in the band's membership would not have been welcomed by either audiences or critics: "[T]hree from [Redman's] troupe are white, they have to leave the musical superiority to their brown-and-black comrades though."[35]

The band played dates in several towns in southern Germany for the US Army but was unable to extend the tour into Czechoslovakia and England, in the latter case because the British musicians' union barred them from playing in London and other cities in retaliation for the ban imposed by the American Federation of Musicians on English performers in the US. The last concert took place on November 30, 1946, in Munich, Germany, and the band was then dissolved.

The December 28, 1946, issue of *Billboard* announced that "Don Redman and several of his sidemen who played with him on a recently completed 11-week tour of European countries are staying over in France for a six-week vacation" while the remainder "of the orksters [show biz press slang for musicians in a jazz orchestra] returned to the United States on the Queen Elizabeth." The poor rate of exchange was blamed for putting "a damper" on plans for "a more extensive" stay, but on the whole, the tour was recognized as "the initial post-war appearance of American musickers on the Continent" and pronounced to be "solid box office."

What the *Billboard* story got wrong was that some of those who stayed behind would not be vacationing but rather getting to work right away playing in Paris nightclubs and recording for France's two leading jazz labels, Swing and Blue Star, among them pianist Billy Taylor. "The '46 tour with Don Redman was only supposed to last six to eight weeks," Taylor said. "We wound up staying eight months." Taylor said that Redman "sent part of the band back home and retained a small combo of about seven pieces, which he took into a nightclub call Le Bouleur ('The Bowler'). It was a very fancy eating club and we had something like a two month engagement there and we played . . . from whatever period that was past the New Year. . . . So we celebrated New Year's Eve in that little club."[36] According to Taylor, although the group played some bebop, "[p]eople came and danced to what we were playing . . . they danced a lot to what we did." This group included, in addition to himself, Redman, Glenn, and Byas, Buford Oliver on drums, several trombone players—Tyree Glenn and Quentin "Butter" Jackson, and Nathan "Nat" Peck—and Jean Bouchéty on bass. Don Redman "rearranged some of the material that" his band had played on the tour "and wrote some new material for that instrumentation" as well, according to Taylor. Then, Taylor said, Redman "decided that he was going to continue to write, and got an offer to write some for movies and to do some other kind of writing," so the Byas/Redman cell divided.[37]

Unlike Taylor, who returned to America with his wife, Byas decided to remain in Paris. "It was sad in some ways," Taylor said. "Don didn't get enough credit because I don't think Don was ever in the right place at the right time. When he went to Europe, he came close to receiving the kind of celebrity he was looking for—over there. At one point he came up to me and said, 'I'm not going back. People don't treat me right at home, and these people treat me just fine. I'm going to stay here.'" And he did, becoming "a big fish in a small pond."[38]

But not at first. In May 1947, an article in a Belgian magazine reported that Byas was a featured guest with the orchestra of Guy Willox (stage name of Guy Dirickx) when they performed at the Casino in Knokke, Belgium, but then returned to France because he had exhausted the possibilities for further work in Belgium after three months. A writer who went only by the name "Jacq" reported in his "Notes of an Alligator" column in the *Hot Club of Belgium* magazine that Byas fronted a combo in a small club in Brussels backed by musicians who accompanied him "frightfully" with a young man "who pretends to play drums" drowning out his tenor sax. The sparse audience "doesn't listen and doesn't care," Jacq wrote. "It is the only serious engagement he found during his time there; he otherwise played only for tips."[39]

Byas nonetheless had a great impact on Belgian musicians during his time there, including Bobby Jaspar, whose band, the Bob Shots, was among the first—if not the first—among native European bands to play bebop. Local musicians made efforts to find Byas gigs, but they were up against a unique cultural requirement. The owner of a dance hall who was looking for a saxophone player wanted one who could double on accordion for tangos. "Does he play the accordion, this Don Byas?" the man asked.

"No," Byas's friend replied, "but this is the famous Don Byas, from the Don Redman orchestra."

"If he doesn't play the accordion," the owner said, "I'm not interested."[40]

CHAPTER 9

Don, Sam, Carlos

Born "Carlos Wesley," self-christened "Don" for stage purposes, known as "Sam" to bandmates, sometimes referred to as "Spots" for his ability to fill any spot "whatever the situation, if you needed a guy who could play"[1]—the subject of this book formed an identity of his own that he made up as he went along; he was his own improvisatory solo.

A triracial boy born in the provincial city of Muskogee only a few years after the Oklahoma territory was admitted to the United States, he went on to become a bon vivant in Europe, then settled down to become a *huisvader* (family man) in the Netherlands. He claimed to have been the first American jazzman to relocate to Europe, and while this was not technically correct,[2] he was the biggest name to have moved there permanently at the time; Sidney Bechet (born 1897) didn't settle in France until 1951.

Byas seems to have been a bit of a polymath, at least in the arts; in addition to his musical talent, he drew and painted, made woodcuts, and was a potter as well.[3] "He would have liked to become an artist," his widow said,[4] and among the materials she left to the National Jazz Archive of the Netherlands when she died are several charcoal sketches and oil paintings by him, some of which reflect his Hispanic heritage (one depicts a bullfighter) however attenuated the link between him and those roots may have been. He told an interviewer in 1965 that he loved to read both poetry and prose, then identified two writers he particularly enjoyed, Edgar Allen Poe and what sounds like (and was transcribed as) "Swearingen." Byas then goes on to ask the interviewer, "I don't know if you remember his *Ode on a Grecian Urn*," indicating that he is referring to John Keats. "Only the title," comes the reply, and Byas proceeds to recite the last lines of the poem (almost entirely correctly) from memory: "Beauty is truth, truth, beauty. That is all you know in this world, and that is all you need to know."[5]

Byas can be forgiven for confusing Keats with Joseph Severn, a friend of Keats who produced the best-known portraits of the poet. Duke Ellington, another musician who was also an artist, was said to have synesthesia, a condition in which stimulation of one sense triggers a perception in another. In Ellington's case, he heard sounds as colors and saw colors as sounds, and Byas seems to have been similarly gifted/afflicted. When asked, in reference to the Keats poem, "Do you feel a musical symbolism in it when you read it, when you recite it—the end of a brilliant solo?" Byas replied, "Of course, poetry is music, and so is prose, it's all music."[6] Perhaps Byas also perceived aesthetic stimuli on a continuum; the thought of the poem recalled to him both the name of the artist who drew Keats as well as its enduring final lines.

During the course of his life, Byas became fluent in a number of languages and picked them up quickly. In addition to English, he spoke good Dutch, learned French fluently, Spanish, a little Portuguese and Italian, and even Catalan, which he learned from Tete Montoliu; he became a European, a cosmopolitan.[7] Within hours after arriving in Denmark, he had composed a song in Danish, "Jeg Elsker Dig" ("I Love You"), which he proceeded to sing "at the top of his voice as the bus rolled through Sweden, Germany, Belgium, Switzerland . . . on to Paris."[8] This facility with foreign tongues notwithstanding, Byas's announcements of songs at gigs were thought to be "disarmingly charming" as he went back and forth between English and Dutch.[9]

Byas was farsighted and wore glasses; he may have been vain about their effect on his appearance, as the author has found only a few pictures of him performing in them. The extent of his visual deficiency is not known, although it was serious enough that, when he left a party with pianist Teddy Wilson one night and forgot his glasses, he returned to a thirteenth-floor apartment to retrieve them. When the host didn't answer the doorbell, Byas crawled out a window in the staircase, inched his way along a narrow molding on the outside of the building and into the apartment, where he found a pair of glasses. Then, rather than exit by the door, he returned in his spider-like fashion along the outside of the building and back through the window he'd crawled out of. The next day, he discovered that he had taken the host's glasses, not his own.[10] As for his tastes in music, they were (small "c") catholic in range. He said that he liked "the more modern" European classical composers, such as Bartok, Shostakovich, Prokofiev and Stravinsky ("very, very much"), Debussy, and Ravel.[11]

He enjoyed "dammen" (the game known as "checkers" in American English), playing in a café close to his home, and he played at an expert level, sometimes bemoaning the fact that he couldn't find anyone to give him a good game. "I am almost a champion checker player," he told an interviewer in 1965. "I've been trying to find someone to give me a decent game of checkers, which is difficult."[12] He also liked to play a card game called "klaverjassen," literally "clover" for the card suit of clubs, plus "jas" (the jack), one of the highest-ranking trump cards.[13] He was competitive at any game he played, including ping-pong. "When we were touring [in Europe with Don Redman after World War II ended]," pianist Billy Taylor recalled, "we had access to a ping-pong table in this castle the Allies had liberated. My wife was a very good player. Don thought he could beat her. It turned out she beat him several times, and he had to scuffle to keep up. He never lost his cool."[14]

He loved to fish, both with a rod in the canal in front of his house at the Admiralengracht, where he caught carp, and with a speargun in the Mediterranean. He was a member of the Club des Chasseurs Sous-Marins de France, a social club headquartered in Paris, during 1952 and 1953 when he was living in Paris, and he spent so much time in the waters at St. Tropez that he came to be known as "Piad" among local fishermen; the word is French slang for the hermit crab that has no shell of its own and makes do "with any empty shell it finds on the bottom of the sea." "They called me that because I was always skin-diving, searching on the bottom of the sea for something to shoot at" with his speargun, Byas said. "I was more often on the bottom of the sea than on top . . . and 'piad' is only found on the bottom of the sea."[15] Despite his skill at spearfishing, he was self-deprecatory: "[The fish] run away when they see me," he told a reporter in a 1958 interview publicizing the Cannes Festival du Jazz. "Fortunately I often meet some who are suicidal. I only have to stretch out my harpoon and they come along to impale themselves. It allows me not to come back empty-handed, which would be very vexing."[16] In a 1955 French episode of the television show *Télé Paris*, Byas appears at a Le Tropicana gig clad only in his swimming trunks with his spearfishing gear, then leads a local band in a hot version of "Tea for Two."[17] His frequent bandmate, Hezekiah Leroy Gordon "Stuff" Smith, gave a concise thumbnail sketch of Byas's proclivities in this direction: "Don is one of these deep sea divers, who likes to go under the water, with his rubber suit on, and catch fish with a spear. I told him, 'Go on down there, Jack, I ain't coming with you. You understand me?'"[18]

In the winter, he would skate (in Alpe d'Huez, when he and Jopie were in France) and tried the sport of curling as well. One photo taken during the winter months there shows him relaxing with Jopie outside an inn with someone in a polar bear costume behind them, and in another, he is operating a large snow-blowing machine. He liked to play billiards at Arti and at a neighborhood café called The Meeting Point.[19] In Amsterdam, the Dutch would boast about seeing Byas and Ben Webster together in order to impress visitors with the importance of the local jazz scene, but in the view of Dutch tenor Hans Dulfer, this was lip service: "'Perhaps we'll see him pass by on his motorbike at Dam Square,' we lied," or say that Byas and Webster had been seen "walking together in town to go and play billiards . . . or to have a beer at Reguliersbreestraat." Of the two men, Webster was accorded more consideration by the Dutch because he remained in their eyes an American, while Byas had, for better *and* worse, become one of them; he "spoke good Dutch, had a Dutch family, and didn't feel the urge to be an American in Amsterdam," Dulfer wrote.[20] Byas got around on a moped, a small motorcycle common on the streets of Amsterdam, and he was sufficiently comfortable astride it to mischievously exempt himself from traffic laws of general application; one day in January 1971, his friend tenor Johnny Griffin was rehearsing at the Paradiso in Amsterdam with bassist Ruud Jacobs and drummer Han Bennink when the trio heard a roar and turned to see Byas riding into the club on his vehicle.[21]

When Byas first came to Europe, he was "a frail and gangling youth," according to Inez Cavanaugh, and "the more robust fellows were always teasing him and calling him 'skinny.'" In response, he became fanatical about exercise—particularly swimming and weight lifting—and "developed into a hardy and healthy chap with arms of steel." He is shown in the Dutch documentary about him pumping iron on what appears to be an early version of the Nautilus-style weight-lifting machine, with weights worked by pulleys, and he taught weightlifting to a boy in his neighborhood with whom he would play checkers.[22] In a 1965 interview, he told jazz writer Mike Hennessey that he had "lifted 120 kilos" (approximately 265 pounds) and that he had nineteen-inch biceps. "Imagine that," Byas said, "a little runt like me."[23] He would often greet friends whom he hadn't seen in a while—and people he'd just met—by inviting them to punch him in the gut as hard as they could to see how fit he was, but his devotion to fitness was more than just a matter of physical vanity; he pursued diving in part to improve his breathing capacity, and he did finger exercises in order to have "perfect physical mastery of the keys" of the saxophone.[24] "It's very good for blowing the tenor, all that holding your breath," he said of his practice of staying underwater for long periods of time.[25] He built up his fingers by training with lead weights on them, which strengthened his grip and increased his digital speed. His grip became so strong that he could squeeze the bell of his saxophone and make it bend (although he admitted that the one he played was made of a special soft metal).[26]

Byas's obsession with fitness was driven in part by masculine emulation, the drive to best his contemporaries, perhaps fueled by the "Napoleon complex" that men who are short in stature sometimes suffer from: "Byas could never accept being less than the best at anything he attempted," Inez Cavanaugh said. Danish tenor saxophonist Jesper Thilo recounts the story of how one night, while Byas was a member of a group he was playing with in Copenhagen, other band members decided to have a push-up contest between sets. When Byas walked in and saw the winner about to be congratulated, he said, "I can do that with one hand!" Byas dropped to the floor and proceeded to do ten (quickly), five more (less quickly), and finally (and slowly) twenty one-armed pushups in all.[27] Sometimes, the desire to impress one's male companions exposed jazz critics to physical risk; one night at a Count Basie concert at the Free Trade Hall in Manchester, England, Byas told jazz writer Steve Voce (after more than a few drinks) that he was a karate expert, "despite the fact that" (in Voce's words) Byas "was about knee-high to a mushroom." Byas claimed that, even though Voce was the bigger man, he could throw him over the bar without hurting him or breaking any glassware. Just as Byas was about to demonstrate, Voce was able to hand him off to British jazz critic Eddie Lambert and excuse himself to go hear the Basie band.[28]

Byas became an expert cook, serving up (it was said) gourmet fare as a way to many a woman's heart. He was "a perfectionist, capable of an astonishing patience in front of the stoves of his friends," according to jazz producer Pierre Voran. In addition to the fish he caught, he was a specialist in southern cuisine, American "Soul Food."[29] His daughter Carlotta says that her father made an excellent lemon meringue pie. In 1958, when he was interviewed before his appearance at the Festival Européen du Jazz in Cannes, a photo caption in *Le Petit Varois* said that "before chasing the fish of the gulf, Don Byas reassured his wife 'I will return in an hour, prepare the soup, I'll bring the fish.'"[30]

Byas insisted that he was of Cherokee heritage on his father's side, and since he was born and raised in Oklahoma, there was no reason to doubt him on this score, as was sometimes the case with other jazzmen; Johnny Hodges used to pull people's legs (most notably, those of jazz writer Stanley Dance) by claiming Native American ancestors, while other musicians, such as white trombonist Jack Teagarden, claimed Native American blood in order to pass among Blacks when they wanted to. Teagarden was rumored to be descended from Cherokees, but this wasn't true; his only connection to the tribe was that his paternal great-great-grandfather won former Cherokee land in a lottery.[31] As reported by Ellington trumpeter Rex Stewart, when Teagarden began to hang out in Harlem, it "caused quite a few uplifted eyebrows among those Harlemites who resented Teagarden's Texas brogue and appearance." Black trombonist Jimmy Harrison "would declare that Jack was more Indian than Caucasian, which made everything all right."[32]

Cherokee folklore, like that of many other Native American tribes, recognizes a "trickster" figure, a contradictory and unpredictable persona who occupies a position between two poles, and Byas's personality certainly seemed at times to be that of a trickster, whether drunk or sober. Trumpeter Bill Coleman said Byas "carried two dumbbells with him in an airplane bag" when the two toured Italy in 1958. "Whenever we arrived at a hotel that was up-to-date enough to have a porter," Coleman recalled, "Don would tell him to take the small airplane bag and we would all be waiting to watch the shocked expression on the face of the guy when he lifted it."[33] Buck Clayton was an observer of this side of Byas on several occasions when the two were members of Count Basie's band. "One night in Utica, New York, [trumpeter] Ed [Lewis] and I got into a fight after going to a party," Clayton recalled, even though he didn't "even remember why we were fighting." Apparently, Byas "had been baiting" the two on, and soon they "were out of the car and fighting on sleet." After much ineffectual swinging at each other because of the slipperiness of the ground, police arrived, and both Lewis and Clayton ended up in jail—but not Byas.[34]

When Byas was in France for the 1949 Jazz at the Philharmonic Tour of Europe, the musicians were invited to a dinner at the home of André ("Pepé") Persiany, a French pianist who had been added to the tour. Appreciative of the meal since the bus only stopped to eat between 11 a.m. and 1 p.m., Clayton bought a bouquet and asked Byas—who had become fluent in French since leaving America—to write a speech for him that he could give to honor Persiany's mother. Byas "scribbled out something on a piece of paper," then "went in the bathroom with" Clayton to rehearse it. When Clayton thought he was ready, he returned to the dining room and gave the speech that Byas had written; it included the line, "Madame Persiany, we enjoyed that wonderful dinner so much that we hope you will accept these flowers and stick 'em up your ass."[35]

And then there was the time in Rotterdam, when—after standing on his head for ten minutes and drinking "a range of tropical stimulants," according to Dutch tenor Hans Dulfer—Byas bet his drinking companions he could play Thelonious Monk's "'Round Midnight" backward. The bet was accepted, but Don had left his tenor in Amsterdam; drummer Candy Finch said that James Moody had a tenor and was staying at the hotel—but no one knew his room number. So Byas started randomly calling rooms at around 4:00 in the morning, saying that he wanted to speak to James Moody. "A higher staff member of the hotel had to make an end to it," Dulfer said, and so his chance to hear "'Round Midnight" played backward was dashed, but Byas's reputation as a two-continent trickster was cemented for good.[36]

Byas enjoyed alcohol, and it was a part of his equipment maintenance; he soaked his reeds in cognac rather than water,[37] but no negative inference should be drawn from this practice as other saxmen have soaked their reeds in vodka, beer, and other forms of liquor to make them more flexible. He worked to control his drinking, but he was often a backslider. Inez Cavanaugh said that Byas refrained from "strong drink" after he arrived in Europe, and this is consistent with his statement to jazz critic Dan Morgenstern that he declined opportunities to return to America to play because "he was fearful that reunions with old friends would lead to renewed drinking."[38] These claims should probably be viewed with some skepticism, however. According to Morgenstern, Byas's "pride led him to turn down the offers for club and recording work he did get," and he "was soon reduced to near inactivity. He sat in now and then, playing marvelously, but there was no steady work, and he started to drink again. When he drank, his stubbornness turned to mulishness."[39] According to Bill Coleman, in 1958, Byas "told [a group of musicians touring Italy with him] that he had stopped drinking since he had married a Dutch girl." He came into a restaurant where Coleman was dining with his wife Lily and offered to buy a round of after-dinner drinks; Coleman and his wife decided on grappa, a potent Italian distilled spirit that ranges from 35 to 60 percent alcohol content, and Byas had one as well. "Later, when we came to the theater," Coleman recalled, "we saw that Don had had quite a few grappas: he was worse than an American Indian when he drank."[40] During intermission, the organizer of the tour came to Coleman and asked him "to go and get Don because he was raising hell at the bar, taking his clothes off and showing everybody his musculature. People were laughing at him."

Coleman finally persuaded his bandmate to return to the stage and finish the concert, which he was able to do despite his condition until he got to the coda of his feature number, "Laura." "It was very special and there was a certain phrase he played before the trio made the last chord with him," Coleman said. "But . . . Don was so high that he could not find the phrase for at least three minutes. He was running exercises all over his tenor and the musicians were waiting and looking at him anxiously." The drummer held his sticks in the air, and Michel Hausser, the vibraphonist, "had his mallets ready to hit the last chord. Finally, after what seemed like a lifetime, Don found the phrase, the musicians hit the chord with him, and everybody breathed a sigh of relief. But Don didn't take another drink the rest of the tour."[41]

Other times, Byas's drinking would cause trouble that extended beyond music. In the late 1960s, Dutch pianist Jack van Poll recalled, there was a club in Breda (in the southern Dutch province of Noord-Brabant) called "de Ritz." After a successful first set, Byas was "the hero of the night" and began to drink heavily, at which point he started to make romantic advances toward the owner's wife, Adje, thinking she was an unattached barmaid. When he tried to pull Adje over the bar, the owner "appeared in a flash, grabbed him by the neck and threw him outside among a number of messily parked bicycles." A few months later, at another gig with van Poll, Byas hardly remembered the incident.[42]

Some musicians tried to reform Byas, such as drummer Art Blakey, who played opposite him in April 1972 for a week at the Swing Jazz Club in Turin. By then, Byas's health was failing and his consumption of alcohol had increased, perhaps out of despair as he saw his days dwindle down. "I understood him," Blakey said.

[H]e was tired . . . Over 60 years old [actually, just 58], and he just went back to drinking a fifth of vodka a day. Some days he'd pay $100 a bottle, because he couldn't get it in some countries. You can't stand up under that. I talked to him about it. We sat in a park in Milano all afternoon, I gave him a lecture, and after I got through, he was kidding and said, "How can you tell me anything? I've lived longer than you." I said, "You sure have, and you know more than I do." He said, "I sure do, so I'm doing it the way I want to do it." He just got disgusted.[43]

Most musicians tolerated Byas's antics, but not all of them. One night, while jamming with fellow tenors Paul Gonsalves and Dexter Gordon, Byas—again under the influence of drink—got it into his head that he could play better nude. "I wanna play naked!" he shouted and took off his shirt. Cooler heads prevailed before he could get all his clothes off.[44] Dizzy Gillespie, who added Byas to his pioneering bop group while he and Oscar Pettiford waited for Charlie Parker to arrive from Kansas City, disputed Byas's claim that he could "play good drunk or sober."[45] Gillespie said Byas "couldn't play shit when he got drunk, but, man, when he was sober!" One night, when Byas showed up intoxicated, Gillespie was

> sitting and looking at him. [Byas] was playing a solo and slobbering all over his horn. I kept looking and going tsk-tsk-tsk. He says, "What the fuck you lookin' at?" . . . I said, "I'm just looking at you." He says, "Wha's wrong?" And I said, "You ain't playin' shit." He says, "Well, you're not doin' so hot yourself." I said, "Well I'm doin' the *best* I can; I'm sober." He says, "Fuck you!" I said, "Fuck you." He says, "Mother-fuck you." And I told him, "Don, if you think for a minute that I won't take advantage of you while you're drunk, you've got another think comin'. You're drunk and if you get up and act like you wanna do somethin', I'm gonna smash you. I'm gonna take advantage of you—you're drunk, you can't do anything. You can't fight."[46]

The conflict on this point of decorum notwithstanding, the two made up. Dizzy said Don "started to cool down" after this exchange and that the Onyx combo "was really a beautiful group" despite the occasional clash of personalities.

On the other hand, Byas's mouth won him many friends and admirers. "Another trait of his was his inexhaustible chatter," wrote Pierre Christophe.

He was known as the premier teller of fish stories in the Old Port of Marseille, where he recounted his exploits—using either a pole, harpoon or speargun—with good humor in his vigorous adopted French.[47]

As for drugs, he is reported to have been a marijuana user, but later in life, he nonetheless held pot smokers who came to hear him in contempt because he didn't think they listened to the music. He didn't want to work at one particular club, his widow recalled, because of "[a]ll those smoking pot and half-asleep junkies."[48] Byas certainly never succumbed to heroin, but for a mundane—not a moral—reason; he was terrified of hypodermic needles and resisted even medicinal injections.[49] "So many musicians have been so stupid on the narcotics question," he said in 1967. "These guys have a distorted conception that narcotics helps them play better. This isn't true at all. The big error they make is that they get high, feel good, and think they are playing great. It's all in the mind."[50] There is at least one tale of Byas trying "uplifting pills"—probably amphetamines—with adverse consequences. The band with whom he was working in Denmark at the time consisted of Kenny Drew on piano, Al Heath on drums, Palle Mikkelborg on trumpet, Torolf Mölgaard on trombone, and Hugo Rasmussen on bass; the group was about to board a bus to play in Aabenraa, Denmark, when Byas "spread his arms and legs like a jumping Jack" and refused to get on. Three men were able to push Byas onto the vehicle, but he remained recalcitrant, attacking and screaming at the others. Drew tried to calm him down but failed, and when the group stopped for something to eat, Byas frightened a red-haired girl who minded a shop for her parents, pulling down food and drinks from the shelves in a manic manner. After he consumed the food on the bus, Byas "started sleeping like a dead man, with his face looking deathly pale," talking all the while. When the bus arrived in Aabenraa, he was able to replicate with Hugo Rasmussen the tenor sax-bass duo numbers with Slam Stewart from his Town Hall concert and perform the rest of the program, but he looked very tired after coming down from his high.[51]

Byas loved to jam, getting a kick both from the spontaneous format—by comparison to playing from charts with Andy Kirk, Count Basie, or other big bands—and from the competition. He would approach opportunities to mix it up with other tenors like a pool shark hustling a mark by pretending to be unprepared or less skilled than he was or to have forgotten his sax. "Everywhere he went, he took his tenor with him, hoping there'd be a possibility to jam," said Dutch tenor Hans Dulfer. "On such occasions, he once told me, he used shrewd tactics. He always thought it would get very 'good' if he didn't have his horn with him," so "he'd secretly put his sax in a club's cloak room and come in grumbling how stupid he had been to leave his horn at home."[52] Byas was described by Teddy Reig,[53] a self-described "jazz hustler" who produced his Savoy sessions, as a "headhunter."

> He and (pianist) Clyde Hart used to walk up and down 7th Avenue looking for action, and whoever was playing anywhere, Don would run them out. He never wanted to go home. He never carried his horn in a soft bag, always in a heavy case, and in the early morning hours, he'd be draggin' that box along on the ground like a trunk. He'd be loaded by then, but still ready for action.[54]

As to the horns Byas used, he is known to have owned at least four different saxophones during his life: the first was a Conn at the time when that brand was known as "the standard of excellence."[55] His next was a Selmer "Radio Improved" Balanced Action model, which he—like many others—adopted after Coleman Hawkins played it on "Body and Soul." "Balanced action" saxes were introduced by Selmer in 1935; the term referred to a new system of keywork in which the bell keys were placed together on the right side of the bell, and advertisements touted the faster keywork that this arrangement made possible, saying it enabled musicians to play "25% faster." The term "radio improved" is more nebulous but may refer to the fact that the Balanced Action line had "a bigger bore throughout, giving you some added volume with less effort."[56] As tenor James Carter put it,

> Byas got a Selmer, Dexter [Gordon] got a Selmer, Illinois [Jacquet] got a Selmer on account of that's what Hawk was playing. [Hawkins] came back [to America] with this horn and all of a sudden the floodgates opened. I mean, mad publicity about [Hawkins] being met by Selmer when he got off the boat. Selmer was perceived as the premier brand from then on, and Byas took his with him when he traveled to Europe in 1946 with Don Redman, only to switch to a Dolnet sax in 1950. Dolnet is a French manufacturer that, at the time at least, was perceived as "third-tier" behind Selmer and Buffet Crampon.[57]

The tale of these two saxophones, the Selmer now owned by Carter and the Dolnet that Byas used during the last years of his career, will be told in a later chapter.

As the sixties came to a close, Byas faced questions as to his position on the rising tide of protests in America about civil rights and the Vietnam War and why the style of music he produced didn't reflect it. In 1969, he was asked by drummer/jazz writer Arthur Taylor if he "ever felt any kind of protest in [his] music," and Byas replied angrily, "I'm protesting now," even if—as an expatriate from America during the most tumultuous years of the civil rights movement—there were other, more direct ways of expressing anger than he had chosen. "If you listen you will notice I'm always trying to make my sound stronger and more brutal than ever. I shake the walls in the joints I play in. I'm always trying to sound brutal without losing the beauty, in order to impress people and wake them up. That's protest, of course it is. I've always felt like that." Then, making the political the personal, Byas turned the question around and gave a response that transmuted the theme of societal wrongs into one of personal resentment. "The point is how long will people keep me waiting before they come in. I'm wondering if things will finally come my way before I pop off."[58] In 1970, he went further—or was more blunt—in response to a Dutch interviewer: "Protest in music?" was the question, and Byas replied, "No, I don't agree. You won't achieve anything with that." "So jazz is just a form of escapism?" the interviewer persisted. "I don't see that you can achieve anything with fighting and protesting. You have to ensure that the audience gets to know what jazz is again. African influences . . . . I think that's a very good idea."[59]

The line of questioning reveals the age-old fault line between pagans and Puritans, the former believing that a thing of beauty can be enjoyed for itself, the latter believing art must be subservient to moral doctrines. The coming of bop gave rise to a good deal of thinking that was "rooted in ideas (and politics) that often [had] little to do with jazz or its development," according to Todd Bryant Weeks, biographer of Oran "Hot Lips" Page. Bop was a radical musical movement, and much was made of the novelty of the "dress, language, social behavior, and race politics" of the musicians who created it, "[b]ut it was a *music* first and foremost, and much of the political ramifications came later as a result of controversy stirred up by promoters and the music press in an attempt to push bop as a commodity."[60] Byas had his foot in both camps, swing and bop, but he resisted the attempt to force him to cut his clothes to fit the fashion of the day and the implied denigration of the hard rows he and others of his generation had to hoe before later lionized musicians. Like an elder scolding youngsters who don't know how tough things were back in the day and how much progress has been made as a result of the efforts of prior generations, Byas defended himself, saying, "My form of protest is to play as hard and strong as I can. In other words, you did this and you did that, so now take this!"[61]

Byas's defensiveness on this point may have a personal explanation. He was, in round numbers, only a quarter Black and may thus have been unwilling to take on a burden of rebellion imposed by the temper of the times that fell only partially on his shoulders. Throughout his life, he denied that his decision to stay in Europe was based on the racial climate in America. While acknowledging that race relations were more moderate in Europe than the United States, he said, "[D]iscrimination had nothing to do with it,"[62] and his wife confirmed that he didn't stay in Europe because of prejudice against his skin color.[63] It is thus inaccurate to say, as Gunther Schuller did, that America "could not ... provide the kind of environment in which" Byas "could pursue [his] art and craft in dignity and security."[64] When he left the US in 1946, Byas said, "I was one of the most recorded jazz musicians. In fact, I did too much recording. I'd walk into a studio and the engineer would say, 'Oh no, not you again.' ... I made an awful lot of money. My phone was ringing all the time."[65]

Byas would not have been the first jazz musician of African American heritage to declare his independence from the Black roots of the music he played. Jelly Roll Morton, some of whose ancestors were African American slaves, would spuriously claim that "all my folks came directly from the shores of France," and he "took pride all his life in his own patrician features."[66] Morton would say that the Black women who worked in the brothels of New Orleans "had lips looked like bumpers on a box car,"[67] and he denigrated Game Kid and other "rough blues pianists" who played in them because their "music was so simple and repetitious."[68] Morton considered his "downtown" New Orleans roots, his training, and his music more refined than those of the "uptown" musicians, "fresh off the plantation" who "really didn't have anyone to teach them" and "just played like they felt and sang."[69] Morton's musical talent was encouraged by his parents; there was a piano in the house (among other instruments), and he received instruction from several teachers.[70] His paternal grandfather had been a contractor (sometimes inflated to "architect") of "some wealth and prominence" in antebellum New Orleans, but his father was a bricklayer, perhaps reflecting the general decline in economic status suffered by the next generation of free persons of color in New

Orleans. Similarly, Byas's father Walter would list his occupation as "Engraver (temporary)" on his firstborn son's birth certificate, perhaps expressing his ambition to rise above that station.

The tenacity with which Morton and Byas would cling to social distinctions and pursue refinements in their lives and chosen art forms may have reflected anxiety over social status. Alan Lomax describes Morton's parents as "bourgeois," and Byas's upbringing may be similarly characterized. His family owned, rather than rented, the house he grew up in, and he said his parents were strict even though both were "artistic," his mother a piano teacher, his father a jeweler who "not only traded in precious stones" but "could also set them and make jewelry."[71] When Morton was interviewed by Alan Lomax late in life, he spoke in "a resonant, authoritative voice,"[72] just as Byas, in videos from his European years, speaks in a formal, almost affected tone. There are several other curious parallels between the two men's families: Morton's half-sister claimed they had a Jewish great-grandmother, as Jopie Byas claimed of her in-laws; Lomax notes that "[m]any persons . . . on looking at some of Jelly Roll's photographs, wonder about the possibility of Native American ancestry," just as Byas's mother was Cherokee. To top off the parallels between the two, some of Morton's ancestors on his father's side from Saint-Domingue (a French colony in the area of modern-day Haiti) were "well known as jewelers or goldsmiths," like Byas's father.[73]

Pianist Hampton Hawes, no stranger to controversy himself (he is the only jazz musician ever to request and receive a presidential pardon[74]), expressed this theory of rebellion in another guise by words of admiration for what an older generation of musicians had accomplished before him with their art: "I believe that when they look back one day and see cats like Bird and even older cats like Sidney Bechet and Don Byas," Hawes said, "they're going to realize that musicians were the true revolutionaries in their own quiet way."[75]

CHAPTER 10

Spanish (and Portuguese) Tinge

Jelly Roll Morton said that in "New Orleans Blues," "one of [his] earliest tunes . . . you can notice the Spanish tinge. In fact, if you can't manage to put tinges of Spanish in your tunes, you will never be able to get the right seasoning, I call it, for jazz."[1] Given his father's Spanish heritage, one should not be surprised to find Spanish tinges in Don Byas's music or to find him playing with Latin musicians in jazz and non-jazz settings.

Following the Don Redman tour, Byas was a member of two groups comprised of veterans of that band (and others as needed) that recorded and played gigs in Paris nightclubs after most other musicians in the Redman band had gone back to America or moved on to other jobs. For their first date at Salle Pleyel, the group consisted of Byas, Herbert Lee "Peanuts" Holland on trumpet, Tyree Glenn on trombone, Don Redman on alto sax and clarinet, Billy Taylor on piano, Buford Oliver on drums, and French bass player Jean Bouchéty. For a subsequent job at Le Beaulieu, Inez Cavanaugh (vocals), J. J. Tilché (guitar), and Nat Peck, an American trombone player who had played with Glenn Miller's band, were added.[2] "By January 1947, the small combo we formed caught on, and toward the end we ended up in Holland with Tyree Glenn and Don Byas," Billy Taylor said. "We changed guitarists and used another bassist and drummer. We mixed the groups up a bit. We were all there at the same time so guys on the recordings were together, working separately."[3]

Ultimately, Tyree Glenn and Peanuts Holland would be the only Americans other than Byas to remain in Europe. Glenn and Byas had played together with the bands of Charlie Echols, Eddie Barefield, and Benny Carter; they had most recently been bandmates in Eddie Mallory's group, except for a period when Glenn was out of commission as a result of a band coach crash.[4] Like Byas, Glenn had artistic interests outside of jazz; after he left the dance band business, he "entered the radio-TV field" and was an occasional actor on a New York television station. Glenn used a plunger for "wah-wah" effects on the trombone in the manner of Joe "Tricky Sam" Nanton of the Duke Ellington Orchestra. After the Redman tour, he went to Sweden but later returned to the US, where a job as a temporary replacement for Lawrence Brown in May 1947 turned into a four-year stay with Duke Ellington's orchestra.[5] Peanuts Holland, like Byas, found life in Europe congenial and remained there. He had been a member of the band at the Jenkins Orphanage in Charleston, South Carolina, which produced, in addition to him, other noteworthy trumpeters, including William "Cat" Anderson, Augustine "Gus" Aiken, and Cladys "Jabbo" Smith. The orphanage was founded in 1891 by Rev. Daniel J. Jenkins, who was inspired to help abandoned African American children he encountered; three years later, Jenkins launched the school's first orphan band using discarded instruments, particularly brass horns, which, it was believed, helped students build lung power to ward off tuberculosis. Holland toured as a single or occasionally with his own small group and would play with Byas on a number of occasions after relocating.[6]

In a sort of cooperative enterprise, Byas, Glenn, and Holland recorded three numbers in one session in Paris on December 4, 1946—"Working Eyes," "Peanut Butter Blues," and "The Mohawk Special"—that were issued under each of their names: the first under Tyree Glenn and His Orchestra, the second as Peanuts Holland and His Orchestra, and the third under Don Byas and His Orchestra, all on the Swing label. The arrangement reduced studio costs, but what, if any, benefit the record company gained by this market differentiation is unclear. It may have benefited the musicians, as the leader of a group is generally paid a higher fee than the sidemen. Holland and Glenn were omitted from a fourth number recorded at this session— "Gloria," a composition by Byas that was issued under his name alone.[7] After his death, lyrics were added to this piece by Claude Nougaro, a singer/poet.

Byas would appear on other records with Glenn and Holland made during this period: a session under Glenn's name on January 13, 1947, that included Holland, Billy Taylor, Buford Oliver, and French musicians, and one on February 17 in the Netherlands with the group called Tyree Glenn-Don Byas and Their Orchestra, as well as recordings with a quartet under his name (Billy Taylor, Buford Oliver, and French bassist Jean Bouchéty), and a six-piece ensemble he called his "Ree-Boppers."[8] (In the battle for linguistic supremacy between "bebop" and "rebop" as the name for the new music that developed out of younger musicians' dissatisfaction with swing, "bebop" ultimately prevailed; a slang dictionary defines "rebop" as "n. = bebop. *Archaic, replaced by 'bebop' and 'bop.'*"[9]) Glenn and Byas made these recordings while they were booked for a long-term stay at Dancing Parkzicht, a Rotterdam dance hall; they were fired from the gig after a few weeks because their music was found to be "unsuited for dancing." Patrons expected a steady stream of tangos, foxtrots, and waltzes of a few minutes each, but Byas, Glenn, and their sidemen gave free rein to their jazz sympathies, playing songs for over twenty minutes with lengthy solos.[10]

Byas would travel to Belgium in the spring of 1947, where he was booked to play a number of concerts. While there, he made a radio broadcast on March 23 from Le Venétien in Liege with Bobby Jaspar, who played clarinet and tenor sax, along with the latter's band, the Bob Shots.[11] Jaspar, a native of Belgium born in 1926, was the rare case (at the time) of a European jazz musician good enough to make it in America; he relocated to the US from Paris in April 1956, married singer Blossom Dearie, and remained in the States for most of the rest of his life, playing with trombonist J. J. Johnson, trumpeters Miles Davis and Donald Byrd, and pianist Bill Evans, among others.[12] From late March through April, Byas was the feature attraction at jam sessions sponsored by Le Hot Club de Belgique; "professional" musicians were invited to bring their instruments to participate—apparently, the club wanted to discourage amateurs who couldn't keep up with Byas from joining in. One of those who participated was Belgian Raoul Faisant, who apparently gave Byas all he could handle in a "combat des chefs" of the tenor sax. At least one observer said that Faisant was the winner ("Faisant sortira vainqueur," i.e., "Faisant emerged the winner").[13] After a recording session in Paris on June 12, 1947, Byas traveled to Barcelona in the summer of 1947; he would not return to France until late in December 1948.[14]

It was Armand Molinetti, a French drummer,[15] who talked Byas into going to Spain. Molinetti had played at a recording session of Byas's orchestra on June 12, 1947 (the two would play together again as members of various combos led by Roy Eldridge[16]), and was under a contract with the Bernard Hilda orchestra. While Byas had been able to keep himself busy after the Redman tour, the Hilda job offered him the prospect of steady work without extensive travel. Hilda was a Russian-born Jewish musician who had fled to Spain with members of his orchestra when the Nazis invaded France in 1942.[17] He had then signed with the Spanish record label Belter SL and established a name for himself as a bandleader.

Byas's sojourn with Hilda began on June 20, 1947,[18] at the Copacabana nightclub in Barcelona; Byas was listed as a featured artist on promotional materials (along with American singer Jane Morgan) in recognition of his stature as a master jazzman among journeymen. Hilda was a typical "front man" of the day, singing and playing violin; the band was "not a jazz orchestra, but rather a sophisticated ballroom ensemble, including a violin section."[19] According to Spanish jazz critic Alfredo Papo, Hilda never claimed that the music it played was jazz. (Byas apparently didn't fool Papo—or perhaps others—with his self-bestowed title of "Don"; throughout his article giving his highly favorable "*primeras impresiones*" (first impressions) of Byas, Papo put "Don" in quotation marks of doubt.) Byas arrived on the scene with high expectations in the minds of those who had read the glowing reviews of European critics who covered the 1946 tour with Don Redman. "When he picks up the sax to play a solo," Papo wrote, "he looks like a boy, a boy with a sweet and calm look. But suddenly, velvety flames come out of his instrument. . . . With an astonishing balance and tranquility, sinuous and warm phrases emerge from his sax of a prodigious richness."[20] Had he wanted to, it is apparent from his reception in Spain that Byas could have stayed there and had a successful career playing "sweet" music with Hilda, but—like Johnny Hodges, who had a standing offer to join Lawrence Welk's orchestra but always remained with Duke Ellington—he needed more room and jazz interest to settle down. "Despite the good arrangements and smooth style of the band, there is little room for soloists," Jordi Baulenas wrote of the Hilda orchestra; Byas was given "some space in numbers such as 'I Got Rhythm,' 'Always,' and 'My Man'" that the band recorded in August 1947 for (Spanish) Columbia records, but he was playing in a league below his level of talent.[21] After a few months, the Hilda orchestra moved from the Copacabana to the somewhat less luxurious Parilla nightclub in the Barcelona Ritz Hotel.[22]

On Wednesdays, when the evening's scheduled program ended, Byas and the Hilda rhythm section would jam with local musicians in sessions that would often last into the next morning. "A few of them were successful, others quite eventful," Papo wrote, "either because the police burst in at four in the morning, or because Don had been drinking a bit too much."[23] They were sometimes joined by a young pianist (at the time just fourteen) named Vicenç Montoliu i Massana "Tete" Montoliu, the son of a Barcelona symphonic woodwind player. Tete Montoliu was born blind in Catalonia, Spain, in 1933, and according to one source, Byas lived for a time with his family.[24] Montoliu's early work with Byas did not immediately result in notoriety for the younger man; he would go on to study music in Barcelona and jam with jazz musicians in that city's clubs and eventually play professionally there. Montoliu was noticed by Lionel Hampton one night playing in a pub and joined his band as it toured through Spain and France.[25]

Byas was also heard on Radio Barcelona playing with pianist Miguel Ramos and guitarist Georges Capitaine in the weekly program "Club de Hot," and he recorded in mid-August with the Hilda Orchestra, soloing on "Quisiera Saber," "Sonar En Ti," "Infiniment," and "Siempre Siempre."[26] "These are not jazz items," notes Jan Evensmo, "but pleasant dance music, and they could have easily been made a decade earlier. Nevertheless, [Byas] blows his brief soli nicely."[27] Byas's drinking caused his relationship with Hilda to deteriorate, however, and he was dismissed when he showed up drunk for a matinee performance at the Arenas cinema.[28] Byas remained in Barcelona following his dismissal, and on October 11, 1947, he recorded with Las Estrellas de Ritmo y Melodia (The Stars of Rhythm and Melody) for the Odeon record label along with fellow American George Johnson on alto sax. The session resulted in "Byas Jump," the "first number with a (slight) bebop flavor to be recorded in Spain,"[29] and "Janine," a torch song for a woman Byas had loved and left behind in Belgium. He was invited by the Salon Bolero to join its "Blanco y Negro" revue, and on October 24, he, along with Inez Cavanaugh, Timme Rosenkrantz's vocalist girlfriend, was added to the show.[30] As always, while in Barcelona, Byas sought out the challenge of afternoon jam sessions to slake his competitive thirst before a night's performance, first at the Bolero and later under the auspices of the Hot Club of Spain at the Saratoga and the Bar Oasis with local musicians, including Belgian pianist Vicky Thunus. Byas was particularly pleased with the playing of the latter, telling a reporter for *Ritmo y Melodia*, "Man, he's gone."[31]

Byas would move on to Madrid in January 1948, where he played gigs in restaurants with small groups, one of which—the "Sicilia-Molinero restaurant in Madrid"—was "a rather solemn and unlikely environment for the saxophonist."[32] A month later, Byas and his friend Louie Williams—a dancer and singer—played at the Madrigal, a Madrid tea salon (*tetería*). He then was added to Luis Rovira's orchestra for a residence at the Madrid "party hall" Pasapoga; Rovira would arrange recording dates while Byas was working for him, the first of which for Columbia resulted in "Chicago Boogie" (a Rovira original), "The Man I Love," "To Each His Own," and Byas's "Riffin' and Jivin." In April, two more sides were recorded: "Manana Sera Tarde" ("Tomorrow Will Be Too Late," but for some reason translated as "I Can't Get Up the Nerve to Kiss You"), and "La Pena de Perder" ("The Pain of Losing").[33] Byas also wrote a song for Rovira, "Azucar en el Café" ("Sugar in Coffee"), no recordings of which have been found by the author. Two numbers Byas recorded in Lisbon with Rovira—"Ai Mouraria" (referring to the Moorish quarter of Lisbon) and "Lisboa Antiga" ("Old Lisbon")—were traditional Portuguese songs and were outliers for Byas as he typically recorded only standards or jazz numbers. Portugal was then governed by União Nacional (National Union), the sole political party allowed to function at the time. The National Union was a nationalist group "set up to control and restrain public opinion," and while it was said by its leader António de Oliveira Salazar to be "the antithesis of a political party," it is possible that Rovira and his group were required to record these songs for patriotic reasons.[34]

In March 1948, Byas performed with Rovira's group at a jazz festival, III Festival de Jazz in Madrid at the Cine Proyecciones, and then the group gave a farewell performance at the Pasapoga in Madrid before returning to Barcelona. They remained there until October, playing at the Monterrey restaurant and the Club de Ritmo de Granollers (the Rhythm Club of Granollers, a city in central Catalonia about thirty kilometers northeast of Barcelona) before a month-long excursion into Portugal, where they made recordings and performed at Cinema Eden and the Chave d'Ouro in Lisbon, home base of the Hot Club de Portugal. After a short stay in Madrid, the group was back in Paris in December 1948.

Byas would return to Portugal two decades later, in 1968, to play at Luisiana Jazz Club in Cascais and at the 2nd Festival Internacional de Jazz at Teatro Avenida in Coimbra. During this trip, he would record an album of *fado*, a Portuguese musical form somewhat comparable to American blues, with singer Amália Rodrigues.[35] One source suggests that the album was his idea, saying, "In 1968, American sax tenor virtuoso Don Byas visited Lisbon and invited [Rodrigues] to revisit some of her classics in a duet with him on the sax," but this is doubtful; it is more likely that the session was organized with the singer in mind, Byas was invited to back her, and he took the job for the money.[36] While the album may appeal to fans of *fado*, the conventions of the genre—"a solo vocalist as central figure, instrumental accompanists and audiences in a communicative process using verbal, musical, facial and bodily expression"[37]—make the addition of embellishments by a tenor saxophone awkward. Byas does his best to emerge from behind the overwrought vocals, but Rodrigues deploys the conventions of the genre—namely, "mournful tunes and lyrics . . . about the life of the poor, and infused with a sentiment of resignation, fate, and melancholy"[38]—so powerfully that the poor 5'7" sax man in his midfifties is no match for her.

The Byases would return to Spain and live there in 1961, when "he had several engagements."[39] These included appearances in Madrid at the Whisky Jazz Club and I Festival Mundial de Jazz in Barcelona; a one-night stand at Teatro Calderón and a two-week residency at the Kit-Kat at the rate of 1,400 pesetas a night (roughly $165 at the time, and $1,680 in today's dollars);[40] a two-night stand at Teatro Calderon; and a three-week engagement at the Whisky Jazz Club in Tossa de Mar in August.[41] In each case except the last, Byas would work with pianist Tete Montoliu. Montoliu would say that Byas "encouraged me a lot and let me accompany him on the piano on many occasions. He never said it was terrible to play with me, although this surely must have been the case."[42] Montoliu was fascinated by Byas's sound and would reunite with him seven years later in Germany for his valedictory album with fellow tenor, friend, and rival Ben Webster called *Ben Webster Meets Don Byas*.[43] A reporter who caught up with Byas at his Madrid gig during this period said that the saxman was indulged by the owner, Jean-Louis Bourbon, with a case of cerveza kept under the bar that was available to him alone; paying customers were only offered more expensive spiritous liquors. Byas played with a Spanish rhythm section as "[a] few teenage couples necked desultorily beneath the soft red lighting." As he sipped his beer, Byas recalled that he had "started the ball rolling here in Spain . . . many years back." He was addressed with mock formality as "The Don," and before he took the stage after a break, predicted that "swing is coming back."[44]

CHAPTER 11

Paris Years

In late 1948, after he had made his final record in Spain, Don Byas moved to Paris, where he began to play with local musicians, both expatriates like himself and touring Americans. He became a familiar figure in Parisian nightclubs where a bartender named Henri Leduc taught him enough French slang to enable him to make time with the women he'd meet there.[1] Despite its occupation by the Nazis from June 1940 through August 1944, when World War II ended, Paris appeared much as it had before the war began; its infrastructure remained intact, having escaped both Allied bombing during the war and German sabotage during its liberation. Hitler had ordered that the city not fall into Allied hands "except as a field of ruins," but German General Dietrich von Choltitz defied his order and did not destroy bridges and landmarks; he said he did not want to go down in history as the man who destroyed the City of Light.[2]

Paris recovered despite the lack of assistance from the French national government, whose resources had been depleted by the war. Aided by the American Marshall Plan, Paris and the nation of France as a whole experienced a period of steady growth, and French record labels responded to increased consumer demand after the privations of the war years. "French record labels like Swing, Pathé, Blue Star, Odeon, Vogue and Royal Jazz thrived," and they "needed music, so they turned to many American jazz musicians who traveled to Paris after the war."[3] Among them was Don Byas.

The first sound of his sax to be preserved in France is from a radio broadcast leading a quartet with pianist Jack Diéval, altoist Hubert Fol, and an unknown drummer and bassist on the program *Jazz Parade* on Radiodiffusion Française ("RDF"), recorded December 26 and broadcast on December 29, 1948, from the Théâtre Edouard VII in Paris. He then hooked up with trumpeter Bill Coleman, who had arrived in Paris with $100, which he promptly lost when he left it in the pocket of a suit he sent out to be cleaned. Coleman had previously lived in Paris from 1936 to 1939, so he knew his way around; he obtained an advance from Charles Delaunay, the French jazz scholar and promoter who was booking him, and managed to survive until he could begin to work.[4]

On January 4 and 5, 1949, Coleman and Byas participated in two recording sessions, the first for the Jazz Selection label and the second for the Swing label, founded by Delaunay; these were Coleman's first recordings in France since 1938. The musicians, in addition to the two Americans, were Bernard Peiffer on piano, Roger Paraboschi on drums, and Jean Bouchéty on bass. The following day, Coleman and Byas played on RDF as part of a group called "Edward's Jazz Band," named after one of the annexes at the Théâtre Edouard VII; it was comprised of the musicians assembled for the Jazz Selection and Swing recording sessions, plus Michel de Villers on alto sax and Georges "Géo" Daly on vibraphone.[5] The records Byas cut for the Swing label sold well; an account statement for the first half of 1947 reflects royalties of 4,777 French francs, approximately $5,363 in US dollars at the time; adjusted for inflation, this amount would be $72,500.

The Hot Club de France helped the group find bookings in "the most important cities in France," and they went on tour, "playing to packed houses," according to Coleman. "The reception was great, the applause terrific . . . . Some jazz fans were following the band from town to town."[6] The tour was extended to Belgium, Switzerland, and Germany, where Coleman and Byas encountered some trouble when an American military policeman ("MP") in Bremen told them they had to leave the area because it was off-limits. Coleman questioned the MP's interpretation of the regulation as he thought that "off-limits" rules applied only to military personnel, not civilians. When the MP remained firm, Coleman told him he "was going to see about it." "Alright, you can see about it now," the MP said and told Coleman and Byas to come with him. Byas objected since he hadn't said anything, but the MP insisted, saying, "Yes, you come along, too." The two were taken in a Jeep to

US military headquarters, where they were detained and questioned, then informed that "off-limits" applied to both military personnel and civilians. After they were released, Coleman said, "Don was really salty with me."[7]

Coleman and Byas—along with various combinations of the other musicians that made up The Edwards Jazz Band—kept up a busy schedule for the first five months of 1949, in Strasbourg, France, on January 14 at the Palais des Fêtes, then on to Switzerland, where in Zurich they played at the Kongresshaus, in Geneva at Victoria Hall, and in Lausanne at the Théâtre Bel-Air, a concert broadcast by Swiss Radio and released as part of the *Swiss Radio Days* archive collection.[8] From there, the group went to Knokke, Belgium, to play for three days in April, where they were on the bill at the casino with several variety acts. These included the Nicholas Brothers dance team, Borrah Minevitch's Harmonica Vagabonds, and a troupe of burlesque dancers from a cabaret on the Champs-Élysées in Paris—known as the "Bluebell Girls"—who proved to be too much of a temptation for Byas. "Don was high and in the process of changing his clothes" when "he decided to chase one of the Bluebell Girls," Coleman recalled. Wearing just his undershorts, Byas went after her at a moment when "the director of the casino happened to be in the hallway of the dressing rooms. He gave Don hell and that killed the chances for us and the band to have a contract for the summer season."[9]

Throughout this period, Byas and Coleman continued to play dates as headliners and to record apart from the Edwards Jazz Band. In February 1949, Coleman was joined by Rex Stewart, Duke Ellington's trumpeter, for a concert at Théâtre Edouard VII with a new cast of French musicians that included Aimé Barelli, reputed to be "the best trumpet man in France. "I believed it when I heard him play," Coleman said, "for he had a big sound, and a touch of Armstrong in his phrasing."[10] On March 3, 1949, Byas performed on an RTF program with a quartet that included Jacques Diéval on piano, Bernard Spieler on bass, and Richie Frost on drums that was recorded for the program *Jeunesse du Jazz*. In the second week of May 1949, both Coleman and Byas appeared at a jazz festival (the Grand Semaine du Jazz) organized by Charles Delaunay in Paris. The event was designed as a sort of United Nations of Jazz and included musicians from a number of different countries, such as Belgium, Sweden, England, Switzerland, and France. Besides Byas and Coleman, America was represented by Sidney Bechet, Charlie Parker, Hot Lips Page, Max Roach, Miles Davis, James Moody, and Kenny Clarke, among others. Byas and Hot Lips Page performed together as coleaders of a septet on several dates in May, and "Byas's solos brought the audience to its feet yelling for more," said a review by pianist Marian McPartland in *DownBeat*.[11] In addition to separate performances by the various acts, there was a jam session among musicians from different countries, a sort of battle royale that seventeen men participated in, including Byas, Charlie Parker, Miles Davis, Sidney Bechet, and Max Roach from America; Jean "Toots" Thielemans from Belgium; and clarinetist Hubert Rostaing from France. After the festival ended, the Edward's Jazz Band was booked into the Vieux Colombier, a club on Paris's Left Bank, but (according to Coleman), "[i]t didn't last long" and "[t]he band broke up after that engagement."[12]

Byas began to play in Parisian nightspots such as Ringside, opened in 1950 and associated with boxer Sugar Ray Robinson,[13] where "you can dance to real gone music," according to a reporter for the *Baltimore Afro-American* advising "black travelers to Europe."[14] Byas recalled that the "'Ringside' club was the big thing . . . modern jazz seven nights a week. That's where it all blossomed. In those days France was the most jazz-minded country in Europe." With characteristic immodesty, Byas said he "was practically responsible for the Paris jazz scene."[15] Byas played there in 1951 with saxophonist James Moody and singer Al "Fats" Edwards when the three Americans were hired to "*renforcer l'orchestre maison*" (reinforce the house band).[16] Trumpeter Buck Clayton remembered his work in 1953 with Byas at the club under successor management in detail:

> I wasn't long in Paris before I was asked to appear at the Blue Note, a jazz club that had been at one time under the direction of the manager of Sugar Ray Robinson. . . . The Blue Note was situated near the Eiffel Tower and was very popular. I was happy to go in there and I signed to go in with Don Byas, Kansas Fields, Pierre Michelot, and Raymond and Hubert Fol, two talented brothers. Mary Lou Williams was playing in a club very near and she would come in some nights and jam with us.[17]

Byas became a regular feature at Saint-Germain-des-Prés, a basement nightclub located at 13 Rue Saint-Benoît memorialized by American humorist Art Buchwald as "one of the famous Left Bank *caves* that one time was supposed to have been haunted by existentialists. There may not be any more existentialists left, but you'll see some fancy jitterbugging by French students. And you'll either be driven out into the street, or right on to the floor, by the loud jazz music."[18] "A lot of good [French] jazzmen came up there," Byas said. "Bernard Peiffer, René Urtreger and Pierre Michelot. But I was the main attraction—they couldn't have made it by themselves."[19] He continued to record as well: on July 7, 1949, he joined fellow tenor sax James Moody, pianist Bernard Peiffer and drummer Richie Frost as the James Moody–Don Byas quartet to record two numbers on the Blue Star label founded by producer Eddie Barclay (*nom de jazz* of Édouard Ruault); the pieces—"Verso (Blue Part I)" and "Recto (Blue Part II)"—were used in the soundtrack of the movie *Une Nuit à Saint-Germain-des-Prés*. Sometime during the summer of 1949, he played with Tony Proteau and His Orchestra on "Autour d'un Récif" ("Around a Reef"), a piece in two parts composed by French jazz critic and composer André Hodeir that was used in the soundtrack of a documentary directed by French oceanographer Jacques Cousteau. (According to one account, when Byas saw the tenor sax part that Hodeir had written for him, he said, "That's a part for a piccolo!"[20]) Finally, on October 10, Byas was a part of the Buck Clayton Sextet that recorded five numbers for the Royal Jazz label, including a Byas composition, "Don's Blues."[21]

On April 12, 1950, Byas was added to the Duke Ellington Orchestra as a "featured soloist" for its European tour after Charlie Rouse left the group.[22] The tour lasted until June 10, where it concluded with a performance at Ernst–Merck–Halle in Hamburg, Germany, and included two stops in the Netherlands: April 28 at Gebouw voor K. & W. in The Hague and April 30 at the Concertgebouw in Amsterdam.[23] With the exception of dates in Casablanca, Morocco, and Mulhouse, France,[24] that he had previously agreed to play, Byas would be with the Ellington band for the duration of the tour. (In Casablanca, Byas was said to have competed against tenor sax Jules "Julio" Pamies in a jam session—for an ox.[25]) Trombonist Lawrence Brown had high praise for Byas, saying, "[T]ruthfully, Don Byas was second attraction to that whole band. He played so much tenor that it was a shame, we should've left him home! Yeah, he really took over."[26] Brown's assessment was shared by audiences who reportedly responded to Byas's solos with "tremendous applause."[27]

In 1951, Byas teamed up with Roy "Little Jazz" Eldridge in Paris on several occasions. Eldridge was a Pittsburgh native who, like many jazz musicians of his era from the vast area west of the Appalachian Mountains and east of the Rockies, got his start playing with traveling carnivals. He graduated to the bands of Horace Henderson, Fletcher Henderson's brother, and a number of bands lost to jazz history, such as Oliver Muldoon, Zach Whyte, and Speed Webb, as well as a group he led under the pseudonym "Roy Elliott." Eldridge first arrived in New York in 1930 and played with the bands of Cecil Scott, Elmer Snowden, Charlie Johnson, Teddy Hill, Fletcher Henderson, and McKinney's Cotton Pickers. Eldridge left the music business in 1938 to study radio engineering, returned to play for a brief stint with Mal Hallett, and then formed his own band.

After this long period as a journeyman, Eldridge came to national prominence as a member of Gene Krupa's band in 1941, and then when that group broke up in 1943, he became a member of CBS Radio's in-house band, played with Mildred Bailey, toured with Artie Shaw, and then led various groups of his own before reuniting with Krupa in 1949. He came to Europe as a member of the Benny Goodman sextet in 1950 and remained on the Continent for eighteen months, playing concerts with Sidney Bechet before connecting with Byas.[28] The two played together at Club Saint-Germain-des-Prés on March 20, when Eldridge was guest soloist with pianist Claude Bolling's band; Byas was at first present only as master of ceremonies, but toward the end of the gig, Eldridge invited him to sit in. On March 28, Byas was part of the Roy Eldridge Quintet that cut four songs for the Vogue label, along with Bolling and his rhythm section of Armand Molinetti on drums and Guy de Fatto on bass. The two appear with pianist Claude Bolling in a short film made in early 1951—"Autour d'une Trompette" ("Around a Trumpet")[29]—and were part of an all-star jam session at the Palais des Beaux-Arts in Brussels that included James Moody on tenor, Kenny Clarke on drums, and local musicians.[30]

While he continued to freelance with groups such as the Saratoga Jazz Hounds and Nelson Williams' All Stars, Byas was sufficiently established on the Continent by this time to be invited to play at most European jazz festivals and to secure recording contracts under his own name, leading groups styled either as his orchestra or a combo that went by the name "Don Byas et Ses Rythmes" (and His Beats). The orchestra recorded for the Blue Star label in April 1951, and the Beats recorded first for Vogue and later Blue Star.[31] Byas was already known for his lush approach to ballads, but at least one critic (Marc Myers) is of the view that "once Byas was liberated from American labels and their formulaic A&R men, he was free to be himself, to record as he pleased. The result was a long stretch of beautiful, passionate ballad playing."[32] When looked at from another perspective, it may be more accurate to say that French producers, knowing their customers, were inclined to emphasize

Byas's romantic side. As the *Baltimore Afro-American* told its readers who were thinking of visiting France, "Don't get excited when you see a couple locked in each other's arms in the street. It doesn't mean what you think. The French just like to kiss—and don't stop to pick time nor place."[33] French jazz critics sometimes took a purist line and "rebuked [Byas's] taste for attractive melodies, and also criticized his sidemen for their discretion, although they hadn't been asked for anything more than support."[34] The reaction in America was similar; an unsigned review in *DownBeat* found the music from a 1947 Blue Star recording date to be "undistinguished" and said, "[T]he occasionally able Byas has rarely sounded more competently dull than on this set."[35] As is usually the case, the reviews had no effect on his records' sales, but Byas didn't need the goad of criticism to explore new territory.

When he wasn't leading his own group, Byas reconnected with Dizzy Gillespie as a member of the latter's quintet (March 27 and April 6, 1952), sextet (March 25, 1952), septet (April 7–8, 1952) and octet (March 29–30, 1952), the last-named at the second Salon International du Jazz in Paris.[36] The recordings are reflective of Gillespie's fondness for Latin music. "I always had a feeling for Latin American music,"[37] he said in his autobiography, and on several of these sessions, he added Humberto "Canto" Morales on congas.[38] That said, the song "Sabla y Blu" ("Sandy and Blue") is a mock Spanish transliteration of its scat-sung bop refrain ("Sa-blue-E-Be Blue"), rather than an actual phrase from the Romance language. In April 1952, Byas would travel to Italy, playing in Bergamo, Milan, and Turin as part of Gillespie's Octet, and would record with Gillespie's Septet in Paris at Schola Cantorum; the latter was probably the most unlikely studio the two would ever play in as the school was founded in 1894 to provide instruction in sacred music, particularly plainsong such as Gregorian chant, although it later developed into a general music conservatory.[39]

While Byas's "Beats" often included Americans on rhythm instruments (Benny Bennett, Bill Clark, or Richie Frost on drums, Art Simmons on piano, and Joe Benjamin on bass), he had to rely on European musicians to fill out the group, leading some to assert that his work suffered as a result. His obituary in *DownBeat* said that "Byas' European recordings mainly presented him as a ballad soloist, often with indifferent accompaniment,"[40] but it wasn't so much the melodic instruments as the rhythm sections that his later work suffered from. "Truthfully," he confessed in a 1965 interview, "the only thing I miss [after having lived overseas for two decades] are those American rhythm sections." In answer to the question, "After all these years, how does" he "get on with Continental accompanists?" he responded:

> Well, it's always a bit of a drag having to play with different sections all the time. It takes a while for a section to get together, to get to feel each other, even for top American musicians. If you have to change sections each job you do, as I have to very often, it makes the work more difficult. And I find that the European rhythm sections are not up to par with American sections.
>
> This isn't because they're not accomplished musicians individually. But they don't seem to be able to play collectively as a group. American rhythm sections do play together, and this gives you a chance to get something going. The point is that American rhythm sections, if they're good, don't have to have been playing together before.[41]

Decoding Byas's diplomatic rhetoric into straightforward language, one can safely assign to the term "American" the connotation "African American" and to "European," "Caucasian." When he said this, discussions of jazz had begun to hide behind euphemisms that only six years before would have been recognized as doublespeak. In 1956, when *The Dictionary of Jazz* by Hugues Panassié and Madeleine Gautier was first published in English, translator Desmond Flowers said in his prefatory note, "The cool musicians of today will not be found in the pages of this Dictionary. As M. Panassié makes clear in the lengthy critical entries in this book, jazz means for him the music of the American Negro," and accordingly, "[a]ll musicians given an entry in this Dictionary are of the Negro race unless stated to the contrary."[42] There was probably no need for Byas to be so circumspect as the readers of *Melody Maker*, the publication that employed the interviewer, no doubt saw through his ruse and wouldn't have cared if he'd been more forthright. As his widow said, however, he was "a man who was not at all aware of his race," and so he may have gone out of his way to express his views in a color-blind manner to avoid giving offense. As to how Byas coped with the different feel of the two types of rhythm sections, he said, "[T]he way I overcome that is by kind of holding myself back and not doing things that might be too difficult, which is not good, of course, but that's the only way to do it."[43]

In the summertime, Byas limited his schedule to jobs in Saint-Tropez on the French Riviera from his first arrival in France until 1961.[44] He became a fixture at a nightclub founded by Boris Vian in 1949 as Club Saint-Germain-des-Prés-La

Ponche (after the Club Saint-Germain-des-Prés in Paris and the La Ponche neighborhood of St. Tropez), which was later renamed Le Tropicana. Byas's widow described the place as "an expensive nightclub," although from photos, it does not appear to be particularly luxurious. While in St. Tropez, she said, he "was working until 4 o'clock in the morning, rested a bit and was in the water for the rest of the day," indulging his enthusiasm for swimming, fishing, and diving. "Don loved underwater fishing," she said.[45] For Byas, Saint-Tropez became a place where he could combine work and play; "every summer," his wife said, "four months, blowing in the sun."[46]

Byas would appear in a French documentary, *Jazz Jamboree*, of the 1953 Festival International des Arénes de Lutèce in Paris. In the film, directed by Jean-Pierre Richard and Edgar and Georges Roulleau, Byas plays "Lady Be Good" with alto sax player Michel Attenoux and his orchestra. Sidney Bechet gets top billing, with Attenoux and other French musicians (André Réwéliotty, Claude Luter, Raymond Fol, and Bernard Zacharias) getting subordinate credits, but Byas isn't mentioned in the movie database listing.[47] Bechet had moved to Paris in September 1925 to perform in *Revue Nègre* with Josephine Baker and remained there until 1929, when he was convicted of shooting three people in a failed attempt to hit banjoist Gilbert "Little Mike" McKendrick on December 20, 1928. Bechet was arrested and sentenced to prison and returned to America after he was released. When he returned to France in 1949, he played the role of jazz's "patron saint," helping young European musicians learn New Orleans–style music as part of a revival of traditional jazz, and it was at this time that he got to know Byas. In June 1951, Bechet was on his way to a music festival in Clamart, a few miles south of Paris, when he injured his head in a car accident. Byas was "called on to deputize at the festival, but after a few days' rest, Bechet was back in action."[48] There is a bust of Bechet in Juan-les-Pins, Antibes, on the French Riviera, erected in 1960 and thought to be the first public monument to a jazz musician in the world, so the producers of *Jazz Jamboree* can be forgiven if they placed him ahead of Byas in the film's credits, as he had a prior claim on the affections of the French. When Bechet died in Paris in 1959, Byas was among a group that included tenor Lucky Thompson and drummer Kansas Fields that mourned him at Gabby & Haynes, a Black-owned American restaurant in Paris and a popular hangout for jazz musicians.[49]

In 1953, Byas recorded with Tony Proteau and his orchestra and this time, the influence was genuine, with all titles rendered *en Français* as compared to the *faux*-Spanish bebop jive of Dizzy Gillespie's "Sabla y Blu." One critic called the Byas–Proteau collaboration "an ambitious orchestra with rather sophisticated arrangements" while noting that the "sophistication tips over into artificialness."[50] In December of that year, Byas would reunite for a second and last time with Mary Lou Williams in Paris to record an album on the Vogue label with Alvin "Buddy" Banks on bass and Gérard "Dave" Pochonet on drums as "The Mary Williams Quartet featuring Don Byas." It was, says Williams's biographer Linda Dahl, "arguably the best recording of her stay in Europe, with Don Byas providing sweet-and-sour poetry with his tenor saxophone on her bop blues 'O. W.' and on a softly shimmering duet in the yearningly lovely ballad 'Why?'" (Williams would subsequently use "O. W."—whose meaning is unknown—as the introduction for her "Mass for Peace," also known as "Mary Lou's Mass," surely the most unusual Introit in the history of the Roman Catholic Church.) For Williams, it was a time of transition; in 1954, she walked out of a gig at Le Boeuf sur le Toit, a Parisian club that had been a center of intellectual life in the 1920s but that had lost its former cachet. "I just stopped playing," she would say much later, leaving her purse on the counter along with her fee for the night. Dave Pochonet, who was in love with Williams, was not playing drums that night but was with her. He returned to the club, retrieved her belongings, then persuaded her to leave her hectic life in Paris and join him at his grandmother's house in the French countryside. She would subsequently convert to Catholicism and, for a time, withdraw from the jazz scene to write sacred music. Dahl notes that "there was a sheen of sadness that overlaid the recording" of the album, "an accurate reading of Mary's state of mind."[51] She was troubled by many things in her life at the time; the debts and taxes she owed, the recent deaths of Charlie Parker and her gay expatriate friend pianist Garland Wilson among them, so the presence of Byas—the former lover with whom she'd had a stormy affair—should not be viewed as a proximate cause of her distress. That she and he had reconciled is, if anything, confirmed by the fact that, as Dave Dexter put it in his liner notes to the album, "on six of the songs she insisted that Byas be showcased more prominently than she."[52]

Byas would wrap up his time as a resident of Paris recording with French pianist and singer Beryl Booker and playing radio dates with Swiss pianist Géo Voumard. There were also more small group sessions with his "rythmes" comprised of an interchangeable cast of characters that included Martial Solal and Maurice Vander on piano; Pierre Michelot on bass; Pierre

Lemarchand, Roger Paraboschi, or Benny Bennett on drums, and "Fats" Sadi Pol Lallemand on vibes.[53] The pattern for the rest of his musical career took shape: while he would sometimes record with other leaders' groups, ranging in size from small combos to big bands and orchestras, in person, he would work "mainly as a single in jazz clubs throughout Europe."[54] He was a loner and a man always on the move; too mercurial to last long with any one employer, too restless to form a band of his own that would remain together for more than a few recording sessions.

The next phase of his life was about to begin, as he would move to Amsterdam to be with the woman he loved.

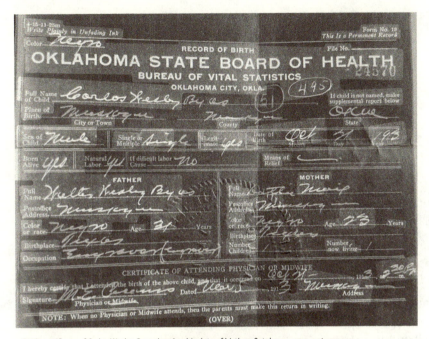

1. Birth certificate of Carlos Wesley Byas showing his date of birth as October 21, 1913, not 1912.

2. Carlos Wesley Byas, far right, with his mother—Dottie Mae Weaver Byas—holding her youngest son, Walter Jackson ("Jack") Byas. Her second son, Vincent ("Vint") Weaver Byas, is seated on the stairs to the left. The other woman in the picture is probably Dottie Mae's sister, Bernice I. Jones; Dottie Mae had two other sisters, but Bernice Jones was the only one who continued to live in Muskogee, Oklahoma. Taken after August 1918, when Walter was born. Courtesy of Nederlands Jazz Archief.

3. Walter Wesley Byas, Don Byas's father, in his jeweler's shop. Courtesy of Nederlands Jazz Archief.

4. Dottie Mae Weaver Byas. Courtesy of Nederlands Jazz Archief.

5. Carlos Wesley Byas in elementary school; he is the third from the left in the bottom row. Courtesy of Nederlands Jazz Archief.

Photo of Carlos Wesley Byas's 1930 graduating class from Manual Training High School. He is the second from the right in the top row; name is misspelled "Byars." Courtesy of Oklahoma Historical Society.

7. Byas (first name given as "Donald") shown as a member of Eddie Mallory's Orchestra, *New York Amsterdam News*, February 12, 1938. Courtesy of New York Public Library.

8. Don as a member of Andy Kirk and His Clouds of Joy playing at Skidmore College's "Beaux Arts Ball" in February 1939. George S. Bolst Collection, Department of Special Collections, Lucy Scribner Library, Skidmore College.

9. Don Byas and Dick Wilson in a publicity photo when they played in Andy Kirk's orchestra. Felix E. Grant Jazz Archives, University of the District of Columbia.

10. Don Byas and Dizzy Gillespie pick out ties to clash appropriately with their hats. Courtesy of Nederlands Jazz Archief.

11. The Don Byas Sextet at the Verona Café, Brooklyn, New York, January 1946 (Herbert Hawkins photo). The other musicians are Sylvester "Ves" Payne (drums), Scoville Brown (clarinet), Leonard Gaskin (bass), and Bud Powell (not shown, piano). Leonard and Mary Gaskin Papers, 1923–2006, Archives Center, National Museum of American History, Smithsonian Institution.

12. Byas backing Dinah Washington at the Brooklyn Academy of Music, Spring 1946. The other musicians are Sylvester "Ves" Payne, Bud Powell (piano), Leonard Gaskin (bass), Scoville Brown (clarinet), and Leonard Hawkins (trumpet). Leonard and Mary Gaskin Papers, 1923–2006, Archives Center, National Museum of American History, Smithsonian Institution.

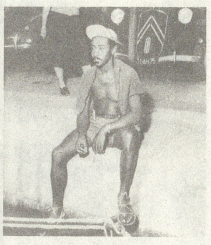

Sur la Ponche et dans les alentours, Don Byas est admiré pour deux raisons : La première, sa valeur de saxophoniste et ses qualités de pêcheur sous-marin. Si sur son instrument il grimpe au plus haut de la gamme, il ne craint pas de descendre au plus profond des gouffres méditerranéens. Une nuit après son travail au « Club » où il fait be-boper les transfuges de Saint-Germain-des-Prés, on l'occusa d'avoir voulu violer Tabou, une explosive beauté blonde à la chevelure garçonnière. Sur plainte des « Forbans », la police enquêta. On interrogea la victime. En réponse elle éclata de rire. « Si j'ai poussé de grands cris dans la rue, c'est que Don me chatouillait dans le dos. »

3. Photo of Byas from *V-Magazine*, September 23, 1951, recounting an incident in which he tickled a woman in the street. Courtesy of Nederlands Jazz Archief.

14. Byas performing at Sheherazade Club, Amsterdam, probably October 1952. On trumpet is Frank Williams, and on bass is Dick Bezemer. It was at this club that Byas met Johanna "Jopie" Eksteen. Courtesy of Nederlands Jazz Archief.

15. Byas's membership card in Club des Chasseurs Sous-Marin de France, 1952. Courtesy of Nederlands Jazz Archief.

16. Byas and Johanna "Jopie" Eksteen on their wedding day, February 16, 1955, Amsterdam. Courtesy of Nederlands Jazz Archief.

Byas in Amsterdam, date unknown. Courtesy of Nederlands Jazz Archief.

Operating a snowblower at a resort in Megève, the French Alps. Courtesy of Nederlands Jazz Archief.

19. Byas and Stuff Smith with the Rose Princess of the Molde Jazz Festival, Norway, August 6, 1966. Courtesy of AB Fable Archive.

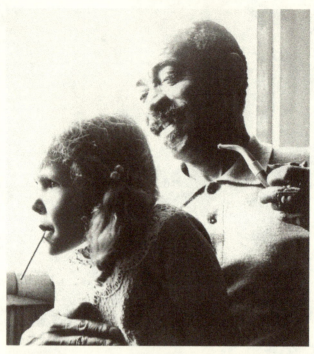

20. Byas at home with his daughter, Carlotta. Courtesy of Nederlands Jazz Archief.

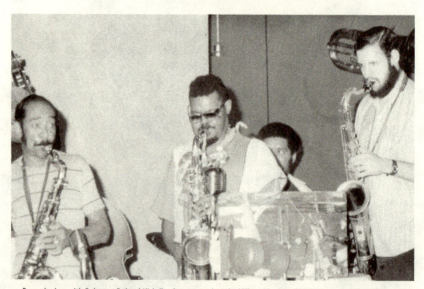

21. Byas playing with Rahsaan Roland Kirk (both tenor sax) at the Village Vanguard in August 1970. The other musicians visible in the photo are Sonny Brown (drums) and Peter Arthur Loeb (tenor sax). Photo by Neal Graham. Courtesy of Nederlands Jazz Archief.

22. Byas, late in life. Courtesy of Nederlands Jazz Archief.

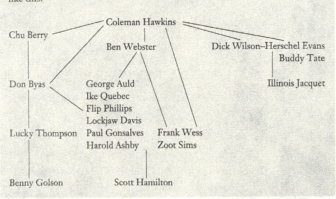

23. Chart by Whitney Balliett, jazz critic for *The New Yorker*, tracing the evolution of the tenor saxophone and Don Byas's direct descent from Coleman Hawkins, from *Whitney Balliett: Collected Works: A Journal of Jazz, 1954–2000*. Courtesy of the estate of Nancy Balliett.

24. A panel from Lionel Pailler's "bande dessinée" (comic strip) about Byas: he is shown in a bar complaining, "Everyone wants to hear my 'Laura'!" From *Don Byas* by Lionel Pailler (BD Music, 2015).

25. Byas and Ben Webster, drinking and having a good time. Copyright 1972, Estate of Sepp Werkmeister.

CHAPTER 12

Amsterdam Years

Don Byas met Johanna Eksteen in 1954[1] when he was living in Paris but playing dates outside of France. The first appearance on his tour was at the Stadtcasino in Basel, Switzerland, on April 21, then on to a performance at the Concertgebouw in Amsterdam on April 28 as The Don Byas Quartet opened for Nat "King" Cole. Byas was backed by Wally Bishop on drums, Cees Slinger on piano, and Henk de Jong on bass in the first set. Slinger and de Jong were late substitutions because Byas's regular sidemen on their instruments—Art Simmons and Alvin "Buddy" Banks, respectively—were stuck in Paris due to a railway strike, but they arrived in time for the second set. The main attraction on the bill was Cole, who, while he started as a pianist playing in small jazz combos, had by that time become "an international show business name" on the strength of his singing.[2] Cole was backed by John Collins on guitar, Charles Harris on bass, and Lee Young, Lester Young's brother, on drums.

Following that gig—and before he was due in Paris for the Salon International du Jazz at Salle Pleyel in the first week of June—Byas played several dates arranged by promoter Lou van Rees at the Sheherazade and Hollywood clubs in Amsterdam. At the former club, he met Johanna Eksteen, known to friends as "Jopie," a familiar form for "Johanna" in Dutch. She was born in Amsterdam on May 28, 1928, and was thus approximately twenty-six years of age—around fourteen and a half years younger than Byas. She had been seventeen when World War II ended and "dove into the bustling nightlife of Amsterdam" after five years of German occupation. She worked at the Filmtheater Desmet in Amsterdam and, after work, would go out with friends to jazz clubs. She enjoyed hearing the band of Piet van Dijk, a saxophonist, which included trumpeter Ado Broodboom,[3] and she would dance to the music of Kid Dynamite, the stage name of Lodewijk Rudolf Arthur Parisius, a Surinamese/Dutch tenor saxophonist who played both jazz and Surinamese "kaseko" music, a rhythmically complex genre with instrumentation similar to that of a small American jazz combo.[4] She would listen to jazz on the American Forces Network when she got home each night—"Real jazz until three or four in the morning," she recalled.[5]

Jopie said that she went to Sheherazade with a male friend when they heard that Byas was playing there. Don saw the two and asked the boy if Jopie was his girlfriend; when he was told that they were just friends, he made his move.[6] At intermission, while waiting at the ladies' room, Jopie met Byas as he was standing "at the cloak-room." Byas asked her if she would like "to go upstairs afterwards," and Jopie declined—vehemently. "[A]re you crazy, of course not," she replied, because she'd "always thought that upstairs [at Sheherazade] was some kind of brothel, but it was just used for having a drink after the gig." Despite rebuffing Byas's first pickup attempt, Jopie returned the next night and, this time, accepted Byas's invitation. "I thought, gee, I'm right here with the crème de la crème, everything you only dream of," she said. When the Sheherazade gig ended, Byas found work at another Amsterdam club, enabling him to prolong his stay in the city, then went on to a gig in Groningen, about ninety miles away. When he received an offer to play a three-month tour of Germany, he asked Jopie to go with him. What, exactly, was he proposing, she wondered; "Courtship? Engagement?" She had "to laugh heartily at this" and concluded it was "mostly adventure"[7]—but she was up for it. She joined Byas for a job in Hilversum, about twenty miles southeast of Amsterdam, then went on to Germany.[8]

As to why Jopie won Byas's heart where others before her didn't, a constellation of factors may have contributed to their attraction to each other and to their marriage, which lasted his lifetime. Like Byas, Jopie came from a modest background; her father was a captain on the Baltic Sea with an accent that reflected his upbringing in Zwolle; he "spoke an 'h' where it didn't belong and let the 'h' drop away where it should have been," according to a 1993 magazine article. She was short, like Byas, and thus fit the conventional model by which a man should be as tall or taller than his mate. She was blonde and attractive, and she was already a fan; at the time they met, she "had all his records," Jopie recalled. "I also had many by other musicians, but of Don I had almost everything."[9] Thus, on the night they met, she "went [to Sheherazade] and only had eyes for Don."[10]

The couple made Paris their home base at first, but they spent much of the first years of their lives together on the road, traveling from one job to the next. "We had a wild life, but we also spent a lot of time in hotels in Paris," Jopie said, as well as private clubs. "It was like being an emigrant. One had to take everything with you all the time, winter clothing, summer clothing, records. And pack and unpack every time."[11] A notice in a Dutch newspaper described the couple's nomadic calendar: in the winter, they lived in the "French wintersport centre Megève"; in the summer, they could be found in Saint-Tropez; in the spring and autumn, they were back in Amsterdam.[12] In addition, there were gigs in Alpe d'Huez, in France, where Byas tried curling one winter, and in Saint-Tropez, where he went skin-diving around the pirate ship used in the Errol Flynn movie *Captain Blood*, among other adventures. When in these vacation spots, Byas's workload wasn't always rigorous; he would sometimes play short jazz sets as the headliner, alternating with a band that provided music more suitable for dancing.

When the couple was living in Paris, Byas said he "was earning only enough to pay the hotel and food bills," and "both he and his wife were strangers" there,[13] so they decided to move to Amsterdam. On stationery of the Hotel Sèvres Vaneau, 86 Rue Vaneau in Paris, Jopie Byas wrote out a list of common expressions in Dutch for her husband to study in preparation for the move, including "Where have you been?" ("Waar ben je geweest?"), perhaps anticipating that there would be nights when he would not come straight home from a gig, and "What do we have for dinner?" ("Wat eten we?"), a question she had no doubt heard before and knew he would ask in the future. An official Dutch document relating to Jopie indicates that she began living at 145 Elandsstraat, Amsterdam, 1st floor, in May 1954, after spending a year in Paris, and that the couple married on February 16, 1955, in Amsterdam. A similar document for Don indicates that he moved into the apartment in March 1955.[14] In addition to his marriage, February was a busy month for the groom; he played in Geneva at the Grand Casino and at La Tour with le Quartet Michel Gaudry, as well as performances in The Hague at Gebouw voor Kunsten en Wetenschappen and at Concertgebouw, Amsterdam, with the rhythm section of the Tony Vos Quartet.[15] A column from a correspondent in France that appeared in a Baltimore newspaper in October 1955 said, "Don Byas hasn't been seen around in a year," bemoaning the fact that many American jazzmen couldn't find enough work in Paris to keep themselves busy and had to go on the road to Switzerland and Denmark.[16]

Jopie Eksteen's apartment was located in the Jordaan, a neighborhood known then and now for its lively music scene; an annual festival there honors the neighborhood's musical tradition, and at the intersection of Elandsstraat with the Prinsengracht, there are memorials to five local pop musicians[17] (but so far none for Byas). Originally an older working-class neighborhood, the Jordaan has been gentrified over the years as property values rose and working-class residents moved out. It is now one of the most expensive residential areas in Amsterdam, but when Don and Jopie lived there, it was still bohemian—one could hear *arias* sung out apartment windows—and affordable for a musician with an irregular income and a young wife who is only known to have worked in low-wage jobs. Their first apartment was on the first floor, rear, of 145 Elandsstraat, and they would move to a presumably nicer space on the third floor in the front of that building in January 1956.[18] Except for a one-month period from August to September 1960, when they listed their address as "Monte Carlo, Monaco," this is where they would live for the next decade. The third-floor apartment was described as small but homey by a reporter who visited it in the spring of 1963: "The living room is occupied by a pair of huge red-plush armchairs and a self-built bar. On the wall hang a number of woodcuts, which Byas makes in his spare time." Byas said that he had good relations with his in-laws: "My wife's family are always stopping by in our apartment to play cards or watch TV," he told a reporter in 1967.[19]

Byas had a reputation as a difficult person to deal with as a performer, but this trait does not appear to have carried over into his private life with Jopie. Ronnie Scott, London jazz club owner, said of Byas that he was "a man endowed with an epic kind of arrogance" and paired him with Lucky Thompson, who resembled him in this and other respects: "Lucky Thompson and Don Byas could be difficult, but they were such great players that you learned to live with their outsize egos and prickly temperaments."[20] In Scott's view, sometimes the high-handed attitudes of American musicians were justified: "Generally speaking, the Americans were entitled to act in a superior way, because many of them *were* musically superior to their European colleagues; but there were certain American jazzmen who clearly took a delight in humiliating European rhythm section players and who seemed more concerned to swagger and to emphasise the discrepancy between their playing and that of their accompanists than to achieve a musical compromise."[21] Scott's view of Byas may be colored by the labor-management mold that necessarily shaped their relationship; pianist Billy Taylor, eight years younger than Byas, called him "one of the great musicians who were working" in New York when he first came on the scene who "buoyed" his spirits: "You ask if I was accepted? They were so supportive . . . they knew about swinging . . . that's the kind of music that led into bebop. Prez and Don Byas and people like that, and they were very like Dizzy, they were very quick to show us, all of us, not just me, what they thought was correct."[22]

Jopie Byas described her husband as "charitable" and slower to anger than other American musicians whom she had encountered. "Don was always nice socially, kind and friendly,"[23] she said. By contrast, she had "seen other blacks," according to Igor Cornelissen, "who, if the piano was out of tune, immediately started bleating"—but not her husband.[24] On another occasion, she would acknowledge that others had formed an unfavorable impression of her husband and that it might even be somewhat justified: "When we were in France they used to say that sometimes, but it wasn't true. I never noticed anything like it. Perhaps people were jealous—although a little bit of arrogance wasn't strange to him."[25] Dutch musicians who played with Byas said he was easygoing—perhaps because he had mellowed in his later years. Drummer John Engels "played many times with Don Byas" and said the two "got along very well with each other musically."[26] Eric Ineke, another Dutch drummer, said Byas "was very nice to me" when he "was a young dude." (He was twenty-three years old, and Byas fifty-seven, when they played together in 1970.) "I felt very comfortable and learned a lot," Ineke said. "It meant a lot to play with one of the great masters of the saxophone."[27]

What was the split on a typical local gig when Byas was the headliner and hired a rhythm section of piano, bass, and drums to fill out his "rythmes"? Receipts from Paradiso in Amsterdam from a November 8, 1968, performance show Byas getting a cut of 57 percent, the pianist (Cees Slinger) getting 16 percent, and the bassist (Rob Langereis) and drummer (Peter Ypma) each getting 13.5 percent. Byas's take from the night amounted to about one hundred dollars adjusted for inflation.[28] The calendar for the first year of Byas's married life contained engagements of this sort in Geneva, as well as "guest artist" spots with the Géo Voumard Trio at Teatro Kursaal in Lugano, Switzerland; the Quartett Michel Gaudry in Geneva; and a gig in Brussels with Martial Solal on piano, Benoît Quersin on bass, and Jean-Louis Viale on drums. There were recording sessions in Paris as well, with Fats Sadi on vibraphone, Maurice Vander on piano, Pierre Michelot on bass, and Benny Bennett or Roger Paraboschi on drums; this group recorded eighteen numbers over three days in May 1955 in Paris.[29] These sessions—heavily weighted toward ballads—were a reversal of form from bebop to swing, but on the other hand, they don't suffer from the inadequacies of European rhythm sections that Byas complained of on other occasions.[30]

The itinerant lifestyle of a jazz musician was compounded in Byas's case by the lack of venues in the Netherlands or at least those that could pay him enough for him to forego dates that required long travel. Many of the jazz clubs that operated in Holland in the 1950s and 1960s were volunteer operations with minimal budgets, and the pay for musicians was probably dependent on each night's gate receipts. There were commercial clubs in Rotterdam, The Hague, Leeuwarden, and Groningen where Byas played with some regularity, but these offered him mainly short-term work, while the engagements he could secure in other countries—where he remained a foreign attraction—typically lasted several days to several weeks. When he went to France (for example), he said he would play "first a festival, then engagements in two expensive French nightclubs. In each I play three weeks. Look, that's France, you can make a living from that."[31]

Further, his self-established price was high, and it cost him some work. In the years after World War II, the Netherlands was slow to recover from the Nazi occupation, which had resulted in a decline in living standards; as a result, in the postwar years, the Dutch did not have a great deal of disposable income to spend on entertainment. In addition to jobs where he was headliner, Byas found work as a supporting act, such as one at Concertgebouw in Amsterdam on June 7, 1958,[32] opening for Sarah Vaughan, who invited Byas back onto the stage to perform on her final number, "How High the Moon,"[33] and a date backing his former Basie bandmate Jimmy Rushing in Paris on November 12 of that year in Paris. There were larger jazz shows, such as Norman Granz's Jazz at the Philharmonic tour, and he was able to earn some money from radio performances in the Netherlands but not much; around $75 per performance or about three-quarters of what he could make for a one-night stand in an Amsterdam nightclub. Foreign countries, he said, were the way for him to make money, so he needed to go to Scandinavia, Germany, Italy, and elsewhere in Europe to get paid what he thought his music was worth.

In his adopted country, Byas faced competition from American musicians whom venues felt they had to hire when they passed through since they would only be around for a short time. He was now viewed as a native of the Netherlands and no longer unique, someone you had to catch when he came to Amsterdam, which forced him to go further afield to command the fees that he felt he was entitled to. Byas "lived too long in the Netherlands," saxophonist Hans Dulfer said. "He already spoke Dutch well, had a Dutch family and was not necessarily an American in Amsterdam." So no "TV movies, no bartenders" giving him a wink if he wanted to cadge a drink, "no radio or TV guys, no sound amateur hunters to tape when he had the hiccups—and above all no work!"[34] He was no longer viewed as an exotic import of African American music in his adopted home for which jazz fans would pay premium prices; because demand for him was low, club owners asked him, in effect, to play for a "local discount."

As a result, during his seventeen years of residence, Byas made only one record in his adopted country, an EP titled "Blues by Byas." It consists of two songs that he played at a live performance in Nijmegen in October 1962[35] and was released by the Philips label, but only as a result of the initiative of a private group, not the record company itself; the concert itself was a benefit to finance the interior of a new student parish church as part of a fundraising campaign referred to as "The Holy Deed," and so it is unlikely that he received a premium fee for his appearance.[36] While his opportunities in other countries were better, over time, they dwindled as well. When he first came to Europe, "he had a lot of work" because "[a]fter the war, all those American musicians came to Europe and were received like kings," Jopie Byas said. Eventually, when European musicians learned from the American expatriates, "they began a boycott. If French could do the same, they would hire French instead of Americans, so the playing circumstances changed."[37]

On June 26, 1964, with two children (Dottie Mae and Ellie Mae), the couple moved to the first floor of 48 Admiralengracht, a more expensive area but one where presumably they had found a larger apartment that they thought they could afford. Two more children would follow in 1965 (Carlotta) and 1969 (Carlos Wesley Jr.), and the couple's itinerant lifestyle came to an end. "Before, I went with him on all tours, but when the children were born, that was over," Jopie said; Byas became, in her words, "really a home-staying person, never went out" when he wasn't traveling for a job. Once the couple "could tell each other that" they "could make it on a slice of bread," Jopie said, but with children, the money became tighter. "[C]hildren keep their mouth open, they have to. When you have children, you got to make money."[38] Where before, Don would get around Amsterdam on his 50cc DKW motor bike, he joked that he had to "buy a car with this family of mine."[39]

"I am my own impresario,"[40] Byas said in 1963, and he watched the bottom line, both financially and artistically. "Maybe I should not have added a piano," he said of a 1969 festival, the Hammerfeld Jazzfest in Roermond. "With just a bass and drummer, you can go in all directions, with a piano you are too stuck."[41] He had expressed his reservations before about the use of piano as a rhythm instrument. "Most piano players—they seem to get in my way, even though they're playing marvelous piano."[42] Byas was caught between artistic principles and economic constraints and made the fateful decision to sacrifice the former for the latter. "Today one can't ask Americans" to play, he said in a candid moment, because "they demand so much more than Europeans. And that's how it should be. Jazz is American music and America is the top in jazz."[43]

The couple's financial situation wasn't helped by Byas's refusal to work for less than what he thought he was worth. "We could have been rich," Jopie said. "After jazz became less popular," with the rise of rock and roll, "he could have had a lot of work, but he didn't do that. Good or nothing, no compromise."[44] He also turned down work that he considered beneath him, such as weddings and parties or in clubs where people didn't come to listen. "He thought Paradiso was below his station," Jopie said, although this may have been grousing in his old age, as he played there a number of times over the years. "Arti on the Rokin was more upscale. Don did a performance there with Ben [Webster]." Byas's selectivity meant he worked less than he could have. "[H]e wouldn't play, that's why he was fishing so often," his widow said, but she was faced with a dilemma, as she didn't want to ask him to compromise, either. "What should I do?" he asked her, and she found it "difficult to deprive him of ideals." Those ideals included refusing "gigs that paid only 25 cents under his minimum price," according to Dutch tenor sax Hans Dulfer, then taking his sax someplace and jamming for free.[45] "If I tell you we have had a particularly difficult time," Jopie said after he died, "you can safely believe me."[46]

Byas's move to Europe in 1946 took him out of the sights of American producers and jazz writers, but his decision to relocate to Amsterdam from Paris made things worse. During the period from 1955, when he first settled in Amsterdam, until his death in 1972 (seventeen years), he participated in twenty studio recording sessions, and only nine were made with him as leader or coleader. In contrast, during his nine years in Paris and Spain (1946–1955), he participated in forty-two studio sessions and was leader or coleader on nineteen of them.[47] While this decline may be explained in part by changes in taste—from swing to bop, from jazz to rock—the difference between being a leader and a sideman on a record may be measured in terms of both prestige and money; the leader typically makes more money than the sidemen, and the record is issued under his name. Depending on marketing power and bargaining savvy, the leader may also earn royalties—while sidemen typically do not. Byas and his widow did receive some royalties on his compositions both during his life and after he died, despite her claim to the contrary, but these were not great and often required more than minimal effort to collect. A letter from the French performing rights organization Société pour l'Administration du Droit de Reproduction Mécanique des Auteurs, Compositeurs, Éditeurs, Réalisateurs et Doubleurs Sous-Titreurs[48] to Byas dated February 27, 1973 (six months after he died), states that they had remitted 229.29 French francs to his bank account; this represented $52 at the time, and approximately $370 adjusted for inflation. A fax dated March 9, 2001, from the Dutch performing rights organization Buma/Stemra[49] to Jaap Lüdecke, an alto saxophonist and flautist who assisted Jopie Byas after Don's death, reveals other problems: Byas didn't copyright many of his works and didn't join European performing rights organizations that could have collected royalties for him, despite being urged to do so before he died.

While Byas presumably commanded a higher fee than other members of bands when he was a "featured" addition to a group, he was nonetheless in the position of a hireling rather than a boss most of his time in the Netherlands, a reversal from the days when he first arrived in Europe. When compared to his output in the period beginning in mid-1943, when he parted ways with Count Basie, to September 1946, when he left America for Europe, the decline in the demand for his services is thrown into even sharper relief; during those three final years in America, Byas played in fifty-nine recording sessions and was leader of seventeen. In his last year in the States, he participated in twenty sessions and was leader on half.[50]

A musician's overhead to play in Europe was greater than in New York where, as Byas put it, "52nd Street was unbelievable, a small street with 20 clubs within 200 meters and big names everywhere."[51] His first engagements after moving to the Netherlands took him from Geneva, Switzerland, to Paris; to Baden-Baden, Germany; to Saint-Tropez on the French Riviera; then to

Lugano, Switzerland, to play with the Géo Voumard Trio. Back to Paris for both short-term work—a one-song job backing The Platters, a doo-wop group, on "Indiff'rent"—and steadier engagements: six recording sessions with Eddie Barclay et son Grand Orchestre, with arrangements by Quincy Jones,[52] some numbers from which were used to produce an album of Billy Eckstine singing French songs, *Mr. B in Paris*, then back to Amsterdam in June 1958, to play with the Arvell Shaw Quartet at the Concertgebouw.[53]

Neither Jopie nor Don were financially savvy. According to Art Blakey, they didn't apply for government benefits to which they were entitled until five years after they became eligible, although whether Blakey was in a position to know the availability of Dutch government benefits and the requirements to fulfill in order to qualify for them is suspect.[54] After her husband died, Jopie received—too late—notice that he had been awarded the paid teaching position that he had sought as a steady source of income to support his family, long after other, less influential musicians had received such sinecures.[55] She worked occasionally as a waitress during the marriage.

Byas faced the financial consequences of his move to Europe as a whole and the Netherlands in particular with a mixture of resignation and disappointment. "It's no good coming to Europe with the expectation of making a lot of money. . . . Sometimes I feel a little disgusted at the money situation, but you can't have your cake and eat it. I never expected to be a millionaire anyway."

He rationalized his meager cash flow by pointing to his escape from what economist Thorstein Veblen referred to as the "conspicuous consumption" practiced by Americans for reasons of status in excess of their needs. "In the States," he said,

> You may make more money, but you spend it faster. If I make $500 a week and the guy next door to me has a beautiful home, I have to fix mine up the same way as his—otherwise people look down on me. If he buys a $15,000 Cadillac, I have to buy one too. Buy why should I, if I prefer to have a little Renault?[56]

Based on a comment made after his death, Jopie Byas wasn't bitter about her husband's willingness to live less grandly than they could have. "I only regret that the children never saw their father in action in the Concertgebouw,"[57] she told one interviewer, although they heard his music on the radio. "They don't know anything about jazz," Jopie said, "but when a record of his is played on the radio, they call 'Ma, you have to turn on . . . Daddy's record.'"[58] Don told an interviewer that his son "has it in him to be a musician, too,"[59] but he has not been heard of in this regard to the author's knowledge. Jopie told another interviewer that her children were "all very musical. It's a pity I cannot pay for music lessons."[60] The children were not eligible for government scholarships because they were American nationals, not Dutch.

The bottom line, for Byas, was happiness and peace of mind. "It is a calmer scene," he said in 1967. "There's more time to live. Things move so fast in the States, and if you don't keep up, you're lost in the shuffle. Here in Europe you just relax and live because that's what everyone else does. But in the States you have no time to live."

In the Netherlands, Byas said,

> When I'm home, it's like a vacation. I have a wonderful time with my children, and I go fishing and swimming. The people in Amsterdam love me because I speak their language and have adopted their way of life. If you really try to understand people, and speak their language, you get along much better . . . If you want a peaceful, comfortable life without too many headaches, then Europe is fine.[61]

Balancing what he gained in terms of peace of mind and well-being against greater fame and fortune, as he looked back in his later years, he was comfortable with his decision. "The best musicians in America don't live to be older than 40," he said. "I am sure I would already be dead if I had stayed there."[62]

In his heart, he retained fond feelings for America, but his head counseled him that he couldn't go home again. "I'd never give up my American citizenship," he said late in life, "[b]ut I'm happy in Amsterdam, and it wouldn't be practical to take my family back to the States." Perhaps thinking of the rhythm sections that he missed in Europe—from Jo Jones and Walter Page in Kansas City to Kenny Clarke and Oscar Pettiford on 52nd Street—he said, "There's no place in the world that could really take the place of my home country."[63] But it was too late; a 1959 review in a Cleveland newspaper of one of the Eddie Barclay sessions for which Quincy Jones provided the arrangements had the following to say about the expatriate sax player thirteen years after he left America: "Those who can remember the name of Don Byas might be happy to hear that Don is blowing his tenor on a new Quincy Jones that was recorded in Europe."[64]

CHAPTER 13

The Sixties

In 1960, when Don Byas had been an expatriate for fourteen years, he reconnected in France with drummer Kenny Clarke, whom he knew going back at least to a recording session the two played on with Teddy Wilson and His Orchestra backing Billie Holiday in September 1940.[1] Clarke was nicknamed "Klook" by onomatopoeia from one of his trademark bop drum licks that irritated a former boss, bandleader Teddy Hill, who reproduced it phonetically as "klook-mop."[2] Clarke had moved back to Paris on the basis of an idle conversation in New York one night in 1956 with Michel Legrand, the French composer/arranger. Clarke told Legrand that he missed Paris (he had played there with both Edgar Hayes and Dizzy Gillespie), and Legrand replied, "Hey, you want a job? All you have to do is say yes."

Clarke accepted the offer by proxy to join the band of Legrand's uncle, Jacques Hélian, but he doubted that it was serious until, one by one, the pieces fell into place: first, a one-year contract arrived from Hélian, which Clarke signed and returned; then, a one-way, first-class ticket to France on the SS *Liberté*, a former German-flagged ship that was given to a French company as reparations for the sinking of the SS *Normandie*[3] in World War II. Clarke got on the boat and, two days after sailing from New York, a cable arrived with $200 spending money from Hélian. The offer was real.

"This time I'm going to stay a long time," Clarke told Thelonious Monk.

"You're crazy, man," Monk told him. "You can't leave New York. There's no scene over there." But as the boat train pulled into Paris, Clarke was greeted by a band of friends and fellow musicians welcoming him to the Continent by serenading him with bop anthems. "Europe had been waiting for a long time for a first-rate drummer," wrote Michael Zwerin.[4]

Clarke moved on from his one-year gig with Hélian to concerts, a steady three-year job as house drummer at the Blue Note Club, recordings, and a film soundtrack with Miles Davis—*Ascenseur pour l'Échafaud* (*Elevator to the Gallows*), directed by Louis Malle and starring Jeanne Moreau.[5] He was thus in demand and stayed busy and, like Byas, he was happy even though he made less money. "You learn to slow down over here," he said. "Things manage to get done anyway."[6]

Byas had been playing radio dates with the Kurt Edelhagen Orchestra in Germany when he connected with Clarke, first in Köln/Cologne on February 25, 1960, to record the extended play 45 rpm record *Don Wails With Kenny*, which contained "Tampico," "Bell Hop," and "More Than You Know." Then on March 20, 1960, he was part of an Oscar Pettiford/Byas/Clarke radio recording that included five titles: "Blues It," "Indiana," "There Will Never Be Another You," "Don't Explain," and "Blues in the Closet." In August 1960, Byas and his wife were in Monte Carlo for a job that included pianist Frans Elsen and other musicians unknown.[7] The gig was at the Knickerbocker Club, opposite the Monte Carlo casino. During this time, the couple lived in a house owned by the grandchildren of Émile Waldteufel, concertmaster for Empress Eugénie circa 1850. One of the other tenants in the building was Aaron Bridgers, an American jazz pianist who was Billy Strayhorn's lover from 1939 until Bridgers moved to France in 1947.[8]

Then in the first week of October, Byas played club dates at the Metropol Restaurant in Oslo, Norway, with trumpeter Rowland Greenberg (who had played with Charlie Parker in Sweden in 1950), tenor Mikkel Flagstad, and local sidemen; performed on a radio broadcast with the Kjell Karlsen Big Band; and recorded a song—"Scarabee"—with the Norwegian Jazz All Stars for the movie *The Passionate Demons*, which didn't make it into the final soundtrack.[9] On October 12, Byas was part of a memorial concert held in Paris for the benefit of the widow of Oscar Pettiford, who died in September in Copenhagen. The group assembled for the occasion included Americans Lucky Thompson, Stan Getz, Kenny Clarke, and Bud Powell, and Frenchmen

Guy Lafitte, Luis Fuentes, and André Persiany, among others; they played "the evergreen classics of jazz" at the Champs Élysées Theater.[10]

At this point, Byas connected with Norman Granz's "Jazz at the Philharmonic" tour as it made its way through Europe. Conceived by Granz in 1944 as a means of keeping the jazz of the swing era alive, JATP (the acronym by which it came to be known) presented staged jam sessions, pitting top instrumentalists with and against each other in an attempt to recreate on the concert stage the competitive atmosphere of the late-night cutting contests where musicians try out new ideas, learn from each other, and expand the boundaries of the art form. Granz had produced his last JATP concert in the US in 1957 and thereafter carried the concept to Europe and Japan, all the while generating content for his record labels Clef, Norgran, and Verve. Musicians were happy to subordinate their star status for the greater collective good of JATP because Granz "paid top money . . . they traveled first class" and stayed in "the best hotels," according to Dizzy Gillespie.[11] Moreover, Granz refused to use segregated venues and insisted that hotels where the tour booked rooms accept all his musicians, regardless of race. As a result, the difficulties that Black musicians typically faced finding food and lodging on the road at that time in the United States were not an issue when they traveled with JATP.[12]

Byas joined JATP for the first time on November 19, 1960, for a performance at the Concertgebouw in Amsterdam, at which he played alongside Roy Eldridge on trumpet, Benny Carter on alto sax, Coleman Hawkins on tenor, Lalo Schifrin on piano, Art Davis on bass, and Jo Jones on drums. The group played a ballad medley of "These Foolish Things" with Hawkins featured, "Laura" with Carter soloing, "The Man I Love" with Eldridge featured, and "I Remember Clifford" with Byas soloing. They would play a similar medley at two other concerts on the tour (Konserthuset, Stockholm, and Salle Pleyel, Paris). In addition, the Duke Ellington theme "Take the 'A' Train" was regularly given a workout in jam session style.[13] Carter's solo on Byas's big hit "Laura" was a rare violation of his policy not to play numbers closely associated with other saxophonists. At a 1977 performance in London, Carter declined to play Duke Ellington's "Sophisticated Lady" because it was "so closely associated with Johnny Hodges" and "the audience was expecting to hear it as Johnny did. I knew I couldn't satisfy those who wanted it played as Johnny would have done it. And to do it that way would not have satisfied me."[14]

Perhaps because he had lived in Europe for five years (from 1934 to 1939), Hawkins adopted a man-who-has-seen-it-all-before attitude on the JATP tour, sleeping soundly while those who hadn't traveled to Europe before strove to take in landmarks and scenic vistas; trumpeter Nat Adderley and vocalist Jon Hendricks began to take photos of him as he slept through one tourist attraction after another, and drummer Jo Jones hung the nickname "Snooze" on him.[15] Despite the rest he was getting, his playing was inconsistent: "[O]n some performances Hawkins was lackadaisical . . . yet, on the very next night, inspiration took over and he blew solos that eclipsed the efforts of everyone in the esteemed cast," wrote John Chilton, his biographer. Byas, by contrast, nearly a decade younger, was never out of form. "Hawkins appeared little interested in the proceedings and played far below his best," wrote critic Max Harrison in *Jazz News*, and he "was badly cut by Don Byas, whose long European exile from good American rhythm sections has not weakened his powers in the least."[16]

While Byas always paid homage to Hawkins and cited him as his first inspiration, he wasn't intimidated by him on the bandstand or reluctant to blow his own horn, literally and figuratively. "I was the only one of that sort of Hawkins school who had modern ideas with it,"[17] a claim that other heirs of the Hawkins estate (such as Lucky Thompson) would have disputed had they heard it. Byas was even willing to place himself higher than Hawkins when he felt he was superior to the elder saxophonist; he once told Eddie "Lockjaw" Davis that "Coleman Hawkins could never play really fast; his tone was just too big."[18] Byas may still have been smarting, many years after the fact, from long-ago faint praise by Hawkins. In August 1941, Hawkins was asked to name his twelve favorite tenor saxophonists by *Music and Rhythm* magazine; he included Byas, but in seventh place—behind Ben Webster, Chu Berry, Lester Young, George Auld, Charlie Barnet, and Bud Freeman. "Don Byas's strongest point is execution," Hawkins had said. He "is young and has plenty on the ball."[19]

Despite the invidious distinctions drawn between him and Hawkins by critics and the bravado tone of his own remarks, Byas was discouraged—at the age of forty-seven—when the tour ended. "Over here [in Europe] there's no competition," he said, perhaps daunted by the all-star talent he'd been up against with JATP. "You know, I always had the dream to be the world's greatest tenor player," he said. "I doubt if I ever will make it now. I have no regrets."[20] But Cannonball Adderley, reporting on the JATP tour in the New York *Amsterdam News*, demurred: "Don Byas, the legendary tenor-saxophonist, has faded somewhat in popularity here in the United States, for he has resided in Europe for the past fifteen years," Adderley wrote. "However," he continued, "he met the same sort of responses from the continental audiences [on the 1960 JATP tour] that the more popular American stars received."[21]

After radio recording dates in March 1961 with the Kurt Edelhagen Orchestra in Cologne, Germany,[22] Byas traveled to Madrid in May 1961 to perform at Spain's First World Festival of Jazz with pianist Tete Montoliu and a local drummer and bassist. His performance was considered a triumph over a typically poor rhythm section with "pudding-stirring drumming and uninspired bass playing." Byas himself was described as "cosmopolitan" in his bow tie and silk tuxedo, his cool demeanor all the more impressive since the group was working a split shift, leaving the festival "to play the midnight set at the 'Whiskey and Jazz Club,'" where they had been appearing throughout the month. Byas was on the bill with Buck Clayton's All-Stars, a group put together for the occasion that included—in addition to Clayton on trumpet—Buddy Tate on tenor sax, Emmett Berry on trumpet, Oliver Jackson on drums, Earl Warren on alto, Gene Ramey on bass, Dicky Wells on trombone, and Sir Charles Thompson on piano. Clayton indicated a desire to reassemble the group for a tour of Europe and expressed dissatisfaction with the tour that Byas had completed the preceding fall, saying, "That J.A.T.P. gig was no tour, man, it was an insult!"[23] While it is not clear exactly what Clayton meant by this remark, from the context, he seemed to believe that it should have had a more extensive schedule into countries other than just Sweden, Holland, France, England, and Germany.

As 1961 came to a close, Byas and Bud Powell were brought together by Julius "Cannonball" Adderley in Paris for an album issued as *Don Byas/ Bud Powell—A Tribute to Cannonball*. This was a misnomer as the original album contains no tribute to Adderley; he acted only as producer, although a warm-up version of "Cherokee" on which he played was added to a later CD version.[24] Nonetheless, Byas was one of Adderley's models when he first started out; before he switched to alto, Adderley "wanted to play tenor after selecting Ben Webster, Lester Young and . . . Byas as his idols," according to a 1956 interview.[25] While Byas and Powell had "played together on numberless occasions going back to the mid-40s," according to the liner notes by Gary Giddins, they had not previously recorded together. Powell had moved to France in 1959, and with Kenny Clarke and French bassist Pierre Michelot, he formed a trio called The Three Bosses. For the *Tribute to Cannonball* session, Powell, Clarke, and Byas teamed up with trumpeter Idrees Sulieman (*né*

Leonard Graham) on four of the nine tracks. Byas and Sulieman knew each other from the early forties when they both played in Kansas City. "The music went from four to twelve at the Kentucky Club" there, Sulieman recalled. "I met Ben Webster, Don Byas there."[26] The five pull off a sympathetic mix of bop and swing that Giddins says is representative of both "Before [Charlie] Parker [in the person of Byas] and After Parker" as to Powell.[27]

The sixties saw several musical trends begin that would adversely affect the market for the styles of jazz—swing, bop, and romantic ballads—that Byas was known for. Ornette Coleman would release *Something Else!* in 1958, *The Shape of Jazz to Come* in 1959, and in 1960, his *Free Jazz: A Collective Improvisation* gave a name to the genre that he and others like him were playing. Late in life, Byas would express great irritation with subsequent practitioners of free jazz who abandoned the rhythmic pulse of swing. "They call it free jazz, but free jazz doesn't exist. Jazz can never be free," he said, echoing Robert Frost's crack that free verse was like playing tennis without a net. "Jazz has to swing to begin with. It has to have a certain rhythmic movement that will make your foot tap along when you listen." When it was pointed out that these same criticisms had been made about bebop in its early years, he demurred. "Bebop was another way of playing the same things. Bop was always swinging. You could always dance to it and you could always hear a certain musical theme. But these days, you don't even know what song they're playing." That, he said, was why jazz "is no longer interesting to the masses. . . . I think it's so cold, so without a heart" that it isn't "music anymore. Only sound. For me, a sound isn't necessarily music. You can throw a rock through a window—that also makes a sound, but that doesn't mean it's music."[28]

So the one-time member of the avant-garde had been moved to the rear, but that is not to say that Byas was wrong; not all change is progress, and it is certainly the case that change—however much it may seem to be an advance past former boundaries—that results in less revenue is not good for jazz musicians. In a curious footnote to Byas's frequently expressed aversion to the jazz that came after swing and bop, he is reported by Valerie Wilmer to have told Albert Ayler's drummer Sunny Murray that "he had wanted to play like Ayler since he was a boy." Byas, she wrote, "whose lifetime obsession was with strength, intensity and fullness of tone, was filled with admiration for the sheer honesty and freedom he detected in the approach of" Ayler.[29] Since Byas was nearly a quarter-century older than Ayler (born in 1936) and thus could not have listened to Ayler as a boy, it is not clear what Byas meant by this remark; he had frequently expressed in strong terms his distaste for free jazz, as in a 1970 interview in which he said "Ayler, Shepp? That's wrong, that's not possible. People should be able to dance comfortably and easily to jazz. To me, jazz is eighty percent dance music."[30] At least one musician who played with Byas expressed the opinion that, given his oft expressed distaste for free jazz, Byas was playing the trickster again and was pulling Wilmer's leg.[31]

A second change that cut into the market for swing jazz in Europe was the revival of traditional New Orleans-style jazz repackaged as "Dixieland." "To most connoisseurs, Dixieland was music played by white bands, striving without a great deal of success to copy the genuine New Orleans style of the coloured people," wrote Hugues Panassié and Madeleine Gautier in 1959. "Dixieland . . . enjoyed the most fantastic popularity throughout the United States . . . a popularity accounted for by the fact that the bop and cool bands had so belaboured the ears of the public that the music—usually vulgar and easy to listen to—of most 'Dixieland' bands came as a relief."[32] The fad spread to the Netherlands: "It got bad after 1962, 1963," wrote Igor Cornelissen, a journalist who was also an amateur trumpeter. "There was music enough but seemed as if there was no room left for the real swing musicians. Enough Dixieland with banjos and tubas getting gigs. That killed Don."[33] Jazz at the forefront had become more complex, less danceable, and a reaction that skipped over the immediate past and went back to a sentimentalized version of early New Orleans jazz set in. "Don was a jazz musician and that means that to love it you have to know a little bit about the music. It is not a sing-along, or forties and fifties golden oldies," Cornelissen wrote, so audiences that yearned for a simpler form of music but were too old for rock 'n' roll could spend their money on a more readily digestible form of jazz that emphasized lively—some might say hyperactive—entertainment over lyrical beauty and harmonic complexity. Byas was caught between the past—Dixieland—and the present, in which the avant-garde musicians made his style seem out of date but not old-fashioned enough to get nostalgic about. Still, he maintained that he'd be proven right in the long run. "Believe me, swing is coming back," he said in 1961, sounding a note like a religious crank predicting an imminent aesthetic rather than moral revival. "One day the new Messiah's going to come along and then they'll all sit up and take notice."[34]

A third shift that adversely affected jazz musicians of Byas's generation in the sixties was demographic, the expansion of the market for rock and roll, which began to supplant jazz in the early sixties among young people.

It goes without saying that the young are more likely to spend their disposable income on music than their parents, who have mortgages and children to provide for, and that they will generally favor musicians closer in age to them than the ones their parents listened to. In 1962, *Billboard* reported that sales of jazz records had increased over the past three years and that some jazz singles and albums had even become pop hits.[35] On February 9, 1964, however, the Beatles appeared on *The Ed Sullivan Show*, a nationally televised variety program, and jazz's market share would begin a slow decline that has continued to the point where jazz now places behind European-style classical music as the least-popular genre, a doleful confirmation that jazz is, as its devotees have long maintained, America's classical music.

Finally, it should be noted that by the 1960s, Byas had been in Europe for a decade and a half and in Amsterdam for five years, so he was no longer new to the scene. As London club owner Ronnie Scott put it, "The problem was—and still is, to a certain extent—that native musicians tend to be taken for granted, however brilliant they may be, so people [do] not exactly flock" to see them,[36] a sentiment echoed by jazz writer Mike Hennessey who wrote, "It is a well-known jazz fact that familiarity breeds indifference." Byas was accordingly "careful to keep [his] status in Europe"—as Sidney Bechet had done before him—in order "to maintain his 'exotic' prestige."[37] When an interviewer asked him in 1965 how he divided his home life and his musical career in Amsterdam, Byas said, "I don't work in Holland . . . I live there and go in and out on tours."[38] In Holland, Byas said, "I tend to be regarded as a Dutch musician. So I work principally in Scandinavia and Germany. And I raise my price every year. . . . You have to do it that way if you want to keep on being regarded as a star. Musicians are only as good as the amount of money they can command. As soon as their money drops, their prestige drops."[39] While this strategy has a marketing expert's cunning to it, it is not clear that it was successful; Byas is said to have been compelled by circumstances to work as a mailman in Amsterdam in the late sixties and early seventies, a fact that was not widely known, presumably because he worked to conceal a fact that would have undercut the appearance of success he thought was necessary to get paid what he was worth.[40]

While it would not be entirely accurate to say that Byas drifted through the sixties as a result of these changes, his pace began to slow down. In 1962, he played on television with organist Lou Bennett in the documentary *Harlem sur Seine*. He played club dates in Stockholm, Sweden, with local musicians and at the Scala in Aarhus, Denmark, with tenor Brew Moore and the Erik Moseholm Trio. He played dates in Paris at Trois Mailletz and The Olympia, personnel unknown, and with the Bud Powell Trio from the Det Ny Casino in Aarhus, Denmark. The Trois Mailletz engagement was perhaps a disappointment typical of the doleful decade: "I possess a photograph . . . of a poster stuck to the door of the club," wrote jazz critic Anthony Barnett. "It reads: 'Don Byas, World famous saxophonist, HOT JAZZ Sweet—Swing—Modern.'" Inside the club, however, Barnett noted that Byas played "three numbers each set, accompanied by a group of mediocre musicians, amidst the talk and laughter of students and tourists. But Don Byas retained an exemplary dignity in his music and himself."[41]

In three studio sessions in May 1962 at Studio Hoche in Paris, Byas recorded material that was used for the Polydor album *Amoureusement Vôtre* with Jacques Denjean et Son Grand Orchestra and with a quartet composed of himself, George Arvanitas on piano, Pierre Sim on bass, and Christian Garros on drums. Then, another iteration of the Don Byas Quartet played at the Concertgebouw de Vereeniging in Nijmegen, the Netherlands, whose performance was recorded and released as an EP (extended play record), *Blues by Byas*. The two titles on it were the familiar Charlie Parker composition "Billie's Bounce" and Byas's tongue-in-cheek tribute to the Norse god, "Old Norse Baldr,"[42] with "Byas to Baldr."[43] There was a five-night stand at the Metropol restaurant in Oslo; first, four nights with pianist Einar Iversen, Bjørn Pedersen on bass, and Jon Christensen on drums, then New Year's Eve with The Big Chief Jazzband.

The year 1963 was worse. Byas played dates in Koblenz, Germany, and Copenhagen, Denmark, in January that were recorded live; the first on January 3 included Americans Bud Powell, Idrees Sulieman on trumpet, Jimmy Woode on bass, and Joe Harris on drums, then two more on January 13 and 14 with Danish musicians Bent Axen on piano, Niels-Henning Ørsted Pedersen on bass, and William Schiöpffe on drums.[44] Then a jam session on January 15 at Jazzhus Montmartre in Copenhagen that included Don Cherry on cornet and Dexter Gordon and Albert Ayler on tenor saxes. Then a gap of nearly five months before Byas went to Stockholm, Sweden, for a club date at Gyllene Cirkeln from July 4 through 6 with the Almstedt-Lind Quintet: Ove Lind clarinet, Nils Engström piano, Rune Gustafsson or Nicke Wöhrmann guitar, Gunnar Almstedt bass, and Anders Burman drums. Then another three-month layoff before dates in Bergen, Norway, at the Neptun Café. There was also a two-week residency at the Neptun Café in Bergen with sidemen Eivin Sannes on piano, Per Vatne on base, and Ole Jacob Hansen on drums, but it is not clear if Byas played continually through this engagement.

In terms of recordings, a 1962 recording session with Jacques Denjean et Son Grand Orchestra at Studio Hoche that was released as *April in Paris* drew a review in the September 12, 1963, *DownBeat* that the album placed Byas "in what would usually be suffocating circumstances . . . slow ballads with lush, Holly-wooden strings and woodwinds," but that he managed "to rise above them with remarkable consistency. His strong, virile attack, the assertiveness of his big-bodied tone, and the grace with which he moves through his lines all but wipe out the dullness of his surroundings."[45] Harvey Pekar, the underground comic book writer who is also a jazz critic, wrote that the numbers from the January 13 and 14, 1963, sessions in Denmark that were compiled into an album titled *Ballads for Swingers* revealed that Byas's style had "evolved noticeably since he arrived in Europe. His tone has hardened so that his ballad performances are less lush than one who might have heard him since the mid-forties might expect. His major asset continues to be the inventiveness with which he runs chord changes." Pekar said that on this album, "his playing is intricate and has considerable harmonic and melodic freshness, but his phrases are often relatively short and rather abruptly cut off."[46] It was as if Byas was swimming against the current of the stream of ballads that poured out of the sluice gates producers had opened onto him.

In 1964, Byas played just three dates of which a record survives: one in Germany for which no details are known other than that Ton Wijkamp was the pianist, a second at the Rembrandt-theater, Haarlem, the Netherlands, on July 4, 1964. The sidemen for the latter were Pim Jacobs on piano, Ruud Jacobs on bass, and John Engels on drums, issued as *Don Byas Meets the Jacobs Brothers*.[47] Finally, there was a December 2 date in Rotterdam with Nedly Elstak on trumpet, Rob Madna on piano, Ruud Jacobs on bass, and Cees See on drums.[48] Byas blamed rock, and his reaction to the Beatles and the other groups who followed in their wake bordered on the intemperate, probably because he rightly viewed them as an economic threat and not just offensive to his musical tastes. "Terrible, those Beatles," he said in 1964. "They got it all from R&B which we played thirty years ago, without making any money."[49] As rock superseded jazz, nightclubs where jazz was formerly played were converted into discotheques, and jobs for saxophone-led combos dried up—at least for a while.

Then, in the manner of a clothing style that is so dated it becomes fashionable again, business began to pick up a bit; as the saying goes, there is no accounting for tastes, which applies to changes in taste as well. Sun first began to peek through the clouds for jazz with Louis Armstrong's success in the fall of 1964 with "Hello, Dolly!"—a jazzy rendition of a popular song from the Broadway show of the same name that "knocked the Beatles from the number-one spot" on the pop music charts on May 9, 1964.[50] In February 1965, Byas was in residence at the Megève Casino in the French Alps with three sidemen dispiritedly playing "what the French call Musique typique," a "special nightclub brand of background sound which might be cynically translated as 'music for boring yourself to death by,'" according to jazz writer Mike Hennessey. Hennessey, who sat in with the group, said that the band "really took off" when they switched from easy-listening music to jazz, but at the break, Byas "looked anxiously around the tables" and explained that the casino owners "don't like me to play jazz,"[51] so he had to stick to the middle-of-the-road stuff.

At that point, Hennessey noted, Byas hadn't made a record in over a year, but in September 1965, he was booked by Ronnie Scott's Club in London, which lifted his spirits. "It's a wonderful place, quite a lot of character," he said of London, "certainly a new sort of scene for me, altogether different from New York, Paris, all the other big cities," and he praised the Stan Tracey Quartet with whom he was working.[52] While in England, Byas toured with and appeared on BBC Television with alto saxophonist Bruce Turner and His Jump Band, then traveled to Germany for the Berliner Jazztage where he performed twice on radio: first on October 29 with a group that included Ben Webster, Kenny Drew on piano, Alan Dawson on drums, Brew Moore on tenor, and Niels-Henning Ørsted Pedersen on bass, then on October 31 with Teddy Wilson on piano, Peter Trunk on bass, and Cees See on drums at Palais am Funkturm.[53] A performance from the engagement at Ronnie Scott's was issued as the album *Autumn Leaves*, and retrospective liner notes by Les Tomkins noted the ironic foreshadowing of the song used as the title: "We did not know," Tomkins wrote, "as we witnessed the great Don Byas enjoying himself in the company of the excellent Tracey [piano], [Rick] Laird [bass], and [Tony] Crombie [drums], that . . . he was, in fact, in the autumn of his illustrious jazz career. These were his first performances in London; he was to die seven years later."[54]

In the fall of 1965, Byas was called on to pinch-hit for baritone sax Gerry Mulligan as a member of the Earl Hines All Stars, which included Hines, violinist Stuff Smith, trumpeter Roy Eldridge, bassist Jimmy Woode, and drummer Kenny Clarke. Friction developed between Mulligan and Hines over who should lead the group, according to one account; according to another, Mulligan couldn't stand the cold weather and left the tour. Whatever the reason, the group was thereafter dubbed the Earl Hines All Stars; Byas joined them in Helsinki, Finland, and continued on for concerts in Stockholm, Paris, and Brussels.[55] In December 1965, Byas would play a gig at Jazzhus in Copenhagen with three tenors, the other two being Ben Webster and Brew Moore, and a Danish rhythm section of Alex Riel on drums, Atli Bjørn on piano, and Niels-Henning Ørsted Pedersen on bass, before assembling a relatively stable quartet comprised of Riel on drums and Niels-Henning Ørsted Pedersen on bass to play dates through the rest of the year.[56]

In early 1966, Byas would play dates in Germany at the Eden Saloon and Dug's with local sidemen and then perform on a Dutch television program with American jazz drummer Stu Martin[57] in May. In August, he appeared at the Molde Jazz Festival in Molde, Norway, where, as he got off the boat, he was welcomed by fellow American tenor sax Wayne Shorter. Byas signed T-shirts for fans, socialized with musicians and audience members, and took the stage with Art Farmer's quartet when he was invited to do so, but then ended up not playing. He played with a foursome comprised of himself, Kenny Drew on piano, Niels-Henning Ørsted Pedersen on bass, and Alex Riel on drums on August 4 and 6, however.[58] He would close out the year with three dates fairly close to home in the Netherlands in December, all with a group made up of himself, Rob Agerbeek on piano, Rob Langereis on bass, and Peter Ypma on drums.[59]

In 1967, Byas would back singer Carlos do Carmo on two numbers, "The Shadow of Your Smile" and "I've Got You Under My Skin," released belatedly in 1976 as a 45 rpm single, and then appear on four songs with the Vladimir Cosma Orchestra recorded in Paris. Cosma was a Romanian conductor who wrote scores for a number of films, often including jazz musicians such as Byas, Pepper Adams (baritone sax), Sam Woodyard (drums), Stephane Grappelli (violin), and Niels-Henning Orsted Pedersen (bass), among the musicians.[60] Byas would praise Cosma, saying, "He writes better than Quincy Jones and half a word is enough for him, you know what I mean?"[61] After connecting with Ben Webster for dates in Amsterdam (see the next chapter), Byas made a live recording in Switzerland with Sir Charles Thompson, Isla Eckinger on bass, and Peter Schmidlin on drums. Thompson was not a knight but a pianist who, like Duke Ellington and Count Basie before him, was given a title of nobility, in Thompson's case by tenor sax Lester Young, who had a gift for coming up with nicknames for his colleagues. Thompson had passed through the bands of Lionel Hampton and Lucky Millinder, but later than Byas; they did not play together until they were both part of the 52nd Street scene in the early 1940s. Thompson was Byas's kind of pianist, leaving lots of room for his solos, and the two worked well together on this, their only joint recording.[62] In November 1967, Byas would perform with clarinetist Tony Scott at Arti et Amicitiae in Amsterdam and with the Clifford Jordan Quartet at Jazzhus Montmartre in Copenhagen. He would finish up the year with a radio broadcast in Stockholm in a new iteration of the Don Byas Quartet (Lars Sjøsten on piano, Roman Dylag on bass, and Egil Johansen on drums) and then a memorial concert for violinist Stuff Smith, who died on September 25, 1967. The concert was held at the Falkonercenteret in Copenhagen, with the Arnvid Meyers Orkester serving as the house band for the occasion. Smith and Byas had played together many times over the course of their careers, most recently on the troubled Earl Hines tour. Smith had followed Byas on Earl Hines's "Rosetta" at the November 3, 1965, concert at the Palais de la Mutualité in Paris, and the two were in fine form despite the advanced ages (for jazzmen), fifty-two in Byas's case, fifty-six in Smith's.

In 1968, Byas would stay in the Netherlands for several performances, the first for a television broadcast backing (along with the quartet of pianist Pim Jacobs) singer Rita Reys, "Europe's First Lady of Jazz," in the AVRO Studio in Hilversum and the next with Jacobs at the Gebouw De Heuvel in Rotterdam. After recording albums with Ben Webster in Germany and Amália Rodrigues in Portugal, he came back home for performances at Paradiso with new configurations of his quartet and quintet.[63]

In August 1969, Byas—at the age of fifty-seven—received mixed reviews for his performance at the Hammerfeld Jazzfest in Roermond with a group that included Cees Slinger on piano, Ruud Jacobs on bass, and Leo de Ruiter on drums. "Frankly speaking, tenorist Don Byas was so drunk that he would have done better not to appear on stage," the reviewer for *Het Parool* wrote. The account in *Het Vrije Volk* reported that "Don sauntered into the park around 4 o'clock [p.m.] and right away moved to the very first beer-counter he saw, moved to the next counter as fast as he could, and kept to this regular rhythm until he had to go onstage at 23:30. Despite [this], he blew the festival with great enthusiasm into its second day." The critic from *De Nieuwe Limburger* wrote that "[t]he most remarkable figure on Saturday was Don Byas, the

The Sixties   149

57-year-old American saxophonist who, apart from his saxophone playing, also stood out for his overwhelming thirst. One glass after another disappeared into his thirsty throat and the organisers held their breath. When Don begins his appearance at 11:00 he is pretty loaded, but nobody really notices."[64]

When these reviews were read to him, Byas shrugged and complained, "I don't understand what those people have against me." He said he wasn't due to perform until 11 p.m. and that he got to the festival early to have a few beers and hear his colleagues play. He said he hadn't eaten and was walking around "tired and alone." Nonetheless, because he was the main act of the night, he received a fee of $200 (approximately $1,670 adjusted for inflation), which he said was "the largest amount I have ever received for performing in the Netherlands." Perhaps his status as headliner raised expectations in the audience and critics, but Byas took it personally. "I felt like a child who was not really wanted by his mother," he said. "That allegation of drunkenness? Of course I wasn't drunk. I had a few [beers], but I did my job well." He admitted, however, that he "was down. That is perhaps why I am uninspired to play," but he absolved his sidemen of blame: "Nothing but good about my accompanists." Byas said the critic's negative reaction was "small" and added, "By the way, I meet that more here in the Netherlands, never suffered from it abroad." [65]

On November 1, 1969, Byas was in Paris and was asked by Duke Ellington to sit in with his band at a concert at Salle Pleyel on "Diminuendo and Crescendo in Blue," the number that had reignited Ellington's fading career in 1956 at the Newport Jazz Festival when tenor Paul Gonsalves brought a restive crowd to their feet with an up-tempo, bluesy improvisation that revived Ellington's career and anticipated (for better or worse) the lengthy solos that became the norm for jazz once the long-playing record took over as the dominant medium for recorded music. Gonsalves was present at the Paris venue, and Byas may have felt uncomfortable trying to equal his historic performance.[66] Further, he was seven years senior to the Ellington tenor and had to borrow Gonsalves's saxophone; he didn't like playing another man's horn but felt that he couldn't refuse Duke. As a result of these adverse conditions, Byas struggled, and coming off his bad night at the Hammerfeld festival, he may have felt his career was in the doldrums. On the other hand, it may have been that he was exhausted by babysitting duties that Mercer Ellington, who had taken over as manager of the band at that point, asked him to perform.

On the afternoon after the Ellington band arrived in Paris from Lille, France, Mercer Ellington encountered Byas coming down the stairs of their hotel with Paul Gonsalves, who told Mercer he needed "more big bucks to go over to the Left Bank." Not trusting Gonsalves, who was an erratic employee due to his fondness for drink and drugs, Mercer gave Byas four hundred francs (about $70 then and about $565 now) and told him he was in charge.

"Paul was never so disgusted in his whole life," Mercer recalled.

"What!" Gonsalves said. "That's like the blind leading the blind!"

"Don, you heard what I said," Mercer told Byas. "He's to be back here at eight o'clock tomorrow morning to catch the bus."

The next morning, according to Mercer, "[H]ere comes four blind sax players, Paul Gonsalves, Don Byas, Archie Shepp, and, I think, Pony Poindexter."

"See, I told you I'd have him here on time. Here's your change!" Byas said, as he gave Mercer twenty-three francs (meaning the four had spent 95 percent of the money they'd been given).

At this point, Mercer happened to remember that he'd bought Gonsalves a fifth of Johnny Walker Black Label scotch at the duty-free shop in Orly Airport.

"What happened to the Scotch, Paul?" Mercer asked.

"It's not all bad news," Gonsalves answered. "You did get change from the four hundred francs."[67]

On November 14, 1969, Byas participated in a memorial concert for Timme Rosenkrantz in Copenhagen, playing on three numbers—"Blues in B Flat," "Indiana," and "I've Found a New Baby."[68] Rosenkrantz died on August 11, 1969, at the age of fifty-eight. Television footage of the event exists, some of which (without Byas) can be seen on the Ben Webster video *Tenor Sax Legend: Live and Intimate.*[69] Inez Cavanaugh, Rosenkrantz's long-time companion, sang a moving tribute to him, giving personal meaning to the Gus Kahn lyrics of the jazz standard "I'll Never Be the Same":

I'll never be the same—
Stars have lost their meaning for me.
I'll never be the same—
Nothing's what it once used to be.

Cavanaugh had sung with Byas on his first recording date for Rosenkrantz, as well as his 1945 sessions with Don Redman.[70] She left the stage dry-eyed to thunderous applause, and Byas could be forgiven if he had—contrary to his wife's testimony that she thought he would live forever—intimations of his own mortality.

CHAPTER 14

With Ben, near the End

On May 30, 1966, Ben Webster was driven by Anders Stefansen, his Danish booking agent, to Copenhagen's Central Station, where he boarded a train to Amsterdam. Webster's work permit had expired the day before, and according to Stefansen, the saxophonist had to leave Denmark "for three months before he could get in again." When Webster asked Stefansen how he should serve out his time in exile, the agent suggested Amsterdam. Rents and the cost of living were comparatively low there, the jazz community was said to be as enthusiastic as the one in Denmark, and Webster's reputation for excessive drinking that impaired his playing and reliability had not spread to the Netherlands since he had never lived there. Webster decided "to visit the town as a tourist at first, to see if he could get used to the idea of living there."[1] Stefansen told him, "[I]f he went to Amsterdam, I'd call up Don Byas, and he could pick him up when he arrived." Stefansen "put Ben on a train to Amsterdam and called Byas to tell him that Ben was on his way," as if the latter tenor with the unpredictable temper and sentimental side was a parcel he was shipping to him.[2]

Byas arranged for Webster to rent a room with Mrs. Johanna Maria "Mientje" Hartlooper-Koster, a seventy-four-year-old widow, at Waalstraat 77 in the Rivierenbuurt district of south Amsterdam.[3] The room was part of Mrs. Hartlooper's three-room utility apartment up a narrow flight of stairs on the second floor; it was said to be twelve or thirteen feet square with a bed, a desk, a small table, and two chairs. Webster rented the room for about twenty dollars a week; he would buy the food he wanted, and his sub-landlady would prepare it for him. She also washed and ironed his clothes and otherwise filled the void in his life left by the deaths of his mother, Mayme, and his great-aunt Agnes Johnson, who, together, had raised him. Webster was allowed to use the living room, which he "pleasantly colonized," according to one biographer.[4]

Webster and Byas had a relationship that veered from friendship to hostility depending on the two men's respective moods during any given period, which could, of course, be worsened by alcohol. Both were born and raised in the Midwest, Webster in Kansas City, Missouri, two hundred thirty-five miles from Byas's hometown of Muskogee, Oklahoma; both claimed they had Cherokee blood (Byas on his mother's side, Webster on his father's). They probably first met in one of the two bands that they were both members of early in their careers, Bennie Moten's and Walter Page's Blue Devils, and they remained close for many years, with occasional bumps in the road of any long-term friendship. It didn't help that the two were both immoderate drinkers, which tends to magnify small differences of taste and opinion into larger issues, but when sober, they got along fine. Webster "had a racing bike that he never used," according to Dutch tenor Hans Dulfer,[5] and from drinking and lack of exercise, Webster grew heavy, causing violinist Stuff Smith to describe him jokingly as "an old beat up fat cat." "He's a fine boy," Smith added. "He's like a little baby when he hasn't been drinking. But when he's drinking look out, run, run, you hear me, you run! He's the roughest cat you ever saw in your life, hm. But he's still my pal."[6]

Byas's widow Jopie said that Webster blamed him for a late-in-life accident in which Webster broke his leg; she is probably referring to a broken ankle Webster suffered at a 1969 memorial concert in Copenhagen for Timme Rosenkrantz,[7] the man who had first recorded Byas, and who brought him to Europe with Don Redman. However, there was alcohol involved, and there was a backstory.[8] Jopie Byas described Webster as "[n]ot so nice" because he would show up from time to time at the Byas's apartment in Amsterdam whether or not he'd been invited and not always in a sober state. Once, when Byas had to leave Amsterdam to go on tour, he warned Jopie not to let Webster in while he was away. When Webster arrived at the door one day with sweets and toys for her children, she relented. He sat down on a couch, took off his shoes, pulled out his hip flask and began to drink. He refused to leave despite Jopie's repeated requests that he go home, and he began to ask questions she found offensive, such as whether Don had ever bought her a mink coat and taunting her because Don had never bought her a wedding ring. "With Ben Webster there was a lot of screaming," she said. He shouted, "I am a principled man and not for sale!" for no apparent reason. She told him she was going to call a taxi, but it was an empty threat as the Byases didn't have a telephone at the time.[9] Webster took a few more sips, lay down on the couch, and fell asleep. Jopie had to call in four neighbors to wake the heavyset Webster; together, they revived him with wet washcloths, put his undersized hat on his head, and someone called a cab. "No taxi driver wanted to take him home,"[10] Jopie said, but eventually, one was persuaded to haul the huge saxman away.

"Don't tell Don," Webster said as he was escorted out the door.

But Jopie did tell her husband, and as Webster was about to take the stage in Copenhagen in November 1969, Byas made a joke about the incident. "A battle of words ensued and then Ben had to take the stage, quite drunk already," Jopie recalled. "Ben fell and . . . blamed Don because he had made him nervous with that story." Jopie could laugh at the time when she saw Ben performing in a cast, but years later, she would look back on the two men's dustup with sadness "because Ben was so terribly lonely. In a bar he would buy a round of drinks," she said, "then at least he belonged somewhere. Ben was sometimes jealous of Don, who was settled here and drove through the city on his moped and could talk to people." Perhaps out of pity, the Byas–Eksteen family invited Webster to join them for Christmas one year. Don cooked fried apple pie and roast chicken, the recipe for which had seen heavy use since it "had the most grease stains in his cookbooks." There was, according to Jopie, a "Christmas tree in the house and lots of decorations, and a present for everyone"—including Webster. "When there turned out to be something for Ben too," Jopie said, "he cried like a child."[11]

Byas and Webster were rivals on several grounds, musical and non-musical. As to the latter, both men had been lovers of Mary Lou Williams (and both had mistreated her), but Byas ended up happily married, with (at least) five children, while Webster ended his life unmarried, childless, and living alone, although ministered to from time to time by girlfriends, one referred to only as "Mule," the other being Birgit Nordtorp. On the musical side, both played the tenor sax, so any praise received by one within earshot or sight of the other was liable to lead to increased friction. There are fewer available jobs in any given marketplace for tenor saxophonists than, say, accountants, so in the zero-sum world of jazz, each man's success could be perceived as coming at a cost to the other. In the year before he left for Europe, the two participated in several jams where they were pitted against each other, such as one held April 7, 1945, at the Audubon Ballroom and a Memorial Day Benefit Jam at Lincoln Square Center,[12] and Byas was viewed as a coming rival of the more-established Webster. "Ben Webster still tops 52nd Street's tenor tooters," wrote Dan Burley in his Back Door Stuff column for the *New York Amsterdam News*, "but Don Byas is on his neck."[13] After Webster left the United States in 1964, the tables were turned. "Ironically," as jazz musician and writer Michael Zwerin put it in an article in *Esquire* magazine, "his good friend Ben Webster" was "getting some of his gigs."[14]

The two men's musical rivalry dated back at least to the time when Byas overreacted to perceived criticism by Count Basie and ended up getting fired when he pulled a gun. Webster had triggered that incident when he impressed Basie's men playing Byas's sax, and the "event boosted the tension between Byas and Webster .... [a]lthough Ben probably would have liked to avoid it," according to Webster biographer Frank Büchmann-Møller.[15] The two were, for the most part, friendly rivals in jam sessions. "I used to live at the Cecil Hotel, which was right next door to Minton's," Webster recalled, speaking of 1943 when Duke Ellington's orchestra was in New York for a long-term engagement at the Hurricane Club. "We used to jam just about every night when we were off," Webster said. "Lester, Don Byas and myself—we would meet there all the time and like, exchange ideas. It wasn't a battle, or anything. We were all friends."[16]

Tenorist Hal Singer said that in the midforties, Byas "was the big man, even bigger than Hawkins. . . . This was the time when 52nd Street was really jumping and Don had the habit, when his night off came around, of coming back to the Street and drinking at the White Rose," the "popular watering hole at the corner of Sixth Avenue and 52nd St. where many friendships were cemented and/or strained, and the drinks were large and cheap," according to jazz critic Dan Morgenstern.[17] After several hours of drinking, Don would "get the devil in him,"[18] said Singer, and on one such occasion, he began to express himself with some rather mild (to this writer's ears) swearing that nonetheless violated Webster's strict interpretation of the Second Commandment not to take the Lord's name in vain. "Byas was at a table saying Lord this and God that," and Webster picked him up and threw him "the length of a White Rose bar."[19]

The two men had played in Europe together before Webster moved to Amsterdam. On December 9, 1965, they appeared with fellow American tenor Brew Moore and a Danish rhythm section of Alex Riel on drums, Atli Bjørn on piano, and Niels-Henning Ørsted Pedersen on bass at Jazzhus Montmartre in Copenhagen, playing a set of standards.[20] After he got settled in Amsterdam, Webster joined Byas in performing at the opening of Amsterdam's only (at the time) permanent jazz venue, Jazzart, on April 8, 1967. The club was located in rooms at Arti et Amiciae, a private facility for artists and authors; Webster fan Steven Kwint persuaded the proprietors to hold weekly concerts on Thursdays in a large room that had a stage, a grand piano, a bar, and several billiard tables. Byas and Webster dueled in front of a local rhythm section, and there was (according to jazz writer Bert Vuijsje) "some rivalry between the two of them." Byas, as was his wont, strove mightily to outperform Webster, but Webster "put him in his place" with "his tone and expression."[21] Jazz writer Michiel de Ruyter said, "Don was a very quick guy of course, just listen to his duet with Slam Stewart in 'I Got Rhythm' from '45 . . . . Anyway, right at the opening piece, Don grabs the first solo. He goes all over the horn, opens up his whole box of tricks, and when he's finished, he looks at Ben with this look of, 'OK—now your turn.' Ben looks at him sidelong for a moment, waits at least two-and-a-half bars, and then just plays *fffvvvooo, fffvvvooo*—two magnificent sighs. He then looks at Don again for a moment, and that's when he really starts going. Don had had a bit more to drink that night, so artistically, Ben beat him. I thought that was a very fine moment."[22]

As Bert Vuijsje described Webster's cutting session strategy, "Webster usually gave his rival the first solo, let him do his thing, but then resolutely set the musical relations straight: unperturbed, he waited eight measures or so for the applause for Byas' vigorous gymnastics to die down, and then simply started his solo with three serene notes, which definitively established who was the greater musician."[23] This opinion was echoed by jazz critic Martin Williams in 1983, looking back over the two men's careers after they were both gone. He cited Webster and Byas as the two most successful students of Coleman Hawkins's style but ranked Webster higher, saying that Byas didn't succeed in varying the rhythm of his phrases, while Webster, "[l]ong an exceptional soloist . . . became a great one . . . after he accepted the limitations of his fingers and embouchure and became a simple and eloquent melodist."[24]

Byas would get a chance for revenge on May 11, 1967, when Webster, playing on a sax he had borrowed from George Johnson, another American living in the Netherlands, was unable to top a toned-down Byas's effort at Jazzart. According to one reviewer, Byas "dropped his tasteless high shrieking and was generally calmer and more composed, which allowed you to enjoy his rich harmonic variations and robust tone." Webster "apparently had some trouble with" his borrowed instrument and "didn't take any risks trying to outdo Byas."[25] Webster sought to even the evening's score by challenging Byas to a game of billiards, a game at which, a Dutch reporter wrote, "Webster was second to none."[26] There were other collaborations between the two while Webster was in the Netherlands. They played at the Continental Bodega in Amsterdam in early 1967 with Byas's regular rhythm section consisting of Cees Slinger on piano, Rob Langereis on bass, and Peter Ypma on drums, and they can be seen performing fragments of "Perdido" with the same rhythm section in a 1967 documentary.[27]

The idea for a Byas–Webster album was suggested by Joachim-Ernst Berendt, a German music writer and producer, in 1967. Webster and Berendt had been involved in an unfortunate incident on October 29, 1965, when Webster was hungover from drinking with fellow tenors Byas, Brew Moore, Dexter Gordon, Booker Ervin, and Sonny Rollins on the night before they were to appear together as members of a "tenor workshop" at the Berliner Jazztage, a festival organized by Berendt.[28] "Berendt knew nothing of the risk in waking Ben, and started to shake him when the time came for him to go on stage," wrote Webster biographer Frank Büchmann-Møller. "Half asleep, Ben took a punch at him and hit Berendt smack on the chin." Webster apologized and eventually made it to the stage, but he was too drunk to perform well, as were some of the others. Webster was teamed with Byas and Brew Moore, and the end of their session "was chaotic because no one remembered what they had agreed on. After this, each of them was to be featured in a solo tune, and Ben was the first of the three." Pianist Kenny Drew began his introduction of "How Long Has This Been Going On?" but Webster waved him off and began speaking to the audience. Webster was distracted for a moment, and the German master of ceremonies used the opportunity to intervene. He apologized, telling the audience, "I can only say briefly that Ben Webster would like to express his pleasure at being reunited with a couple of his old colleagues, with whom he has played for many years, and I think I should tell our audience at this time that Ben Webster is very happy tonight and in an extremely good mood." Drew began to play again, but Webster called him off and continued talking, forcing the band to begin again several times before Webster "finally started up the tune. He played one tender chorus, but was forced to leave the rest of the tune to the rhythm section." Intent on avoiding further embarrassment, Berendt persuaded Webster to leave the stage during Drew's solo.[29] On this occasion, at least, Byas was better able to hold his liquor than Webster, as a review of the concert said, "Don Byas and Brew Moore made a more sober impression."[30] Webster and Berendt eventually made up, and when Berendt suggested on a train trip through Norway that Webster and Byas record an album together in Germany, Ben agreed.[31]

In early 1968, the two tenors went into the studio in Villingen, Germany, with a rhythm section consisting of pianist Tete Montoliu, bassist Peter Trunk, and drummer Al "Tootie" Heath, with Berendt as producer. "He's trying to beat me with his quick notes," Webster grumbled to jazz writer Henk Romijn Meijer,[32] and the session pushed the two further apart rather than bringing them together. While to this writer's ears, the group's version of "Sunday" (misspelled "Sundae") by Chester Conn with lyrics by Jule Styne, Bennie Krueger, and Ned Miller (misattributed to Chester "Cann" and Bennie "Kreger") is a fine one, what could have been a session for the ages turned out to be a bit of a disappointment, at least to some. After a few numbers, Webster refused to play with Byas; they each recorded a self-composed solo piece, Webster with "When Ash Meets Henry" and Byas with "Lullaby to Dottie Mae." "That record? Disgraceful!" said jazz writer Michiel de Ruyter. "They were both drunk as skunks and produced nothing at all." Jazz photographer Egbert de Bloeme said, "Byas had a very high opinion of himself. And he was a star soloist, of course, but whenever Ben was around, he never realized that he had to be a bit more modest. And if you added alcohol to this mixture, they would both get pretty irritable."[33] In *DownBeat*, Dan Morgenstern pronounced it "jazz of the heavyweight championship class," however, noting the "element of challenge involved in such get-togethers, and on 'Sunday,' 'Perdido,' and especially 'Caravan,' the two masters at times converse heatedly." He concluded that "Byas' style has changed more over the years than Webster's," calling him "a bold and imaginative musician, and a true master of his horn."[34] The album functions as a mileage marker to show how far the two had come from their common point of beginning, starting with the music of Coleman Hawkins. "Stylistically," wrote Webster biographer Frank Büchmann-Møller, the younger Byas "had traveled farthest from his starting point . . . He was also more advanced harmonically than Ben, which is illustrated well in the slow 'Blues for Dottie Mae,' dedicated to his oldest daughter, whereas Ben's two choruses are hushed and kept in lovely phrases."[35]

The last musical encounter between Byas and Webster was the November 1969 memorial concert in Copenhagen for Timme Rosenkrantz. Eddie Barefield, with whom both Webster and Byas had played, was there as a member of a band called The Saints and Sinners. Barefield and Byas were old friends, going back to their days together in California in the mid-1930s. Clarinetist Kenny Davern told the story of having seen the two men encounter each other by chance in the 1960s, take out their horns, and spontaneously run through Frankie Trumbauer's C-melody saxophone chorus from "Singin' the Blues." "Everybody knew that chorus," they told Davern, laughing; it was the lingua franca of saxophone players of their vintage.

But Byas didn't show the same affection for Webster; Barefield recalled the chill between the two when they saw each other.

> [O]ne of the biggest thrills I had was when I walked into this hall that night. Ben Webster was standing there. . . . And we had such a good time talking to each other, because I'd been getting letters from him. And that wasn't enough. I went up on stage, went backstage, and who else do you think was there? Don Byas. I hadn't seen him for about twenty-five or twenty years. I had been to Europe several times looking for him, and he was always someplace else. This was really a great reunion to find Ben and Don there together. The only heartbreaking thing was that they weren't friendly with each other, but I made them get together.[36]

Eventually, Webster wore out his welcome in Amsterdam. He couldn't get his drinking under control, and when he'd been imbibing late at night, he would make long-distance calls to friends in the US, leaving Mrs. Hartlooper with telephone bills she couldn't afford on her pension. (This was another trait he shared with Byas, who, according to Jopie Byas, "never wrote, but . . . spent huge amounts of money on the telephone."[37]) Mrs. Hartlooper "told him it was time for him to start looking for a different place to live," documentary filmmaker and photographer Johan van der Keuken said. Webster searched for an apartment with Dutch friends, but without a regular source of income, he was unable to secure one, and he moved back to Copenhagen.

The sometimes-fraught friendship between Webster and Byas was honored after their deaths by pianist Ron Burton and drummer John Lewis with the composition "For Don Byas and Ben Webster" on their 1974 album *The Waterbearers.*[38]

CHAPTER 15

The Out Chorus

In 1968, Don Byas told fellow jazz musician and writer Michael Zwerin that he was thinking of coming back to the States. "I may do that," he said. "One more trip. One grand tour. I'll make some money, come back and" (according to Zwerin, this next said with a smile) "I'll lay down and die."[1] By the summer of 1969, Byas had formulated somewhat grandiose plans for an eight- to ten-month tour of the US that would be billed as "Don Byas Returns." "The intention is that I will be there with a new format," he said, with a specially composed group "in a large well-known club, with a lot of advertising. There should also be one or two records made of which we hope that one will become a hit."[2] With the support of a Dutch public broadcasting association that proposed to make a documentary of his return to America, Byas returned to his native land in style: "They laid out the red carpet. When I stepped off the plane, there was champagne and the works," he said. "The TV people want to do [the documentary] in the same surroundings in which I became famous," he added, sounding a bit boastful but declining to indulge in false modesty.[3] After a long period of neglect, he was, like Gloria Swanson as Norma Desmond in *Sunset Boulevard*, ready for his close-up.

His homecoming turned out to be less successful than he imagined, however, and his hope for a hit jazz record in the seventies was a bit naive; tastes had moved on from the romantic ballads and scorching bop that he was the master of to electric fusion (John McLaughlin, Weather Report, Herbie

Hancock's *Head Hunters* album, and Pat Metheny) and moody, introspective music by the artists who recorded with the German ECM label (Keith Jarrett, Jan Garbarek, and Eberhard Weber). In a 1972 obituary, *DownBeat* said it "soon became clear" after he returned to the US in 1970 that the triumphant homecoming he envisioned was not to be; his "long absence, coupled with the few new recordings by him available in the US, made it difficult for him to obtain work at the prices he demanded."[4] As jazz critic Dan Morgenstern put it, it was "kind of sad, because nobody remembered him."[5] Because of his "fierce ego, he expected star treatment," which was not forthcoming; he had "counseled and guided a generation of other émigrés, part-time and full-time, and though his long stay abroad had led the Europeans to take him pretty much for granted, he was still *somebody*"—or so he thought.[6]

When Byas arrived in New York for the 1970 Newport Jazz Festival, he stayed in New York's Edison Hotel and tried to pick up some gigs before heading to Rhode Island. He was booked for two nights at the Village Vanguard (a job that Rahsaan Roland Kirk is believed to have helped him obtain), where he led a quartet that included Roland Hanna on piano, Wilbur Ware on bass, and Jo Jones on drums, then played with the Thad Jones–Mel Lewis Band, which had been in residence at the club since the mid-1960s.[7] Portions of these performances can be seen on the Dutch television documentary *Don Byas Come Back*,[8] with Byas playing "Lover Man" with the Jones/Lewis band and "I Remember Clifford" with a group under his name. Kirk and Byas had played together before, in October 1963, in Sweden. At the time, Kirk was playing in Copenhagen, and when he heard that Byas was in Stockholm, he traveled there and played as guest soloist one night at the Gyllene Cirkeln with Byas's combo, which included Jan Carlsson on drums, Sture Nordin on bass, and Gören Lindberg on piano.[9]

On July 11 at Newport, Byas was reunited with Dizzy Gillespie, whose rhythm section backed him on three numbers; "But Not for Me," "'Round Midnight," and Byas's composition "Orgasm" (the latter two may be seen in *Don Byas Come Back*). Byas said his appearance at Newport was "just wonderful! I have never experienced anything like that! The reception and the atmosphere were extraordinarily special. I did not expect this at all—it was very touching, we were all like brothers." Byas said he "hardly slept at all" during the festival. "I didn't have time to sleep. But when I returned to Europe I slept for two days and two nights."[10] Contrary to the view that Byas's "abilities had sadly withered" during his time in Europe,[11] he carries the ball without a break from his sidemen in his Newport performances and is in fine form throughout. Again, like Gloria Swanson/Norma Desmond, he seemed to say that he was still big—jazz got small(er) in his absence. He crowed about the audience's response to his session, saying, "I received a greater reception than Coleman Hawkins in 1939 when he came back from Europe. I never expected that, because Hawkins was bigger than me, or so I think."[12] By his Newport performance, Byas effectively rebutted the rumors that he had remained in Europe because "he was washed up in New York anyway," or "he wanted to be a big fish in a small pond."[13] A reviewer in the *Washington Post* wrote that "[i]n after-hours sessions at Newport, Byas showed he had lost none of the roaring power his work has been noted for," but his set and that of Dexter Gordon were "cut short . . . because of a crowded program," while Ike and Tina Turner, "one of the hottest-selling soul acts" of the day "were given ample time."[14]

After the festival, Byas traveled to Chicago, where he was recorded with a group that included Rufus Reid, Wilbur Campbell, and Jodie Christian on piano for the *Just Jazz* television show on Chicago's public television station, WTTW, coproduced by Dan Morgenstern.[15] He played gigs that Joe Segal, a local club owner and promoter, had lined up for him, including two weekends at The Apartment nightclub on the South Side from July 17 to 18 and 24 to 25, with either Jodie Christian or John Young on piano, Rufus Reid on bass, and Wilbur Campbell on drums.[16] The pay was $250 a night [around $2,000 adjusted for inflation], "a nice amount for a jazz musician who had been away for so long"[17] but from which he had to pay his sidemen; his contract read, "On behalf of the Employer the leader will distribute the amount received from the Employer to the musicians, including himself."[18] A reviewer in the *Chicago Daily Defender* pronounced Byas to be in excellent form at this venue,[19] while John Litweiler, covering the dates for *DownBeat*, noted that he was something of a curiosity due to his long absence from the American scene: "Don Byas is a small, animated man who looks like an elf on leave from Santa's workshop," he wrote.[20]

Byas played two Sunday shows on July 19 and 26 at the Jazz Showcase, a club then located in the North Park Hotel.[21] Female saxophonist/vocalist Vi Redd was performing at the club at the time of the first date and Byas sat in with her,[22] but the two didn't gel; the *DownBeat* reviewer described her set as one of "energetic vocal and alto funk" and said Byas was "out of place in such extroverted circumstances." He "politely offered a brief middle-register solo, then chose to leave the stage."[23] On the later date, Byas played alongside fellow tenors Dexter Gordon and Gene Ammons, a gig that was made into the album *The Chase*—but without Byas, who would not allow the producers to record him because he thought the fee they offered ($300) was too low for both a live performance and a recording.[24] To accommodate him, "they simply turned off the tape recorder when Byas played."[25] After the session was in the can, the three tenor players walked across the street to Lincoln Park, with Byas appearing "fairly wound up," according to an eyewitness.[26] Byas may have been cranky because he was tired; the Saturday night gigs at The Apartment ran until 5 in the morning on the following Sunday, and the job at the Jazz Showcase began at 4 p.m. Sunday, the 26th, a tight fit for a restful sleep.[27] The three tenors drew "unusually large crowds . . . on successive weekends at the North Park," Litweiler wrote, but he added, "I suspect that the majority, like myself, only knew Byas by reputation: absent from the US for a quarter-century, he has only one fairly recent LP available here, and two reissues."[28]

Byas then returned to New York, where he played at Slugs' Saloon, sitting in with Milt Jackson, whose group included Sonny Redd on alto sax and Cedar Walton on piano, then sat in with Kenny Burrell at the Guitar Club, along with Wilbur Ware on bass.[29] In mid-August, he appeared at the "Black Is" festival as a guest artist with trumpeter/composer Calvin Massey and his group, comprised of (among others) Curtis Fuller (trombone), Hakim Jami (bass), and Rashied Ali (drums).[30] Massey held what were considered radical political views; his music was performed at benefit concerts for the Black Panther Party, and he was blacklisted (or, as he put it in a linguistic transvaluation, "whitelisted") by major recording companies, with only one album ever recorded under his name.[31] Massey's music is more strident than what was customary fare for Byas and contrary to his views on the use of jazz as protest, so the old dog must be given credit for his willingness to try a new trick. Byas was then booked at the Village Vanguard for two Thursday through Saturday engagements in August with Rahsaan Roland Kirk. "Added attraction Thurs., Fri., Sat.," the ads in the *New York Times* proclaimed, "DON BYAS."[32] A photo shows Byas playing with Kirk at the club along with Sonny Brown on drums, Henry Mattathias Pearson on bass, and Peter Arthur Loeb on third tenor.[33] He attended a memorial service for fellow tenor Booker Ervin at St. Peter's Lutheran Church on September 4, 1970, then a September workshop with pianist Billy Taylor and a student band for Jazzmobile, a non-profit formed by Taylor and Daphne Arnstein to expand the audience for jazz by mobile concerts around New York City.[34]

Before returning to Amsterdam, Byas worked briefly with Art Blakey's Jazz Messengers even though Blakey already had a tenor sax, Ramon Morris. "I had two tenor players," Blakey said. Byas "was here in the United States and he wasn't working, and I couldn't stand that, so I said, 'Come on, work with me.' Fantastic artist, plus the young guys in the group took advantage of his experience."[35] Blakey paid Byas fifty dollars a night, part of which he paid from his own pocket until it became too expensive.[36] While in New York, Byas also tried to secure a recording contract; Blue Note Records responded negatively to an overture made by or on Byas's behalf, then Prestige Records offered him three hundred dollars, about $2,315 in today's dollars, to cut an album. Byas thanked the label but turned down the offer, which was consistent with his past practice of not working for less than the minimum price he thought he was worth.[37] On November 6, Byas returned to Amsterdam, but not for long.

In January 1971, Byas would reconnect with Blakey for a two-month tour of Japan, where they were warmly received. "In Japan the public is so enthusiastic," Byas's widow said. "They throw their watches and rings and stuff on the stage. Don returned . . . with a beautiful leather jacket he got from a fan who insisted he take it, he liked his music so much."[38] The tour was a grueling one, however, with over fifty concerts in two months. While in Japan, Byas would record another session with strings for Polydor Records.[39] He remains in control of his tone throughout, but the material is aimed at the middle-of-the-road, "easy listening" market and fails to generate much jazz interest. On his way back to the Netherlands, he started out with the Jazz Messengers but "left the group after one US engagement" in March at Club Baron in Harlem.[40] From there, he headed south to Washington, DC, where he participated in the Howard University Jazz Institute, a year-long program that had included other luminaries of the genre, such as Herbie Hancock and McCoy Tyner;[41] he then played a week-long engagement from April 18 to 24 with a pick-up rhythm section at Blues Alley, a Washington jazz and blues club.[42] On May 10, he joined the Duke Ellington Orchestra at Constitution Hall, Washington, DC, in a benefit concert for Wolf Trap Farm Park,[43] the nonprofit music venue located in Vienna, Virginia. At this appearance, after sitting in with the band on "In Triplicate,"[44] Byas played a duet with William Strethen "Wild Bill" Davis, who was then an arranger, organist, and second pianist with Ellington.[45] Davis deserves some credit for the invention of the sax-organ combo, having jointly hit upon the formula in 1948 in Atlantic City, New Jersey, with alto Johnny Hodges when Ellington, the latter's employer at the time, was touring England without his orchestra due to British musicians' union restrictions.[46]

Finally, nearly six months after setting out from the Netherlands like a latter-day pilgrim, Byas returned home. "He came back satisfied," his wife Jopie said, because "Japan is a country grateful for jazz musicians." But, she added, "He was tired, very tired." Byas got a physical exam but checked out of the hospital before he received the results. He performed on September 16, 1971, with the George Gruntz Orchestra (which included a number of fellow expats including Art Farmer, Herb Geller, and Dexter Gordon) at the Zurich Jazz Festival, then, after a layoff of four months, whether for reasons of fatigue or lack of work—he played three last dates in the final year of his life. The first was on February 10 at Pol's Jazz Club in Brussels with unknown sidemen; the second, on March 3, 1972, brought him together again with Tete Montoliu, whom he had first played with when the latter was still in his teens nearly four decades before for a one-night stand at The Boogaloo, a club in Venlo, the Netherlands.[47]

In addition to Montoliu on piano, the group included Henk Haverhoek on bass and Tony Inzalaco on drums. The performance was broadcast and recorded, and the copy made by Bert van Eijck, recording engineer of the Venlo Jazz Society, was deposited in the Netherlands Jazz Archive. Haverhoek described the final scene, at the same time a mournful and convivial affair:

Don had arranged transport for himself [from Amsterdam to Venlo]. Tete and he were happy to be together again. I think some alcohol was consumed, but not excessively. . . .

That day I met Don for the first time and, unfortunately, also for the last. I recall a rather energetic older musician. I was 25 years old and wasn't aware of him having lung cancer. We rehearsed some tunes and agreed on the repertoire that we were going to play, among it a composition by Don: "Orgasm."

We played the following tunes: "But Not for Me," "Misty," "'Round Midnight," "Whisper Not," "I'll Remember April," "Joy Spring," "Tenderly," "Autumn Leaves," and probably some others that I don't remember now. . . . There has been an attempt to put all of it on CD, but Tete justly didn't give permission for it: the quality of the recording wasn't good enough. For instance,

Tete played with a broken little finger of his right hand. It was splinted in a special way.

Don Byas played well. Perhaps not as good as in his high days, but for me it was a great experience. I thought he was in good condition. Better than Ben Webster, who played his concerts exclusively seated (at that time). Therefore, the news of his death later in 1972 came as a surprise to me.[48]

After he began to experience shortness of breath when performing simple tasks such as taking out the garbage, Jopie took Don to the doctor, where an X-ray of his lungs revealed a dark spot, diagnosed as incurable lung cancer. He had a three-day gig in Italy, and the pulmonologist told the couple that if Don wanted to do it and felt up to it, he should make it. He went, but when he returned to Amsterdam at the end of April, Jopie was shocked by his appearance because "he looked so horrible." He had a concert scheduled for The Hague on April 30, 1972, with Dutch musicians, but it didn't come off as Byas had to cancel due to ill health. He lost his appetite and would take only small bites of the foods he had previously liked that Jopie would buy for him, such as sausage. The last time she gave him some, he said, "Bedankt hoor" (thank you) "in that beautiful Dutch" he had learned; she then closed the door to their living room so that he would not see her cry.[49]

On August 24, 1972, at 4:30 p.m., Carlos Wesley Byas died at the age of fifty-eight; the Report of the Death of an American Citizen prepared on October 25, 1972, by Arnold J. Croddy Jr., vice consul in the United States consulate in Amsterdam, did not identify him as "Don"—the name by which the world knew him—as that was the title he bestowed on himself as a young college bandleader. He died at home, 48 Admiralengracht in Amsterdam. The cause of death was listed as lung carcinoma, according to the physician who signed the death certificate, a Dr. Moolhuizen. "The doctor said he had lung cancer and it couldn't be cured," his wife said of the doctor's visit that Byas had left before receiving his results. "I never told him," Jopie said. "He thought he had eternal life."[50] When he "was ill," she recalled, "he was laying on the couch in the living room and didn't know he was going to die, but he had a kind of premonition like, *if I were to leave the room and go to the bedroom, I'd never come back again.*"[51]

News of his demise traveled fast. That night at the Village Vanguard, Dewey Redman, a free jazz saxophonist who mainly played tenor, was performing with Keith Jarrett's American Quartet when the group started a "tune with chords," as Jarrett put it, instead of the modal sort popularized by Miles Davis and John Coltrane in the late fifties and early sixties that was the group's usual fare. Usually, Redman would "ignore the changes, but he got into the chords, and he became Byas that day," Jarrett recalled, "as a sort of tribute."[52] His widow placed a notice in an Amsterdam newspaper in the "Family Messages" section that said, "For the warm expressions of sympathy from neighbors, musicians, friends and relatives on the death of my husband Carlos Wesley Byas, our father and my brother (*en mijn Broer*),[53] I would like to express my sincere thanks." The program handed out at his memorial service similarly contained a collective expression of grief from his widow, his four Dutch children, and his extended family: "After a courageously borne illness my beloved husband, our dear caring daddy, son-in-law, brother, brother-in-law, uncle and nephew has passed away from us." A handwritten exclamation point next to her husband's age at the time of his death—stated as fifty-eight in the program—may have registered his widow's surprise that he was a year younger than she thought.

Byas's occupation was listed on the Report of Death as simply "musician," and his remains were disposed of by cremation at Westgaarde, Amsterdam, on August 29, 1972. His personal effects were left in the custody of his wife; US Passport No. Z726392 issued to him on September 28, 1967, was destroyed by the US Embassy. Copies of the Report of Death were sent to his wife and to his brother Walter, then living in Washington, DC. His three daughters—Dottie Mae, Ellie Mae, and Carlotta—were still living at home with their mother. No mention is made of Carlos Byas Jr. in the report.

After his failed attempt to revive his career in the United States, Byas lost the competitive drive that had fueled his rise from a provincial city in eastern Oklahoma to New York, Paris, and beyond. "He had no lust [for life] anymore," his wife Jopie said. He stayed close to home, where he would receive visitors from the American jazz community from time to time. "Everybody who came to Amsterdam for concerts and so on always came by," Jopie said. "Sonny Stitt, Buddy Tate, he loved that. He loved that they came to visit him."[54] Thelonious Monk stayed in the Byas house, nodding off "with his hat over his forehead," Jopie said. When their daughter asked if Monk was asleep, "he opened one eye" and "she was scared to death." Monk later sent a large floral arrangement to thank the family for their hospitality, demonstrating that even an eccentric jazzman can be a punctilious observer of etiquette. Bud Powell visited; Jopie remembered him as "a pathetic man, completely drugged."[55]

Byas's death was reported in the *New York Times* on August 25, 1972, in an obituary of fewer than one hundred words. While the paper got some of the basic facts about Byas right, it gave his age as fifty-nine, assuming he had been born in 1912; it also identified Don Redman as "Dan" and Art Blakey as "Art Blake" and said that Byas's career began with Lionel Hampton, skipping over his years with lesser-known bands. The Associated Press obituary published across America by its member newspapers also gave his age at death as fifty-nine and repeated the comparison that Byas had long sought to escape, saying that he played "in the style of the late Coleman Hawkins," but its author redeemed himself somewhat, saying that "[i]n his earlier years he was a modernizer of jazz."[56]

Jopie Byas donated scores that her husband had written to the Netherlands Jazz Archive in Amsterdam. "There were about twenty pieces, most unfinished tunes without chords," said Daniele D'Agaro, a tenor saxophonist who has played Byas's unpublished works in Europe and the United States.[57] Byas "worked out the pieces and arranged them for a quintet with Benny Bailey on trumpet," according to D'Agaro.[58] Benny (born Ernest Harold) Bailey was, like Byas, an American jazz expatriate who had played with Lionel Hampton; in 1953, he stayed in Sweden at the end of a tour of Europe with Hampton and remained there for most of the rest of his life, dying at his home in Amsterdam in 2005.[59] D'Agaro did not try to replicate Byas's sound; "Don Byas—who can imitate him? Nobody," he said. "Byas offers interesting musical solutions, vehicles for improvisation. They had a very conscious harmony. Benny [Bailey] said that Byas was formerly called 'The Professor.'"[60] Among the works Byas left behind are "Orgasm," scored for tenor sax and piano; "Dance of the Lotus Blossoms," which D'Agaro said, "sounds a little Horace Silver-ish"; and "My Heart Goes Crazy," said by D'Agaro to sound "like an evergreen, very beautiful. There are even lyrics too."[61] Bailey, who often encountered him at jazz festivals, said he never heard Byas play these later compositions in Europe; "Orgasm" was played at the 1970 Newport Jazz Festival, and according to Jopie Byas, "Duke Ellington heard it and told Don 'I can make something beautiful from that,' but Byas died before they could collaborate on its further development.[62]

At Byas's cremation, pianist Cees Slinger played "'Round Midnight," the Thelonious Monk tune that Don played so many times he claimed to know it backward and forward. A week later, Ben Webster, Don's long-time friend, bandmate, and rival with whom he had tangled often, sent a huge wreath to

Jopie.[63] Claude Nougaro, a French singer, painter, and poet who had achieved popular success by persuading singers, including Édith Piaf, to sing his lyrics,[64] approached Jopie Byas through his publisher with a proposal to add lyrics to Byas's composition "Gloria" and using that song as the starting point to expand into an opera. Enthralled by Byas's music, Nougaro's conception for the melody was romantic (if not sensual), as described by the publisher:

> The theme is the following: it's the dream of a 'catarrhe' (in the South of France . . . Catarrhe were men who live in castles up in the mountains and they strictly obey to a very hard and pure religion; some of them were called 'The perfect'; they live very simply and they did not make love in order to be purer. They were fighted [sic] and persecuted by Catholics). So the song says that the Catarrhe thinks about a woman that he idealizes and she becomes as pure as he is.

Negotiations foundered when the French publisher discovered that Jopie Byas was not, as she thought, her husband's sole heir; because he died without a will, their children came first in the order of distribution from his estate, then Byas's two brothers, and only then her.[65]

After he died, Jopie received one final visit from a musician who had played with Don, a saxophonist who "came to the door . . . claiming that Don had promised him his mouthpiece."[66] After he moved to Europe, Byas used a Berg Larsen 150 millimeter mouthpiece, according to Dutch tenor Hans Dulfer; Dulfer added an exclamation point when he wrote that[67] because a 150 millimeter mouthpiece has a comparatively large tip opening, and consequently, is more difficult to play.[68] One saxophonist referred to this model as "made for someone with lips of steel,"[69] and Dulfer said Byas was very proud of the tone he produced with it; it might indeed have represented an extraordinary feat of strength to play it as Byas did, given the declining state of his lungs as he grew older. Dexter Gordon relates that earlier in his career, in New York, Byas used a less difficult mouthpiece. "[O]ne night at the [Three] Deuces I played [Don's] horn," Gordon said, "and I dug his mouthpiece so much I asked him about it. It was a Linck [sic], metal, an eight [110 millimeter]," which "had a short facing, and . . . blew so easy. So next day I went down to Linck and told them I wanted a 'Don Byas Special.'"[70] Not content to go gently into old age, Byas thus *increased* his degree of difficulty in playing as he grew older in order to achieve the sound he wanted. Whether the mouthpiece the unexpected visitor sought was the Link or Berg Larsen, Jopie knew that her husband had not been fond of him. "But fair is fair," she said, suggesting that she may have given the man what he asked for based on her husband's alleged promise despite her misgivings.[71] She ended up donating photos, news clippings, and other memorabilia from her husband's career to the Netherlands Jazz Archive. The one item missing from her collection? A record of his big hit, "Laura," from his Parisian years, which she loved but didn't own.[72] Jopie outlived Don by thirty-two years and never remarried, perhaps cherishing what he would frequently say to her: "You are the best thing that ever happened in my life."[73] She died November 10, 2004, in Amsterdam.

As for the other woman who played an outsized role in Byas's life—his mother, Dottie Mae Weaver Byas—Jopie Byas said that after her firstborn son hit the road to perform professionally, "he never saw his mother again,"[74] although it appears that she corresponded with him, sending him a picture of her and other women who served as "Grey Ladies," American Red Cross volunteers, that was among his possessions at the time of his death. After his mother's death in Muskogee, Oklahoma, in 1962, the house that she lived in fell into a state of disrepair, and in 1993, the town put a lien on it as a dilapidated hazard to be torn down. The owners were listed as Carlos W. and Walter J. Byas, Don's brother. In 1995, Jopie Byas and her four children, as Don's heirs, signed deeds conveying their interests in the property to Walter J. Byas, who then sold the property—once valued at $65,000—for $1.

When asked near the end of his life if he agreed with the view that American jazzmen deteriorate in Europe because of the lack of inspiration and competition, Byas answered evasively.

> You have many fine musicians in America but they can be divided into two classes: the creators and the imitators. The imitators can play for many years, and play wonderfully well, as long as they stay close to their idols, their source of inspiration. When they are separated, the imitators are lost.
>
> Really, there's no sense in copying someone. It's not worth doing, because even if you do it better than the man you're copying, the one who did it first gets the credit.[75]

From these words, it is clear by implication that Byas considered himself to be a creator, not an imitator, which is why, over time, he came to resent comparisons to Coleman Hawkins. "There have never been but three schools

The Out Chorus 171

of tenor. The first was Coleman Hawkins. The second was Lester Young, and the third was me," he said in 1965 while acknowledging that there was a "possibility of a Coltrane school because he started a big thing." In words that perhaps reflected his insecurity over his place in jazz history, Byas added, "It's a funny thing but a guy like [Leonard] Chu Berry, who was marvelous, led to no school. I'll tell you how you get a school. You're going along peacefully, getting accustomed to the sounds and everybody's happy, then here comes a guy who upsets it. Everybody says: 'Here, wait a minute. What's this. We're not going far enough. That's the cat we should listen to.'"[76] It seems safe to say at this time that Byas's decision to live out his life in Europe, while it may not have dulled his competitive edge, caused him—at least as this is written—to leave no school of followers behind him in contrast to Hawkins, Young, Parker, and Coltrane. He was out of the mainstream in a tidal pool of his own.

Byas has been criticized for sentimentality, "his worst pitfall" in the view of jazz critic Gary Giddins,[77] but the occasions on which he lapsed into the lachrymose are on balance few when considered against the entire body of his work, and he always recovers before he goes too far; he is more of a tease in this mood than a swooning Young Werther. He expressed himself through the warmth of his tone and timbre, but his interpretations of even the most sentimental ballads are generally marked by a healthy restraint; that said, in his opening statement of well-known ballads, he had a tendency to ladle on the schmaltz for the first few bars as if to give his audience a chance to get their oohs and aahs out of the way before he got down to business. "Byas is an unashamed, openly emotional romantic," wrote Dan Morgenstern, who followed him as a young Dane from his first Copenhagen concerts in 1946, "but he never becomes treacly or sentimental. He makes the instrument and the melody sing."[78] It was only at the end of his life, when he was striving to revive his career—on the album with strings he cut in Japan—that he seemed to trim his style to satisfy middlebrow tastes and to be running out of imaginative fuel. By then, however, he was fifty-seven years old and on his lengthy tour with Art Blakey, and so could be excused for a lapse from his prior rigor and his fading energy in pursuit of a financially successful middle-of-the-road album.

As for the saxophone that Byas played in his final years, a Dolnet model, it lay untouched in Jopie's house for some twenty years after his death but is now owned by the Institute of Jazz Studies at Rutgers University in Newark,

New Jersey, purchased from her for $1,500; when timely payment had not been received two months after delivery from Amsterdam to New York, saxophonist Jaap Lüdeke was forced to follow up to Rutgers with a polite dunning letter on Jopie Byas's behalf.[79] The one Byas used before that was made for him in 1950, another Dolnet; Byas had switched to this brand after bringing his Selmer Radio Improved tenor with him to Europe in 1946. According to Dutch tenor Hans Dulfer, the Dolnet that Byas had previously used was stolen at some point, and when Dulfer was approached in the 1980s by a man who offered to sell it to him, he declined, saying he was suspicious of its provenance.[80] Dutch tenor Hans Duffer was approached in the 1980s by a man who offered to sell this saxophone to him, but he declined to buy it because he was suspicious of its provenance.

In the belief that the sax acquired by Rutgers was the only Dolnet that Byas had owned, Carter was at first skeptical when he received an email from a man who said he was proud that Carter was carrying on Byas's legacy and asking if he would be interested in acquiring his first Dolnet. Carter's interest was piqued when he was provided with pictures showing Byas's name on the horn, a different serial number than the one owned by Rutgers, and an octave key with the figure of a snake on it; for Byas, this was a symbol of his Native American heritage that he also added to the Dolnet he played at the end of his life.

Carter agreed to meet with the seller and tried the horn out. "I'm just trying to contain myself," he said to describe the feeling as he took it in his hands. "I put the horn together and I just started playing it and . . . the horn became possessed, literally. There was one point where I actually felt like a finger on top of my finger go down 'cause I was playing the intro to 'Laura.' And I felt like my ring finger on the right hand had something that caused it to go down to show me how to make that gliss[ando] like he used to." Carter had only intended to play one song on the instrument to try it out (a ballad, on the assumption that the sax would be fragile) but "for the next four days my horn didn't even come out of the case," he said. "I played the rehearsal and the gig on [Byas's] horn, and it didn't bat an eyelash. The keys had already been broken in to the point where it was just sublime." Convinced of its provenance and impressed with its condition, Carter began to sound the owner out to see what he would ask for it. The man said, "I wouldn't entertain anybody else but for you—$50,000." Carter didn't bite at the time, but after some research into how much the Selmer saxophone that Coleman Hawkins played on "Body and Soul" had sold for, he came back with an offer

The Out Chorus   173

of half the asking price plus an old German horn that he used for practice, and the sax was his.[81]

Byas gets a brief namecheck ("Mr. Byas blew a mean axe") in the lyrics that Jon Hendricks sings to Thelonious Monk's "In Walked Bud" on the latter's 1968 *Underground* album, a tribute to the 1944 Onyx Club band, but the lone full-length musical tribute to Byas that this author has found is Rahsaan Roland Kirk's "From Bechet, Fats, and Byas." Kirk said, "To me, Don Byas had it all; I think he had it over them all, even Hawkins."[82] While Kirk was a proselytizer for Byas during his life, the "Byas" portions of the aforementioned number are only marginally reminiscent of the older tenor; they are melodically more Kirk than Byas, although they echo Byas's relentless rhythmic attack. After Kirk's death in 1977, Byas's legacy was carried on more by absorption and imitation than outright testimonials; he gradually fell out of style, at least to the extent that one measures fashion by the number of practitioners of an instrument who proclaim themselves to be followers of a predecessor. Tracing a musician's influence may be a vain endeavor, but it is more than mere speculation to say that Byas's sound can be heard in many tenors up to (and perhaps including) the great dividing line between traditional and modern jazz tenor marked by John Coltrane. Paul Gonsalves, born in 1920; Eli "Lucky" Thompson, born in 1924; and Benny Golson, born in 1929, are three that come to mind in the first generation after Byas.

Paul Gonsalves is best known for his long career with the Duke Ellington Orchestra, but he played first with Count Basie's band from 1946 until he joined Dizzy Gillespie in 1949.[83] He was an erratic employee; his fondness for drink and drugs is apparent in a film of the Ellington band in which he leans at a nearly horizontal angle, catching a nap when not gainfully employed by ensemble play or solos. Gonsalves's star turn on "Diminuendo and Crescendo in Blue" at the 1956 Newport Jazz Festival revived Ellington's then-faded fortunes, and it contains in form and content echoes of Byas's memorable 1945 duets with Slam Stewart at the Town Hall on "(Back Home Again in) Indiana" and "I Got Rhythm." Gonsalves acknowledged the older sax's influence: "I always admired Coleman Hawkins, Don Byas, and Ben Webster," he said.[84]

Lucky Thompson replaced Byas in the Count Basie band in 1944 and, like Byas, left after only a brief tenure—less than a year; like Byas, he had a short temper that made him ill-suited for the communal life of a big band. Byas was a member of approximately fifteen bands by the time he joined Basie's, and after leaving the latter, he would play for the rest of his life primarily as a single backed by a rotation of rhythm sections. Thompson played with Lionel Hampton, Hot Lips Page, and Lucky Millinder, as had Byas, and he would play with picked-up sidemen as his career wound down. After leaving Basie, Thompson moved to Los Angeles, where he became one of that city's busiest sidemen, as Byas had been in New York. Like Byas, Thompson eventually moved to Europe (on three different occasions), but he returned each time due to his dissatisfaction with European rhythm sections—again, like Byas. "[T]here are such vast differences in conception in the rhythm section," Thompson said, that it was "impossible to establish the type of impulse to which I could respond most fully."[85] In other words, he missed the sense of swing that fellow Black American musicians could provide, just as Byas had. Byas expressed much the same sentiment as Thompson in 1965: "I'll always miss the atmosphere in the States," he said. "[B]eing away from the source .... [T]he lack of inspiration here bothers me sometimes. I sometimes feel very sad because I have no-one to play with."[86]

Thompson was ambitious to displace Byas as top tenor in the manner of a young buck who picks a fight with an old bull, as recounted by fellow tenor Johnny Griffin. "I remember one night in New York, Lucky Thompson you know always wanted to play more saxophone than Don Byas," Griffin said.

> [W]ell he came in a joint one night when Don was stoned out of his mind; could hardly hold his head up. So Lucky decided it was his night and he gets up on the bandstand and plays beautifully, and you know Lucky Thompson can really play! But Don Byas, he tells some friends of his to pick him up and place him carefully on the low bandstand and to hand him his instrument. Which thing they proceeded to do. Well Don started to play and it was like something I have never heard before—fantastic! Stoned as he was, he played the most tremendous tenor I have ever heard. And poor Lucky, who don't drink or smoke or anything, he just shrugged his shoulders and said with a smile: "Just you listen to that drunken bum there—nobody can ever beat him!"[87]

The similarities between Gonsalves, Thompson and Byas were perhaps best expressed by trombonist William "Dicky" Wells, who said that the three were so alike that Basie could not use them together in the "dueling tenor" format that he first deployed to contrast the light tone of Lester Young with the heavier, Hawkins-influenced style of Herschel Evans. "He wouldn't put

The Out Chorus

175

Don Byas and Lucky Thompson together, or Don and Paul Gonsalves," Wells said. "He aimed for two different sounds and styles."[88]

Benny Golson listed Byas and Thompson as his original influences, according to Leonard Feather,[89] which Golson himself confirmed. "Don Byas is the one that set me back on my heels when I first heard him in person,"[90] Golson said. Like other tenors of his vintage, Golson said that he memorized Coleman Hawkins's solo on "Body and Soul," and also Ben Webster's on "Raincheck" and Lester Young's on "D.B. Blues," but then, "Don Byas walked into my heart, and occupied a large part of the space there. I couldn't believe the velocity with which he moved over that horn, and his huge sound was overwhelming—so natural, not strained or manufactured. Don's articulation was amazing. He played wide intervals, jumping over the notes like skipping up or down a pair of steps."[91] A 1959 review of a Golson album said that a year earlier, he "was sounding like any number of tenor men mostly Don Byas," but that "he seems to have leveled off with an identity of his own."[92]

Sonny Rollins, born in 1929, is another member of the older generation to descend from Hawkins through Byas; only Rollins and Golson are alive as this is written. Jazz critic Martin Williams is of the view that "[a]t least by the mid-forties Byas was as sophisticated harmonically as was Rollins at his peak—witness Byas' version of *I Got Rhythm*,"[93] but this strikes one more as praise of Byas than a suggestion that Rollins's music is excessively derivative. The two had a competitive in-person encounter in 1959. "I came to Holland . . . and played at the Concertgebouw," Rollins said, "and there was a guy waiting on the steps with his horn. That was Don Byas."[94] Byas had heard about Sonny and "wanted to see if he lived up to his reputation," writes Rollins's biographer Aidan Levy. As recounted by Rollins: "We went down to my dressing room, Byas said 'Let me see what you know,'" and the two began playing. "We played and played and were there for quite a while,"[95] Rollins said. "Don Byas was my hero. . . . We played so much and so hard, because it was Don Byas, you know?"[96] Rollins collected Byas's records and considered him "one of the greatest saxophonists of all time. . . . Fortunately, I was young and strong, 'cause we almost played up to the time that I should be getting ready for the concert that night."[97] Rollins began to wonder after a while "if Byas was trying to bust his chops before his Amsterdam debut, but realized by the end of the blowing session that it was a rite of passage."[98] "I wondered whether he was trying to wear me out for my show. You know, sometimes with saxophonists there's that competitive edge. It was a great honor to play with him."[99] As for Byas's place in the history of jazz, Rollins thought of him as a bopper before his time. "Don . . . had the technical proficiency," he said. "He was a bebopper who had roots in the earlier school. . . . Those records he made with Dizzy Gillespie, 'I Can't Get Started,' 'Good Bait'—he was there already."[100] The elder tenor's influence on the younger extended from his instrument to orchestration; when Rollins recorded his "Way Out West" album with just bass (Ray Brown) and drums (Shelley Manne), no piano, it "wasn't for economic reasons"—Rollins was "thinking of Don Byas's duet with Slam Stewart on 'I Got Rhythm.'"[101]

Among the second generation out of Byas, there is Joe Lovano, born in 1952, who, in the words of Whitney Balliett, "has a big tone, not unlike . . . Chu Berry and Don Byas." Byas's most ardent acolyte among the living these days is James Carter, born in 1969, who has said he feels "mad respect" for Byas. Carter is one of the few tenors of today who has resisted the "hard, vibratoless tone" of Coltrane's followers and, in Baillett's early assessment (1995), had "clearly gone back and studied Hawkins and Byas and Johnny Hodges."[102] Carter began by "taping Byas' music off public radio [Jim Gallert's *Jazz Yesterday* show on station WDET in Detroit], listening to it over and over on his Walkman with a determined zeal to figure out every note on his horn," but he "took it further; he absorbed the Byas seriousness and competitiveness, at any tempo." Carter sometimes plays tributes to Byas at his concerts, such as one at the North Sea Jazz Festival in 2006 with the Jazz Orchestra of the Concertgebouw. To Carter, Byas is "the link between Hawkins and John Coltrane."[103]

The further one gets downstream from Byas, the less sure one can be of his influence, so it is useful to return to the source and gauge his impact on those who heard him when he was alive, who swam in his headwaters, so to speak. Musicians sometimes resist the implication that they have modeled their style on someone else and seek to cover their tracks. When alto Talmadge "Tab" Smith, who played with Count Basie, was told that he had a tone like Johnny Hodges, he indignantly replied, "What do you mean, I sound like Johnny? I'm Tab Smith, and that's who I sound like."[104]

One musical relative of Byas is John Coltrane, "out of" Art Tatum, as the horse breeders say. Byas "and Coltrane had the same idea for the same reason," said pianist Billy Taylor. "They both heard Art's seamless runs on the piano. Don was trying to do that on the tenor back then." Byas was, according to Taylor, "way ahead of Coltrane on those sheets of sound,"[105] the term coined by jazz critic Ira Gitler to describe Coltrane's improvisational style.[106]

"He was trying to make the tenor saxophone sound like Art Tatum," Taylor said. Jazz critic Martin Williams places Coltrane squarely in the tradition that produced Byas: "Coltrane owes more to the Hawkins heritage and to a brilliant Hawkins follower like Don Byas, than to Lester Young or any of Young's followers, or to Dexter Gordon or any of *his* followers first or second-hand," he wrote in 1983. "Coltrane's basic rhythmic concept came from Hawkins and Byas, who, in contrast to [Louis] Armstrong, were almost 'European' in their use of heavy and light accents within a 4/4 time context."[107]

According to Byas, he and Coltrane "were tight. Every time Coltrane came to Europe," Byas said,

> the first place he would go, he would ask: 'Where is Don Byas?' Always went where I was playing, never said hello. He'd just come in, sneak in. I don't know how this cat did it. He would sit in the club all night long and never move. I wouldn't know he was there. I'd say to myself, that looks like Trane sitting back there. So when the set was over, I would go and ask, 'How long have you been here?' He'd say, 'I just came in.'[108]

In 1964, Byas told an interviewer that Coltrane played "thoughtfully" but that he didn't like his tone and didn't think of him—yet—as a "pioneer" in the same class as Coleman Hawkins, Charlie Parker, Lester Young, and himself.[109] One anecdote suggests that, despite Byas's claims to friendship, he saw the younger man as a competitor. One night in October 1963, when Coltrane was in Stockholm, he heard that Byas was playing in town as well and dropped by with the other members of his quartet (bassist Jimmy Garrison, drummer Elvin Jones, and pianist McCoy Tyner). The group requested "Stardust" and, at the break, came backstage.[110] After embraces and kind words, Byas suggested that Coltrane try his sax; Byas carried his reputation as a he-man over to his instrument, which he had equipped with the hardest reed and a mouthpiece with a wide aperture. Byas handed the sax to Coltrane, who blew into it but could produce only "a piping sound in the bell." Byas broke out laughing, "knowing beforehand what would happen, and having his self-image as a strong guy confirmed."[111] At the end of his life, after Coltrane had surpassed him in fame and influence, Byas sounded a bitter note: "You'd be surprised how many great tenorists are students of mine," he told an interviewer. "Coltrane, for instance. He imitated my records at home, played them note by note. Only later did he create his own style."[112]

Before Coltrane, there was Charlie Parker, who was young—around four-teen years old—when he met Byas in Kansas City. Byas claimed that Parker "learned a lot from me as far as chord progressions were concerned"[113] while acknowledging that the younger man's primary influence was Lester Young: "Pres was really his boy," he said.[114] The two streams of influence were some-times viewed as tributaries, according to jazz critic Martin Williams: it has been "suggested that [Parker] combined on alto the two tenor traditions: the sophisticated and precise harmonic sense of Coleman Hawkins and his follower, Don Byas; and the rhythmic originality of Lester Young and his follower, Charlie Christian."[115] Having said that, Williams concludes that Parker surpassed Byas, and not many would disagree with that view, includ-ing the author: "Melodically and rhythmically Byas echoed Hawkins; he was an arpeggio player with a rather deliberate and regular way of phrasing. Accordingly, when [he] plays an up-tempo *Cherokee*, his solo is so filled with notes that it seems a virtuoso display, and in an apparent melodic despair he is soon merely reiterating the theme." Parker, by contrast, "broke up his phrases and his rhythm with such brilliant variety that he was able to estab-lish a continuous, easy linear invention, avoiding Byas's effect of a cluttered desperation of notes."[116]

And so, what to make of the man? Don Byas bounced around from band to band, never staying long, never forming a stable unit of his own. He left Oklahoma in search of something that neither California nor New York could provide him; dogged by drink all the while, he burned bridges on his way out of every town but somehow could persuade those who'd sent him packing—Count Basie and Mary Lou Williams being the most notable examples—to ask him back or play with him again. He was a frustrated aesthete—paint-ing, carving, throwing pottery—among men who were unlikely to express themselves artistically except by the music they made. He pursued beauty in female form and lured women through their senses with his cooking and his music: "[t]he beauty of his tone, fluidity of expression, originality of ideas and musicianship," in the words of Inez Cavanaugh,[117] as well as his silver tongue, which took on the tone of a worldly sophisticate as he aged and by the end of his life bore no trace of the red clay of Oklahoma.

He left America—and a lot of money behind—for a life in Europe, where he could, as he put it, take a week off and go fishing for carp and pike. "I never had time for that in America. If you take a week off there, you come back and you're out of a job."[118] Even though the fishing was right out his door on the Admiralengracht, to him, it was a world away from the grind of the road, where he had to spend "three or four months away in Sweden, West Germany, Switzerland or France"[119] to make a living. It was his adopted home where the nomad, who had left his country behind, found peace and happiness among his wife and children.

"When I'm home," he said, "it's like vacation."[120]

EPILOGUE

A final image of Don Byas: he is playing to a sparse crowd in a casino in the French Alps in the mid-1960s. Most of those in the audience are there not to listen to jazz or to any kind of music at all but rather to gamble, drink, and socialize. The music is an afterthought—aural wallpaper—if anyone gives it a thought.

Byas is playing not jazz but what American jazz musicians might refer to as "cocktail lounge music." "Of course I miss playing jazz," he says to a writer present, "but you can't have your cake and eat it," an allusion to the fact that he has tailored his performance to fit the old saying that he who pays the piper calls the tune.

His brand of jazz—if he could find a venue that would hire him to play it—is out of fashion. "I dig Miles, Coltrane and Dexter Gordon—but that's about all," he says. "The rest of the new guys are just thumbing their noses at the public. I hear this stuff and it makes me laugh—they can't kid me. I know what's happening. Ain't nothing happening—that's what. That Ornette Coleman—man, he's a comic strip." Byas is trapped in a no man's land between the past and the present, a member of an old guard whose ranks have been depleted by age, unable to advance against the avant-garde.

He finishes his drink—a screwdriver—and returns to the bandstand to play "Once in a While," a 1937 song by Michael Edwards with lyrics by Bud Green that lends itself to both pop and jazz interpretations. One person applauds. When he finishes the last set, Byas goes back to his hotel room and practices—without making a sound.

"When I practice now it's usually without the instrument," he says. "I lie in bed and play imaginary tenor for hours. I see everything more clearly that way."[1]

ACKNOWLEDGMENTS

The author wishes to thank the many institutions and individuals who assisted in the research for this book, of which the following is an incomplete list.

Most importantly, Dr. Cornelis "Kees" Hazevoet, biologist and jazz scholar, who knows more about the music of Don Byas than any man alive, including the author, and who has generously shared his extensive collection of Byasiana and provided input on the manuscript.

Professor Hugh Foley, Rogers State University, who had the foresight to interview Jay McShann and Ellis Ezell, two Muskogee natives who played with Don Byas.

Agustin Pérez, who provided me with valuable materials and background regarding Don Byas's time in Spain and Portugal.

DownBeat Magazine

The Netherlands Jazz Archive

Ditmer Weertman, Conservator of the Music Collections, Allard Pierson Museum, University of Amsterdam

Muskogee County, Oklahoma, Genealogical Society

Tamiment Library and Robert F. Wagner Labor Archives, New York University

Three Rivers Museum, Muskogee, Oklahoma

Oklahoma Jazz Hall of Fame

Jeroen de Valk, biographer of Ben Webster

James Carter, tenor saxophonist

Hans Dulfer

Eyla Jeschke, for her assistance in translating spoken and written Dutch to English

All errors of fact or omission are nonetheless mine alone.

NOTES

Chapter 1. In the Beginning

1. Record of Birth, Oklahoma State Board of Health, dated November 5, 1913.

2. "Don Byas Come Back," Nick van den Boezem, Omroepvereniging VARA, 1970. https://www.youtube.com/watch?v=1sGQHsSzBgo (hereinafter "Homecoming").

3. Igor Cornelissen, "Het Amsterdamse Leven van Don Byas," *Vrij Nederland*, January 2, 1993.

4. *1936 City Directory of Muskogee, Oklahoma*, 64.

5. *Tulsa Star*, October 24, 1914, 4. This was perhaps the firm of Cochenour–Rygel according to research by David Fletcher, cited in liner notes by Loren Schoenberg to *Classic Don Byas Sessions 1944–1946*, 2 (Mosaic Records LLC 2023) (hereinafter "Schoenberg").

6. Hollie I. West, "Byas: Sweeping Style," *Washington Post*, B7, April 21, 1971.

7. "Run Down and Killed by an Engine," *Tulsa World*, October 15, 1907, 5.

8. Schoenberg, 2.

9. *Muskogee Daily Phoenix* and *Times-Democrat*, April 13, 1962, 2.

10. Fred Coot, Els de Jong, "Remember . . . ! Don Byas 1912–1972, *Jazz/Press*, no. 41: 17, July 8, 1977 (hereinafter "Coot/de Jong").

11. Stanley Dance, *The World of Duke Ellington*, 202–3 (New York: Da Capo Press Inc., 1970).

12. 1900 United States Federal Census, Springfield Ward 6, Greene County, Missouri.

13. 2000 and 2010 US Federal Census statistics.

14. Alain Tomas, liner notes to *Don Byas: New York–Paris, 1938–1955*, Frémeaux & Associés FA 5622, adapted from the French text by Martin Davies (hereinafter "Frémeaux").

15. Diane Westerink, "Manual Training Movement." https://www3.nd.edu/~rbarger /www7/manualtr.html.

16. The decline in value for a house that was larger in size presumably reflects the general decline in the value of real estate during the Great Depression. See Nicholas, Tom, and Anna Scherbina, "Real Estate Prices During the Roaring Twenties and the Great Depression," *Real Estate Economics* 41, no. 2: 278–309, Summer 2013.

17. Federal Census records, 1920, 1930, and 1940.

18. Coot/de Jong.

19. Paul Stebel, "Don Byas," *Swing Time*, no. 18, Summer 1952.

20. Les Tomkins, liner notes to *Autumn Leaves: The Stan Tracey Quartet with Don Byas*, JHAS 613 (hereinafter "Tomkins").

21. Homecoming.

22. Coot/de Jong.

23. "Man Here Blows Mean Tenor," Mike Hennessey, *Melody Maker*, February 20, 1965, 6.

24. Tomkins; Conover, Willis. Bob LaPlante interview with Don Byas; unidentified audio recording, November 2, 1965. University of North Texas Libraries, UNT Digital Library (hereinafter "Conover/LaPlante"). https://digital.library.unt.edu/ark:/67531/meta dc983758/m1/?q=byas: accessed November 6, 2022.

25. Email from Angie Rush, director, Three Rivers Museum, Muskogee, Oklahoma, April 8, 2023.

26. "Muskogee," *The Encyclopedia of Oklahoma History*. https://www.okhistory.org /publications/enc/entry.php?entry=MU018.

27. *Thirteenth Census of the United States Taken in the Year 1910, Statistics for Oklahoma Supplement*, 568 (hereinafter "Oklahoma Supplement").

28. Lawrence Gushee, "A Preliminary Chronology of the Early Career of Ferd 'Jelly Roll' Morton." *American Music* 3, no. 4: 401, Winter 1985.

29. Chris Albertson, "Jelly Roll Morton: Biography and Notes on the Music," Time Life Records, Alexandria, Virginia, 1979, 3.

30. Ross Russell, *Jazz Style in Kansas City and the Southwest*, 187 (Berkeley, Los Angeles: University of California Press, 1973) (hereinafter "Russell").

31. Nathan W. Pearson Jr., *Goin' to Kansas City*, 13, 20 (Urbana, Chicago: University of Illinois Press, 1990) (hereinafter "Pearson").

32. Pearson, 48.

33. Hugh W. Foley Jr., *Oklahoma Music Guide*, 417. (Stillwater, Oklahoma: New Forums Press Inc., 2019) (hereinafter "Foley *Guide*").

34. Foley *Guide*, 44.

35. *Oklahoma Supplement*, 567.

36. Ryan P. Smith, "How Native American Slaveholders Complicate the Trail of Tears Narrative," *Smithsonian Magazine*, March 6, 2018.

37. Patrick Neal Minges, *Slavery in the Cherokee Nation: The Keetowah Society and the Defining of a People, 1855–1867* (New York: Routledge, 2003). See, for example, the Taj Mahal song "She Caught the Katy and Left Me a Mule to Ride," Henry St. Claire Fredericks Jr. (a.k.a. "Taj Mahal") and James "Yank" Rachell. https://en.wikipedia.org/wiki /She_Caught_the_Katy.

38. "African Americans," *The Encyclopedia of Oklahoma History and Culture*, Oklahoma Historical Society. https://www.okhistory.org/publications/enc/entry.php?entryname =AFRICAN%20AMERICANS#:~:text=The%20history%20of%20black%20Oklahomans %20is%20linked%20closely,government%20to%20remove%20Indian%20tribes%20from %20the%20region.

39. Hugh William Foley Jr., "Jazz from Muskogee, Oklahoma: Eastern Oklahoma as a Hearth of Musical Culture," PhD thesis, May 2000, 270, https://shareok.org/handle /11244/336297 (hereinafter "Foley Thesis"). While Ezell suggests his mother was a freed slave, this is unlikely given his birth year, which he says was 1913. It is more likely that the "freed-man" designation applied to the descendants of former slaves who appear to have been

given some form of reparations by the Cherokee Nation. Ezell says, "I've heard from the tribe every now and then, with some money that they had given to Cherokee freemen, just a few cents."

40. Victor Luckerson, "The Promise of Oklahoma: How the Push for Statehood Led a Beacon of Racial Progress to Oppression and Violence," *Smithsonian Magazine*, April 2021.

41. Hennessey.

42. Conover/LaPlante.

43. Kurt Mohr, "Don Byas: Toujours au Premier Rang," *Jazz Hot*, no. 131, April 15, 1958 (hereinafter "Mohr").

44. A photo depicts Ross, Lester Young, and Henry "Buster" Smith as members of the Blue Devils. (Courtesy of Kansas City Museum in care of LaBudde Special Collections, University of Missouri–Kansas City Libraries.)

45. "Jay McShann Relates His Musical Career in a Conversation with Frank Driggs," *Jazz Monthly*, January 1958, 5.

46. Walter Barnes Jr., "Hittin' High Notes," *Chicago Defender*, January 23, 1932.

47. Jonita Mullins, "McShann Kept Muskogee Connections," *Muskogee Phoenix*, Three Forks History, February 9, 2018. Foley *Guide*, 506. https://www.muskogeephoenix.com /news/three-forks-history-mcshann-kept-muskogee-connections/article_79627b05-2573 -53c8-9a6d-5de67a8d4832.html.

48. Foley *Guide*, 506.

49. Foley Thesis, 265.

50. Foley Thesis, 271.

51. Foley Thesis, 269.

52. Frank Driggs and Chuck Haddix, *Kansas City Jazz: From Ragtime to Bebop—A History*, 161 (Oxford, New York: Oxford University Press, 2005; Foley Thesis, 283).

53. John Chilton, *Who's Who of Jazz*, 57–8 (New York: Macmillan, 1985).

54. Gary Giddins, liner notes to *Don Byas/Bud Powell—A Tribute to Cannonball*, Columbia Records 35755.

55. Mohr; Coot/de Jong.

56. "Een Super-Sax-Solist uit Amerika: Don Byas, Veteran, maar Niet uit de Oude Doos!" *SwingTime*, January–February 1980, no. 45.

57. Douglas Henry Daniels, *One O'Clock Jump: The Unforgettable History of the Oklahoma City Blue Devils* (Boston: Beacon Press, 2006); Frank Driggs and Chuck Haddix, *Kansas City Jazz: From Ragtime to Bebop—A History* (New York, Oxford: Oxford University Press, 2005); Ross Russell, *Jazz Style in Kansas City and the Southwest* (Berkeley, Los Angeles: University of California Press); Charles Delaunay, *New Hot Discography* (New York: Criterion, 1948; Pearson).

58. Count Basie as told to Albert Murray, *Good Morning Blues: The Autobiography of Count Basie*, 246 (New York: Primus/Donald I. Fine Inc., 1985).

59. Hennessey.

60. Johnny Hodges, another sax player who began to perform at an early age, "had to work with permission of the government and with [a] guardian" accompanying him, according to saxophonist Benny Waters. *The Key to a Jazzy Life* (Toulouse, France: Self-published, 1985). Mary Lou Williams's mother had to sign papers "backstage . . . with the public notary" for her to go on her first tour as a professional with the traveling show "Hits and Bits." Max Jones, *Talking Jazz*, 180 (New York, London: W. W. Norton & Company, 1987).

61. Mohr.

62. Hennessey.

63. The year is approximate, based on a Holder interview in which he says that he organized his Twelve Clouds of Joy in 1925 and was a part of the band until he was fired approximately four years later. Nathan W. Pearson Jr., *Goin' to Kansas City*, 55 (Urbana, Chicago: University of Illinois Press, 1994).

64. Coot/de Jong.

65. Tom Lord Discography, Andy Kirk, leader.

66. Victor Luckerson, "The Promise of Oklahoma: How the Push for Statehood Led a Beacon of Racial Progress to Oppression and Violence," *Smithsonian Magazine*, April 2021.

67. Jan Evensmo, *The Tenor Sax of Carlos Wesley Byas "Don," Part 1 (1938–1946)*, 2 (hereinafter "Evensmo").

68. DSS Registration Card No. 4385, Carlos Wesley Byas, October 16, 1940.

69. Schoenberg, 1.

70. Frémeaux.

71. The Smithsonian Institution Jazz Oral History Program, interview of Jay McShann conducted by Stanley and Helen O. Dance, December 11, 1978.

72. Bill Cranfield, "Don Byas," *Jazz News*, December 20, 1961, 13.

73. Karl George, Tom Lord Discography. https://en.wikipedia.org/wiki/Karl_George _(musician).

74. *New York Times*, July 21, 1987.

75. Stanley Dance, *The World of Count Basie*, 186 (New York: Da Capo Press Inc., 1980).

76. Coot/de Jong.

77. Frémeaux.

78. Charles Delaunay, *New Hot Discography*, 74 (New York: Criterion, 1948).

79. Conover/LaPlante; Tomkins.

80. Evensmo, 2, says the year was 1933, but the *City Directory of Muskogee, Oklahoma* for 1936 lists Byas as a student residing with his parents and brothers at 610 West Fon du Lac, 64. This could have been a case where a prior year's entry for the family was carried forward due to lack of new information either because the family didn't respond or the publisher didn't inquire.

81. Conover/LaPlante.

Chapter 2. Los Angeles Nights

1. Cee Pee Johnson, Tom Lord Discography.

2. *California Eagle* (Los Angeles, California), Friday, October 12, 1934, 6. "Raybon" Tarrant was possibly Ramon Tarrant, a "powerful and swinging drummer . . . who . . . was also an effective blues shouter." McVea, Jack, Eric Thacker, and Howard Rye, Grove Music Online, January 20, 2002 (hereinafter "*California Eagle*"). https://www.oxfordmusiconline .com/grovemusic/view/10.1093/gmo/9781561592630.001.0001/omo-9781561592630-e -2000284400?rskey=lu1AIi&result=1. "Eddie Garland" may have been a bassist with various groups of Kid Ory's, such as the Sunshine Orchestra and Spike's Seven Pods of Pepper Orchestra, Tom Lord Discography, Ed Garland.

3. Wim Bossema, "Een Amerikaanse Saxophonist Die Te Goed Nederlands Sprak Teruggenvonden Muziek van Don Byas Gereconstrueerd," *de Volkskrant*, February 16, 1996; Bill Cranfield, "Don Byas," *Jazz News* 5, no. 51: 13, December 20, 1961; Kurt Mohr, "Don Byas: Toujours au Premier Rang," *Jazz Hot*, no. 131: 15, April 1958 (hereinafter "Mohr").

4. Mohr.

5. Tom Lord Discography under both "Bert" and "Burt" Johnson; Sammy Price, *What Do They Want? A Jazz Autobiography*, 38 (Urbana and Chicago: University of Illinois Press, 1990).

6. Paul Stebel, "Don Byas," *Swing Time*, no. 18, Summer 1952 (hereinafter "Stebel").

7. Alain Tomas, liner notes to *Don Byas: New York–Paris, 1938–1955*, Frémeaux & Associés FA5622.

8. Stebel.

9. *The Complete Library of Congress Recordings by Alan Lomax, Jelly Roll Morton, Autobiographical Notes from Tempo-Music Files* (1938), 57 (Rounder Records 11661-1888-2 BK01).

10. Steven Isoardi, "*Central Avenue Sounds*," 88–89, booklet accompanying *Central Avenue Sounds: Jazz in Los Angeles (1921–1956)*, R2 75872, Rhino Entertainment Company, 1999; John Chilton, *Who's Who of Jazz*, 109 (New York: Macmillan, 1972) (hereinafter "Chilton").

11. Hugues Panassié and Madeleine Gautier, *Dictionary of Jazz*, 100 (London: The Jazz Book Club, 1959) (hereinafter "Panassié and Gautier"); Paul Howard, Tom Lord Discography.

12. Mohr.

13. Leonard Feather, *The Encyclopedia of Jazz*, 256 (New York: Bonanza Books, 1960); Bill Cranfield, "Don Byas," *Jazz News*, December 20, 1961, 13; Les Hite, Tom Lord Discography.

14. Lionel Hampton with James Haskins, *Hamp: An Autobiography*, 48 (New York: Amistad Press Inc., 1989); Panassié and Gautier, 42.

15. Chilton, 58; Michael Erlewine, Vladimir Bogdanov, Chris Woodstra, Scott Yanow, *AllMusic Guide to Jazz*, 164 (San Francisco: Miller Freeman, 1998); Coot/deJong.

16. Panassié and Gautier, 100.

17. Panassié and Gautier, 43.

18. Delaunay, 353 (Hollywood, California: Criterion Music Corp., 1948).

19. Lionel Hampton, "Show Biz Buzzes," *Pittsburgh Courier*, December 5, 1953, 23.

20. *California Eagle*, Friday, May 8, 1936, 11.

21. *California Eagle*, Friday, November 6, 1936, 10.

22. Barefield is heard on Calloway records beginning in June 1932 and continuing through early 1935, Eddie Barefield, Tom Lord Discography.

23. Fred Coot and Els de Jong, *Jazz/Press*, no. 41: 17–18, July 8, 1977 (hereinafter "Coot/de Jong").

24. Eric Townley, "Hitting the Road" interview with Eddie Barefield, *Storyville 76*, April–May 1978, 150 (hereinafter "Barefield Interview"). The film was released in April 1936: "The Singing Kid." imdb.com, https://www.imdb.com/title/tt0028257/.

25. Stanley Dance, *The World of Count Basie*, 323 (New York: Da Capo Press Inc., 1980) (hereinafter "Dance *Basie*").

26. Mohr.

27. Barefield Interview.

28. Leroy White, Tom Lord Discography; Dance *Basie*, 317.

29. Barefield Interview, 150.

30. Luc Delannoy, *Pres: The Story of Lester Young* (translated by Elena B. Odio), 67, citing unpublished interview, New York, June 13, 1984 (Fayetteville, Arkansas: University of Arkansas Press, 1993).

31. Dance *Basie*, 324.

32. Eddie Barefield, *Tom Lord Discography*.

33. Ira Gitler, *Swing to Bop: An Oral History of the Transition in Jazz in the 1940s*, 48 (New York, Oxford: Oxford University Press, 1985).

34. *California Eagle*, Friday, December 4, 1936, 10.

190   Notes

35. Charles Delaunay, *New Hot Discography*, 518 (Hollywood, California: Criterion Music Corp., 1948).

36. *California Eagle*, Saturday, December 19, 1936, 14 (hereinafter "Delaunay").

37. Barry Kernfeld, "Douglass, Bill [William Vernon]," Grove Music Online, January 20, 2002. https://www.oxfordmusiconline.com/grovemusic/view/10.1093/gmo/9781561592630 .001.0001/omo-9781561592630-e-2000128300. Howard Rye, "Phillips, Gene [Eugene Floyd]," January 20, 2022. https://www.oxfordmusiconline.com/grovemusic/view/10.1093/gmo /9781561592630.001.0001/omo-9781561592630-e-2000666000. Marv Goldberg, Lorenzo Flennoy & The Flennoy Trio, 2017. https://www.uncamarvy.com/FlennoyTrio/flennoytrio.html.

38. *Central Avenue Sounds*, 19, edited by Clora Bryant, Buddy Collette, William Green, Steven Isoardi, Jack Nelson, Horace Tapscott, Gerald Wilson and Marl Young (Berkeley, Los Angeles: University of California Press, 1998) (hereinafter "*Central Avenue Sounds*").

39. Howard Rye, "Scott, Mabel," Grove Music Online, January 20, 2002, Grove Music Online, January 20, 2022. https://www.oxfordmusiconline.com/grovemusic/view/10.1093 /gmo/9781561592630.001.0001/omo-9781561592630-e-2000689700.

40. Bill Cranfield, "Don Byas," *Jazz News*, December 20, 1961, 13.

41. Buck Clayton assisted by Nancy Miller Elliott, *Buck Clayton's Jazz World* (Oxford: Bayou Press Ltd., 1986).

42. Coot/de Jong.

43. Colin Larkin, "Charlie Echols," *The Encyclopedia of Popular Music* (London: Omnibus Press, 4th edition, 2006).

44. *Central Avenue Sounds*, 59.

45. New York, Oxford: Oxford University Press, 1992.

46. London, New York: Continuum, 2001.

47. Los Angeles: Rhino Records, 1999.

48. Storyville, 150.

49. Harold S. Kaye, "Francis 'Doc' Whitby," *Storyville 110*, December 1983–January 1984, 56.

50. *Central Avenue Sounds*, interview of Lee Young by Stephen L. Iosardi, Tape Number I, Side Two, June 14, 1991, Department of Special Collections, University of California, Los Angeles.

51. Cornelis J. Hazevoet, *Don Byas, Part 1: American Recordings, 1938–1946*, 27–34, updated through March 8, 2022.

52. *Central Avenue Sounds*, 63.

53. Tad Hershorn, *Norman Granz: The Man Who Used Jazz for Justice*, 40–44, 97–89 (Berkeley: University of California Press, 2011).

Chapter 3. Women and Children

1. State of Arkansas, Pulaski County Marriage License and Certificate of Marriage, February 10, 1942.

2. Rowe's Notebook, *Pittsburgh Courier*, February 28, 1942, 20.

3. Cheryl Nichols, *Historically Black Properties in Little Rock's Dunbar School Neighborhood*, Arkansas Historic Preservation Program (2013). https://www.arkansasheritage.com /docs/default-source/ahpp-documents/local-historic-contexts/dunbar_new11f1ae89-855f -45ae-9b52-48d61c78f359.pdf?sfvrsn=9ffbbf6b_5.

4. *Arkansas State Press*, December 21, 1951.

5. Igor Cornelissen, "Het Amsterdamseleven van Don Byas," *Vrij Nederland*, January 2, 1993, 70–72.

6. Linda Dahl, *Morning Glory: A Biography of Mary Lou Williams*, 87–88 (New York: Pantheon Books, 1999) (hereinafter "Dahl").

7. Dahl, 47.

8. Dahl, 28.

9. Dahl, 119.

10. Classics 814 (1995).

11. GNP Crescendo GNP 9030 (1974).

12. Dahl, 147, 231.

13. Dan Morgenstern, liner notes to *Don Byas: Savoy Jam Party, The Savoy Sessions*. New York: Savoy SJL 2213, Arista Records, 1976.

14. Cornelis J. Hazevoet, *Don Byas Chronology, 1946–1972 (Updated through April 7, 2023)*, 4, 8. See also inlay booklet to *Bobby Jaspar, Early Years: From Bebop to Cool, 1947–1951, Featuring the Bob Shots*, Fresh Sound Records FRS CD 977, 2019 (Byas "stayed in Belgium for more than three months" in spring 1947).

15. Arthur Goepfert, "Ellington and Goodman Visit Switzerland," *Jazz Journal*, July 1950.

16. Reproduced in insert to *Don Byas–George Johnson: Those Barcelona Days, 1947–1948*, Fresh Sound Records FSR 3001 CD, 1999.

17. Contract between Don Carlos Wesley Byas and Ritmo y Melodia Public dated September 19, 1947.

18. Boris Vian, *Manual of Saint Germain-des-Prés*, 107 (New York: Rizzoli, 2005).

Chapter 4. Influences

1. Arthur Taylor, *Notes and Tones*, 52 (New York: Coward, McCann & Geoghegan, 1977) (hereinafter "Taylor").

2. Mark Berresford, *That's Got 'Em: The Life and Music of Wilbur C. Sweatman*, 73 (Jackson: University Press of Mississippi, 2010) (hereinafter "Berresford").

3. Nathan W. Pearson Jr., *Goin' to Kansas City*, 47–8 (Urbana and Chicago: University of Illinois Press, 1994) (hereinafter "Pearson").

4. Quoted in liner notes by Stanley Dance to *The High and Mighty Hawk*, Felsted Records SJA 2005, 1958 (hereinafter "Dance Liner Notes").

5. Pearson, 47–48. John Chilton says Hawkins was playing "in a 12th Street theatre orchestra" when he signed with Smith. *Who's Who of Jazz*, 139 (New York: Macmillan, 1972) (hereinafter *Chilton Who's Who*).

6. Berresford, 138–40.

7. *Chilton Who's Who*, 138–9.

8. John Chilton, *The Song of the Hawk: The Life and Recordings of Coleman Hawkins*, 147 (Ann Arbor: University of Michigan Press, 1990) (hereinafter "Chilton *Hawk*").

9. Charles Delaunay, *New Hot Discography*, 363 (New York: Criterion, 1948) (hereinafter "Delaunay").

10. Dance Liner Notes.

11. Mike Hennessey, "Man Here Blows Mean Tenor," *Melody Maker*, February 20, 1965, 6.

12. "Crowd of Five Hundred Hears Fletcher Henderson," *Kansas City Call*, December 22, 1933, 11; Driggs & Haddix, 125.

13. *Good Morning Blues: The Autobiography of Count Basie as Told to Albert Murray*, 148 (New York: Primus/Donald I. Fine Inc., 1985) (hereinafter "*Good Morning Blues*").

14. *Good Morning Blues*, 149.

15. Pearson, 80, interview of Eddie Durham.

16. Max Jones, *Talking Jazz*, 192 (New York: W. W. Norton & Company, 1988) (hereinafter "Jones").

17. Jones, 192.

18. Rex Stewart, *Jazz Masters of the 30s*, 69 (New York: Da Capo Press Inc., 1972) (hereinafter "Stewart").

19. Jones, 252.

20. Stewart, 69–70, 149–50.

21. Joachim E. Berendt, *The Jazz Book: From Ragtime to the 21st Century*, 103 (Lawrence Hill Books, 2009).

22. Martin Williams, *The Jazz Tradition*, 82 (New York, Oxford: Oxford University Press, 1983).

23. Billy Taylor interview by Marc Myers. https://marcmyers.typepad.com/my_weblog /page/127/ (hereinafter "Myers").

24. Chilton *Hawk*, 191.

25. Bert Vuijsje, "Don Byas: From Swing to Bop," *Vrij Nederland*, July 11, 1964.

26. Cornelis J. Hazevoet, PhD, *Don Byas, Part 1: American Recordings, 1938–1946*, updated March 8, 2022 (hereinafter "Hazevoet Discography 1").

27. George Hoefer, "The First Bop Combo," *DownBeat*, June 20, 1963. Chilton *Hawk* says the price was $1.10, 214.

28. Chilton *Hawk*, 214.

29. Michael Erlewine, Vladimir Bogdanov, Chris Woodstra, and Scott Yanow, *AllMusic Guide to Jazz*, 508 (San Francisco: Miller Freeman Books, 1998).

30. Hazevoet Discography 1, 37.

31. Jan Evensmo, *The Tenor Sax of Carlos Wesley Byas "Don," Part 1 (1938–1946)*, updated June 3, 2020.

32. Chilton *Hawk*, 206.

33. Chilton *Hawk*, 212.

34. Rosenkrantz, 118.

35. Taylor, 52.

36. Leonard Feather, *The Encyclopedia of Jazz*, 452 (New York: Bonanza Books, 1960) (hereinafter "Feather").

37. Stanley Dance, *The World of Count Basie*, 73–74 (New York: Da Capo Press Inc., 1980) (hereinafter "Dance *Basie*").

38. Taylor, 52.

39. Dance *Basie*, 73–74.

40. Taylor, 53.

41. Taylor, 52.

42. Taylor, 52.

43. James Lester, *Too Marvelous for Words: The Life and Genius of Art Tatum*, 17 (New York, Oxford: Oxford University Press, 1994) (hereinafter "Lester").

44. Alain Tomas, liner notes to *Don Byas: New York–Paris, 1938–1955*, Frémeaux & Associés FA 5622, adapted from the French text by Martin Davies (hereinafter "Frémeaux").

45. Taylor, 68.

Notes

46. Myers.

47. Igor Cornelissen, "The Amsterdam Life of Don Byas," *Vrij Nederland*, January 2, 1993.

48. Gary Giddins, *Visions of Jazz: The First Century*, 623 (New York, Oxford: Oxford University Press, 1998).

49. Dance *Basie*, 217.

50. Taylor, 71.

51. Whitney Bailliett, *Jelly Roll, Jabbo & Fats: 19 Portraits in Jazz*, 37–38 (Oxford, New York: Oxford University Press, 1983).

52. Jim Burns, "Don Byas," *Jazz Journal* 18, no. 9, September 1965.

53. Stanley Dance, liner notes, *The Complete Johnny Hodges Sessions 1951–1955*, 6. Mosaic Records MR6–126, 1989.

54. Frank Büchmann-Møller, *Someone to Watch Over Me: The Life and Music of Ben Webster*, 284 (Ann Arbor: University of Michigan Press, 2009).

55. Stanley Dance, liner notes, *Giants of Jazz* 20 (Time Life Records, TL-J19).

56. Lester, 212.

57. Frémeaux.

58. Polydor Special series, 2482 068, printed in the Netherlands. The rights to this album are licensed through SABAM, a Belgian performing rights organization. "SABAM" is an acronym for "Société d'Auteurs Belge-Belgische Auteurs Maatschappij."

59. *Ben Webster Johnny Hodges Sextet: The Complete 1960 Jazz Cellar Session*, Solar Records 4569895 2011.

60. Kurt Mohr, "Don Byas: Toujours au Premier Rang," *Jazz Hot*, no. 131: 15, April 1958.

61. BASF Stereo MB 20658.

62. Cornelis J. Hazevoet, PhD, *Don Byas, Part 2: European Recordings, 1946–1972*, 24–5 (hereinafter "Hazevoet 2"). Klaus Stratemann, *Duke Ellington: Day by Day and Film by Film*, 321 (Copenhagen: JazzMedia ApS, 1992).

63. *Johnny Hodges: The Rabbit in Paris*, Inner City Records IC7003; Hazevoet 2, 23–24.

64. Hazevoet 2, 73; Ken Vail, *Duke's Diary: The Life of Duke Ellington, 1950–1974*, 366 (Lanham, Maryland and Oxford: The Scarecrow Press Inc., 2002).

65. Alyn Shipton, *A New History of Jazz*, 580. London, New York: Continuum, 2001.

66. Taylor, 71.

67. The source of Berry's nickname is disputed; one school of thought holds that it was derived from his practice of chewing on his mouthpiece, while another attributes it to his mustache in the style of Dr. Fu Manchu, a villain who appeared first in the novels of English author Sax Rohmer beginning in 1912 and was later featured in movies, radio, television, and comic books.

68. Quoted in Dan Morgenstern, liner notes to *Savoy Jam Party: The Savoy Sessions*, Arista Records SJL 2213, 1976. Morgenstern (hereinafter "Morgenstern Liner Notes").

69. Feather, 135.

70. Gary Giddins, review of *Anthropology*, Black Lion BL 160, *DownBeat*, January 31, 1974; Hazevoet Discography 2, 61.

71. Pearson, 46.

72. Loren Schoenberg, booklet included in Mosaic Records, *Classic Columbia, Okeh and Vocalion: Lester Young with Count Basie (1936–1940)*, booklet 2–3, 2008 Mosaic Records LLC; Dave Gelly, *Being Prez: The Life and Music of Lester Young*, 27 (Oxford: Oxford University Press, 2006).

73. Leonard Feather, *The Encyclopedia of Jazz*, 212 (New York: Bonanza Books, 1960).

74. Frémeaux.

75. Hans Dulfer, "In Memoriam Don Byas," *Jazzwereld* 40, no. 14, 1972.

76. "Berg Larsen 150?" Sax on the Web. https://www.saxontheweb.net/threads/berg-larsen-150.90815/.

77. Les Tompkins, liner notes to *The Stan Tracey Quartet with Don Byas: Autumn Leaves*, JHAS 613.

78. Chip Deffaa, *Voices of the Jazz Age*, 35 (Urbana and Chicago: University of Illinois Press, 1990).

79. Monroe Berger, Edward Berger, and James Patrick, *Benny Carter: A Life in American Music* 2, 114 and 115 (Metuchen, New Jersey; London: 1982, The Scarecrow Press and the Institute of Jazz Studies, Rutgers University) (hereinafter "Berger, Berger & Patrick II").

80. Berger, Berger & Patrick II, 182–83.

Chapter 5. Move to New York

1. Bert Vuijsje, "De Come-Back van Don Byas," *Haagse Post*, April 29, 1970 (hereinafter "Vuijsje").

2. Buck Clayton, *Buck Clayton's Jazz World Assisted by Nancy Miller Elliott*, 107 (Oxford: Bayou Press, 1986).

3. Ethel Waters, *His Eye is on the Sparrow: An Autobiography by Ethel Waters with Charles Samuels*, 227 (Garden City, New York: Doubleday & Company Inc., 1951).

4. Donald Bogle, *Heat Wave: The Life and Career of Ethel Waters*, 247 (New York: Harper, 2011) (hereinafter "Bogle").

5. Inez Cavanaugh, liner notes to *Don Byas: A Night in Tunisia*, recorded at the Montmatre Jazzhus, Copenhagen, January 13–14, 1963 (hereinafter "Cavanaugh").

6. Timme Rosenkrantz, *Harlem Jazz Adventures: A European Baron's Memoir, 1934–1969*, adapted and edited by Fradley Hamilton Garner, 117–18 (Lanham, Toronto, Plymouth: The Scarecrow Press, 2012) (hereinafter "Rosenkrantz"); Rud Niemans, "Jazznomade Don Byas Vond Huis en Liefde in Amsterdam-West," *De Telegraaf*, July 3, 1964.

7. Cavanaugh.

8. *New York Amsterdam News*, February 12, 1938, 17.

9. Cornelis J. Hazevoet, *Don Byas Chronology, 1912–1946, Updated through February 7, 2023* (hereinafter "Hazevoet Chronology 1").

10. Rosenkrantz, 113.

11. Dan Morgenstern, text to *Jazz People*, photographs by Ole Brask, 192 (New York: Da Capo Press, 1993) (hereinafter "Morgenstern *Jazz People*").

12. Interview of Billy Taylor NEA Jazz Master (1988) by Anthony Brown and Eugene Holly, November 19, 1993, the Smithsonian Institution Jazz Oral History Program, NEA Jazz Master Interview, 66.

13. Morgenstern *Jazz People*, 192.

14. Alain Tomas, liner notes to *Don Byas: New York–Paris, 1938–1955*, Frémeaux & Associés FA 5622, adapted from the French text by Martin Davies.

15. Cornelis J. Hazevoet, *Don Byas Part 1: American Recordings 1938–1946*, last updated March 8, 2022, 40, 43–48 (hereinafter "Hazevoet Discography 1").

16. Rosenkrantz, 182.

17. Rosenkrantz, 118.

18. Rosenkrantz, 116.

19. "Rosenkrantz Lines Up a Solid Crew," *New York Amsterdam News*, June 11, 1938, 7A.

20. Jan Evensmo, *The Tenor Sax of Carlos Wesley Byas "Don," Part 1, 1938–1946*, last updated June 3, 2020 (hereinafter "Evensmo 1").

21. Rosenkrantz, 120.

22. Vuijsje.

23. Fred Coot and Els de Jong, *Jazz/Press*, no. 41: 18, July 8, 1977; Hazevoet Discography 1, 74.

24. Hazevoet Chronology 1.

25. Tom Lord's Discography, Don Byas; Charles Delaunay, *New Hot Discography*, 464–65 (Hollywood: Criterion Music Corp., 1982).

26. Extreme Rarities LP 1002, Kaydee KD-8.

27. Evensmo 1, 3.

28. Stanley Dance, *The World of Count Basie*, 101 (New York: Da Capo Press Inc., 1980) (hereinafter "Dance *Basie*").

29. *Good Morning Blues: The Autobiography of Count Basie as Told to Albert Murray*, 210 (New York: Primus/Donald I. Fine Inc., 1985) (hereinafter "*Good Morning Blues*").

30. Tammy L. Kernodle, *Soul on Soul: The Life and Music of Mary Lou Williams*, 79 (Urbana, Chicago: University of Illinois Press, 2020). John Williams, Tom Lord Discography.

31. Max Jones, *Talking Jazz*, 197 (New York, London: W. W. Norton & Company, 1987) (hereinafter "Jones").

32. Leonard Feather, *Encyclopedia of Jazz*, 465 (New York: Bonanza Books, 1960).

33. Jones, 194.

34. Frank Driggs and Chuck Haddix, *Kansas City Jazz: From Ragtime to Bebop—A History*, 139 (New York, Oxford: Oxford University Press, 2005) (hereinafter "Driggs & Haddix").

35. Gunther Schuller, *The Swing Era: The Development of Jazz, 1930–1945*, 358 (New York, Oxford: Oxford University Press, 1989) (hereinafter "Schuller").

36. Evensmo 1, 4.

37. Jones, 198.

38. Linda Dahl, *Morning Glory: A Biography of Mary Lou Williams*, 119 (New York: Pantheon Books, 1999).

39. Andy Kirk as told to Amy Lee, *Twenty Years on Wheels* (Ann Arbor, Michigan: University of Michigan Press, 1989).

40. Jones, 198.

41. Hazevoet Discography 1, 8.

42. Photo of record label sent to the author by James Accardi, October 31, 2023.

43. https://www.richardvacca.com/on-february-17-1913/.

44. Hazevoet Chronology.

45. Monroe Berger, Edward Berger, James Patrick, *Benny Carter: A Life in American Music* 1, 313 (Metuchen, New Jersey, London: The Scarecrow Press and the Institute of Jazz Studies, Rutgers University, 1982) (hereinafter "Berger & Patrick").

46. Billie Holiday with William Dufty, *Lady Sings the Blues*, 67 (New York: Harlem Moon/Broadway Books, 1956).

47. Berger & Patrick 1, 313.

48. Selective Service Act of 1940, 50 USC, War and National Defense.

49. Interview with Jay McShann, conducted by Stanley Dance and Helen O. Dance, The Smithsonian Institution Jazz Oral History Program 2; 3, 6, December 11, 1978.

50. Driggs & Haddix, 180.

51. Leonard Feather, *The Encyclopedia of Jazz*, 247 (New York: Bonanza Books, 1960).

52. David Griffiths, interview of Harvey Davis, "Still Very Much on the Scene," *Storyville* 115, October–November 1984, 17.

53. Colin Larkin, ed., *The Guinness Encyclopedia of Popular Music*, 1,110 (1992).

54. John Chilton, *Who's Who of Jazz*, 55 (New York: Macmillan, 1978).

55. Joop Visser, liner notes to *The Dizzy Gillespie Story*, Proper Records Ltd., Properbox 20, 12; Alyn Shipton, *Groovin' High: The Life of Dizzy Gillespie*, 92 (New York, Oxford: Oxford University Press, 1999); Tom Lord Discography, Edgar Hayes.

56. William H. Reddig, *Tom's Town: Kansas City and the Pendergast Legend*, 330 (Columbia: University of Missouri Press, 1986).

57. *Kansas City Jazz*, Coral Records CP 39 (1970). Jan Evensmo lists Byas as playing on "Piney Brown Blues" by Joe Turner and His Fly Cats, Evensmo 1, 4–5, but there is no sax heard on that number and the album cover does not list Byas as a member of that group of musicians.

58. Quoted in Dave Gelly, *Being Prez: The Life and Music of Lester Young*, 73 (Oxford University Press, 2007) (hereinafter "Gelly").

59. Tom Lord's Discography, Paul Bascomb.

60. "How They Stand," *Pittsburgh Courier*, December 28, 1946, 21.

61. Morgenstern *Jazz People*, 165.

62. Les Tomkins, liner notes to *Autumn Leaves: The Stan Tracey Quartet with Don Byas*, JHAS 613.

63. Chris DeVito, Yasuhiro Fujioka, Wolf Schmaler, and David Wild, ed. by Lewis Porter, *The John Coltrane Reference*, 82–92. (New York: Routledge, 2008); J. C. Thomas, *Chasin' the Trane*, photo image (New York: Da Capo Press Inc. 1976).

64. Interview of John Hammond by Michael Brooks, 1974 (private collection); 31.

65. Vuijsje.

66. Evensmo 1, 8.

67. Sinclair Traill, "In My Opinion: Don Byas," *Jazz Journal*, March 1961.

68. Charles Fountain, *Another Man's Poison*, 64 (Chester, Connecticut: The Globe Pequot Press, 1984) (hereinafter "Fountain").

69. Loren Schoenberg, liner notes to *Count Basie and His Orchestra: The Columbia Years, America's #1 Band!* (Legacy Recordings/Sony Music International, 2003).

70. Schuller, 255.

71. Fountain, 65.

72. Dizzy Gillespie with Al Fraser, *To BE, or not . . . to BOP*, 139 (Garden City, NY: Doubleday & Company Inc., 1979) (hereinafter "Gillespie").

73. *The Men from Minton's*, May 1941 (Esoteric ESJ4; ES548).

74. Todd Bryant Weeks, *Luck's in My Corner: The Life and Music of Hot Lips Page*, 136 (New York: Routledge, 2008).

75. Gillespie, 139.

76. Gillespie, 139–40.

77. Hazevoet Discography 1, 12.

78. Hazevoet Discography 1, Evensmo 1.

79. E.g., *Don Byas—Midnight at Minton's*, Onyx Records ORI 208 (1973); *Don Byas—Live at Minton's 1941*, Musidisc 30 JA 5121 (1975).

80. *Good Morning Blues*, 263.

81. "Billy Rowe's Note Book," *Pittsburgh Courier*, December 11, 1943, 15.

Notes

82. *Good Morning Blues*, 263.

83. Dance *Basie*, 124.

84. Gary Giddins, "Weatherbird: The Mile High Mainstream," *Village Voice*, October 8, 1985, 80 (hereinafter "Giddins").

85. Giddins.

86. Gelly, 87.

87. "Billy Rowe's Note Book," *Pittsburgh Courier*, June 26, 1943, 20.

88. Gelly, 87.

89. Gelly, 87, quoting Rutgers Jazz Oral History Project interview.

90. *Jazz Journal*, March 1972.

91. Cavanaugh.

92. "Don Byas on Basie," *Crescendo*, October 1965, 18.

Chapter 6. Life after Basie

1. Paul Stebel, "Don Byas," *Swing Time*, no. 18, Summer 1952.

2. Bill Cranfield, "Don Byas," *Jazz News* 5, no. 51: 13, December 20, 1961 (hereinafter "Cranfield").

3. Ira Gitler, *Swing to Bop: An Oral History of the Transition in Jazz in the 1940s*, 7 (New York, Oxford: Oxford University Press, 1985).

4. Leonard Feather, *The Encyclopedia of Jazz*, 458 (New York: Bonanza Books, 1960) (hereinafter "Feather").

5. Timme Rosenkrantz, *Harlem Jazz Adventures: A European Baron's Memoir, 1934–1969*, 179–80, 175–76 (hereinafter "Rosenkrantz").

6. Todd Bryant Weeks, *Luck's in My Corner*, 166 (New York: Routledge, 2008).

7. "Woody'n You (1943)." https://www.jazzstandards.com/compositions-1/woodynyou.htm.

8. Joop Visser, liner notes to *The Dizzy Gillespie Story, 1939–1950*, Proper Records Properbox 30, 16 (hereinafter "Visser").

9. Ira Gitler, *Jazz Masters of the 40's*, 75 (New York: Da Capo Press Inc., 1966).

10. George Hoefer, "The First Bop Combo," *DownBeat*, June 20, 1963, 19 (hereinafter "Hoefer").

11. "World's Greatest Saxophonist at Yacht Club Nitely," *New York Amsterdam News*, May 13, 1944, 9B.

12. Eric Felten, "How the Taxman Cleared the Dance Floor," *Wall Street Journal*, March 17, 2013.

13. Cornelis J. Hazevoet, *Don Byas Chronology 1912–1946*, updated through August 27, 2016 ("Hazevoet Chronology 1").

14. Feather, 254; Hugues Panassié and Madeleine Gautier, *Dictionary of Jazz*, 110 (London: The Jazz Book Club, 1959).

15. *Eddie Heywood 1944*, Classics 947, Classics Records 1997.

16. *New York Daily News*, May 15, 1944, 247; Hollywood *Citizen-News*, May 17, 1944, 7.

17. Visser, 16.

18. Hazevoet Discography 1, 35–37.

19. Tammy L. Kernodle, *Soul on Soul: The Life and Music of Mary Lou Williams*, 106, citing interview by John Wilson, July 26, 1977, transcript, National Endowment for the Arts / Institute of Jazz Studies (University of Illinois Press, 2004).

20. Hazevoet Discography 1, 38.

21. Frank Driggs and Chuck Haddix, *Kansas City Jazz: From Ragtime to Bebop—A History*, 80, 107–8 (New York, Oxford: Oxford University Press, 2005).

22. Hazevoet Discography 1, 40–41.

23. Michael Erlewine, Vladimir Bogdanov, Chris Woodstra, and Scott Yanow, *AllMusic Guide to Jazz*, 651 (San Francisco: Miller Freeman Books, 1998).

24. Barry Mishkind, "The Story Behind: 'Transcribed,'" *The Broadcasters' Desktop Reference*. https://www.thebdr.net/the-story-behind-transcribed/.

25. Jan Evensmo, *The Tenor Sax of Carlos Wesley Byas "Don" Part 1 (1938–1946)*, 17.

26. John Chilton, *Who's Who of Jazz*, 32 (New York: Da Capo Press Inc., 1985) (hereinafter "Chilton").

27. Hazevoet Discography 1, 44.

28. Hazevoet Discography 1, 46–50.

29. Dan Burley's Back Door Stuff, *New York Amsterdam News*, November 18, 1944.

30. Hazevoet Chronology 1.

31. Chuck Miller, "V-Disc Records (1943–1949), Victory Music, *Goldmine*, February 1999. http://www.chuckthewriter.com/vdisc.html.

32. Hazevoet Discography 1, 49, 54, 62.

33. Dorothy Donegan, classically trained jazz pianist and sometime vocalist, was said to be with "Don Byas' solid jazz band" in a February 1945 newspaper column, but no evidence of her playing with Byas has been found. *New York Amsterdam News*, February 10, 1945, B6.

34. John Shaw, "Billy Eckstine: A Singer Who United the Great Players," *Crescendo International*, April 1970, 14.

35. https://www.discogs.com/release/4276377-Billy-Eckstine-And-His-Orchestra-Mr-B.

36. Hazevoet Discography 1, 76.

37. Ken Vail, *Bird's Diary: The Life of Charlie Parker 1945–1955*, 8 (Castle Communications, 1996).

38. Arthur Taylor, *Notes and Tones*, 179 (New York: Coward, McCann & Geoghegan, 1977).

39. Chilton, 138.

40. Whitney Balliett, *Night Creature*, 131 (New York, Oxford: Oxford University Press, 1981).

41. Husband and wife go to a marriage counselor. "What seems to be the matter?" the counselor asks. "We never talk," the wife says. "Take him to a jazz club," the counselor says. "What good will that do?" the wife asks. The counselor replies "Everybody talks during the bass solo."

42. Feather, 382.

43. Hoefer; Dave Gelly, *Being Prez: The Life and Music of Lester Young*, 86–87 (New York, Oxford: Oxford University Press, 2007).

44. Cornelis J. Hazevoet, PhD, *Don Byas, Part 2: European Recordings, 1946–1972*, 52–3 (hereinafter "Hazevoet Discography 2").

45. Williams, 194.

46. Hazevoet Discography 1, 40, 58; Hazevoet Discography 2, 11.

47. Williams, 194.

48. Alyn Shipton, *Groovin' High*, 129 (New York, Oxford: Oxford University Press, 1999).

49. Hoefer.

50. https://www.discogs.com/artist/4575649-Little-Sam-Orchestra; Hazevoet Discography 2, 57.

51. Hazevoet Discography 2, 58; Jazz Musician Pseudonyms. https://jazzmf.com/jazz-musician-pseudonyms/.

52. https://en.wikipedia.org/wiki/Cozy_Cole; Hazevoet Discography 2, 55–8.

53. Neil Slaven, liner notes to *Big Joe Turner* B, 1942–46, JSP Records JSP7709B, 2003.

54. Hazevoet Chronology 1.

55. Jesper Thilo, *Man ska' ku' se Komikken* (Copenhagen: Lindhardt & Ringhof, 2000). Thilo is a Danish saxophonist.

Chapter 7. Sax about Town

1. Timme Rosenkrantz, *Harlem Jazz Adventures: A European Baron's Memoir, 1934–1969*, adapted and edited by Fradley Hamilton Garner, 177 (Lanham, Toronto, Plymouth: The Scarecrow Press, 2012) (hereinafter "Rosenkrantz").

2. Rosenkrantz, 183.

3. "Season's Best Jazz Bash Financial Flop," *DownBeat*, July 1, 1945.

4. Martin Williams, *The Smithsonian Collection of Classic Jazz*, 68, The Smithsonian Collection of Recordings, 1987.

5. Andre Hodeir, *Jazz: Its Evolution and Essence*, 181 (New York: Grove Press Inc., 1956).

6. Anthony Barnett, "Don Byas; Tenor Saxophonist," *Jazz Monthly*, September 1965, 14.

7. Thomas Cunniffe, "Timme Rosenkrantz and the Town Hall Concert (June 9, 1945). Jazz History Online, March 5, 2019, Best of JHO Archives.

8. *DownBeat*, July 1, 1945, "Season's Best Jazz Bash Financial Flop!"

9. Rosenkrantz, 185.

10. Cornelis J. Hazevoet, *Don Byas: Part 1, American Recordings, 1938–1946*, 60 (March 8, 2022) (hereinafter "Hazevoet Discography 1").

11. "Teddy Wilson, 'Ivory Man, on All-Star Jazz Concert," the *Baltimore Afro-American*, September 29, 1945, 22.

12. Leonard Feather, *The Encyclopedia of Jazz*, 431–2 (New York: Bonanza Books, 1960).

13. https://en.wikipedia.org/wiki/Glad_To_See_You.

14. Slam Stewart, Tom Lord Discography.

15. Hazevoet Discography 1, 63, 65.

16. Hazevoet Discography 1, 61.

17. *Esquire*, February 1946, 56.

18. Perry Gilliard, "Breaking the Ice," *Philadelphia Tribune*, 6, July 30, 1946.

19. "Laura (1945)," JazzStandards.com. https://www.jazzstandards.com/compositions-0/laura.htm.

20. Interview of Billy Taylor NEA Jazz Master (1988) by Anthony Brown and Eugene Holly, November 19, 1993, the Smithsonian Institution Jazz Oral History Program, NEA Jazz Master Interview, 44 (hereinafter "Taylor Interview").

21. John Chilton, *The Song of the Hawk: The Life and Recordings of Coleman Hawkins*, 214 (Ann Arbor, Michigan: University of Michigan Press, 1990) (hereinafter "Chilton *Hawk*").

22. "Nee, de Kern van de Jazz, Dat is de Ritmiek," *Het Parool*, September 25, 1985.

23. Lionel Pailler, *Don Byas* (Paris, Éditions Nocturne, March 2006).

24. *The Seven Lively Arts.* https://www.ibdb.com/broadway-production/seven-lively-arts-1604#People.

25. Gilbert Seldes. https://en.wikipedia.org/wiki/Gilbert_Seldes.

26. Taylor Interview, 59.

27. Cornelis J. Hazevoet, *Don Byas: Part 2, European Recordings, 1938–1946* (March 8, 2022), 55, 58.

28. *Seven Lively Arts.* http://www.sondheimguide.com/porter/seven.html.

29. Fred Coot, Els de Jong, "Remember . . . ! Don Byas 1912–1972," *Jazz/Press*, no. 41: 17, July 8, 1977 (hereinafter "Coot/de Jong").

30. Ira Gitler, *Jazz Masters of the 40's*, 67 (New York: Da Capo Press Inc., 1966) (hereinafter "Gitler *Jazz Masters*").

31. Leslie Gourse, *Straight, No Chaser: The Life and Genius of Thelonious Monk* (New York: Schirmer Books, 1997).

32. Hazevoet Discography 1, 15.

33. Wayne Enstice and Paul Rubin, *Jazz Spoken Here: Conversations with Twenty-Two Musicians* (New York: Da Capo Press Inc., 1994).

34. Coot/de Jong.

35. Alyn Shipton, *A New History of Jazz*, 3, 439 (London, New York: Continuum, 2001) (hereinafter "Shipton").

36. Rud Niemans, *Jazznomade Don Byas Vond Huis en Liefde in Amsterdam-West, De Telegraaf*, July 3, 1964.

37. Gary Giddins, *Celebrating Bird: The Triumph of Charlie Parker*, 110 (New York: Beech Treet Books/William Morrow, 1987).

38. Danny Barker, *A Life in Jazz*, ed. Alyn Shipton (London: Macmillan, 1986).

39. Ken Vail, *The Life of Duke Ellington, 1927–1950*, 75 (Lanham, Maryland, Oxford: Scarecrow Press Inc., 2002).

40. "52nd Street, NYC: Big City Jazz in the 30s," The Jim Cullum Riverwalk Jazz Collection (hereinafter "Riverwalk"). https://riverwalkjazz.stanford.edu/?q=program/52nd-street-nyc-big-city-jazz-30s.

41. Shipton, 404.

42. *Stuff Smith: Time and Again*, Proper Records Ltd. PVCD 118; Tom Lord Discography, Joe Venuti, Joe Sullivan.

43. Riverwalk.

44. Shipton, 406–7.

45. Martin Williams, *Jazz in Its Time*, 188 (New York, Oxford: Oxford University Press, 1989).

46. Hazevoet Discography, 1, 50.

47. Gitler *Jazz Masters*, 74.

48. Arthur Taylor, *Notes and Tones: Musician to Musician Interviews*, 122 (New York: Coward, McCann & Geoghegan, 1977) (hereinafter "Arthur Taylor").

49. Don De Leighbur, "Musical Virtuosos Develop Among Itinerant 'Sidemen,'" *Philadelphia Tribune*, April 28, 1945, 13.

50. Alyn Shipton, *Groovin' High: The Life of Dizzy Gillespie*, 120 (New York, Oxford: Oxford University Press, 1999).

51. Arthur Taylor, 122.

52. Dizzy Gillespie with Al Fraser, *To BE, or not . . . to BOP*, 202 (Garden City, New York: Doubleday & Company Inc., 1979) (hereinafter "Gillespie").

Notes

53. Arthur Taylor, 122.

54. Leonard Feather, *Inside Bebop*, chapter 3 (Kindle edition).

55. Gillespie, 206.

56. Shapiro & Hentoff, 367.

57. Gitler *Jazz Masters*, 186.

58. Hazevoet Discography 1, 51.

59. Taylor, 53.

60. Hennessey Tenor.

61. Driggs & Haddix, 214.

62. Gitler *Jazz Masters*, 22.

63. Robert Reisner, *Bird: The Legend of Charlie Parker*, 20–21 (New York: Da Capo Press Inc., 1977).

64. "Jam-Fests Switch to Spotlite Club," *Pittsburgh Courier*, January 20, 1945, 22.

65. Ken Vail, *Bird's Diary: The Life of Charlie Parker 1945–1955*, 9–10 (Castle Communications, 1996) (hereinafter "Vail Chronology").

66. Leif Bo Petersen, Charlie Parker Chronology 1949, 4, last updated December 21, 2023. https://www.plosin.com/milesahead/BirdChronology.aspx (hereinafter "Petersen Chronology").

67. Gary Giddins, *Celebrating Bird: The Triumph of Charlie Parker*, 102 (New York: Beech Tree Books/William Morrow, 1987).

68. *DownBeat*, July 15, 1945, 1.

69. Petersen Chronology, Vail Chronology 13.

70. "Heat Wave Sessions," *New York Amsterdam News*, February 3, 1945, B11.

71. Ira Gitler, *Swing to Bop*, 76 (New York, Oxford: Oxford University Press, 1985).

72. Petersen Chronology 7; Vail Chronology 14.

73. *Chicago Defender*, "Harlem Notes," August 4, 1945.

74. Chilton *Hawk*, 232.

75. "Nite Life Shenanigans with Bobbye," *Philadelphia Tribune*, March 30, 1946, 14; the author nonetheless mistakenly says the composer was trumpeter Benny Harris.

76. Leonard Feather, *The Encyclopedia of Jazz*, 236 (New York: Bonanza Books, 1960).

77. Hazevoet Discography 1, 71.

78. Gunther Schuller, *The Swing Era: The Development of Jazz, 1930–1945*, 391 (New York, Oxford: Oxford University Press, 1989).

79. Hazevoet Discography 1, 72.

80. *New York Amsterdam News*, September 15, 1945, 21.

81. *New York Times*, December 21, 1944, June 22, 1945, September 24, 1945, and December 30, 1945.

82. Spelled both "Diga Diga Doo" and "Diga Diga Du" on the original Okeh record label.

83. Evensmo.

84. Hazevoet Discography 1, 72; Jan Evensmo, *The Tenor Sax of Carlos Wesley Byas "Don" Part 1 (1938–1946)*, 30; Monroe Berger, Edward Berger, and James Patrick, *Benny Carter: A Life in American Music* 2, 121–23 (Metuchen, NJ, London: 1982, The Scarecrow Press and the Institute of Jazz Studies, Rutgers University).

85. Hazevoet Discography 1, 74–78.

Chapter 8. To Europe

1. O. Harsløf, "For Europeans Only" in *Festschrift für Walter Baumgartner*," Universität Greifswald (2006).

2. "Don Redman Builds Band," *Billboard*, May 29, 1943, 25; "Advance Bookings," *Billboard*, July 15, 1944, 16.

3. G. Montassut, "Redman au Beaulieu," *Jazz Hot*, no. 12: 8, 2nd series, 1946.

4. Cornelis J. Hazevoet, *Don Byas: Part 1, American Recordings, 1938–1946*, 74 (March 8, 2022) (hereinafter "Hazevoet Discography 1").

5. Don Redman: The Little Giant of Jazz. nps.gov. https://www.nps.gov/hafe/learn/history culture/don-redman.htm.

6. John L. Clark, "Redman, Don(ald Matthew)," Grove Online Music Dictionary, January 13, 2014, Redman, Don(ald Matthew), Grove Music (oxfordmusiconline.com).

7. Count Basie as told to Albert Murray, *Good Morning Blues; The Autobiography of Count Basie*, 137–38 (New York: Primus/Donald I. Fine Inc., 1985).

8. Franklin S. Driggs, "Kansas City and the Southwest," collected in *Jazz: New Perspectives on the History of Jazz by Twelve of the World's Foremost Jazz Critics and Scholars*, edited by Nat Hentoff and Albert J. McCarthy, 229 (New York: Da Capo Press, 1974).

9. Armin Büttner, Leif Bo Petersen, Anthony Barnett, Howard Rye, Mario Schneeberger, and Dieter Salemann, *Don Redman's 1946 European Tour* (hereinafter "*1946 Tour* Wordpress"). https://donredman1946tour.wordpress.com.

10. Timme Rosenkrantz, *Harlem Jazz Adventures: A European Baron's Memoir, 1934–1969*, adapted and edited by Fradley Hamilton Garner, 185 (Lanham, Toronto, Plymouth: The Scarecrow Press, 2012) (hereinafter "Rosenkrantz").

11. Thomas Cunniffe, "Timme Rosenkrantz and the Town Hall Concert (June 9, 1945). Jazz History Online, March 5, 2019, Best of JHO Archives.

12. Hazevoet Discography 1, 74.

13. Sarah Vaughan, Boyd Raeburn, Tom Lord Discography. Joop Visser, liner notes to *The Dizzy Gillespie Story: 1939–1950*, Proper Records Ltd. Properbox 30, 26.

14. Jim Burns, "Don Byas," *Jazz Journal* 18, no. 9: 5, September 1965; Ruth Miller, "Mapping Brooklyn," *Chicago Defender*, 19, March 16, 1946.

15. Hazevoet Discography 1, 75.

16. Hazevoet Discography 1, 77.

17. Hazevoet Discography 1, 77.

18. H. Nicolausson, "Svart Jazz/Köpenhamn," *Orkester Journalen*, October 1946, 10. Redman's wife also traveled with the group.

19. Interview of Billy Taylor NEA Jazz Master (1988) by Anthony Brown and Eugene Holly, November 19, 1993, the Smithsonian Institution Jazz Oral History Program, NEA Jazz Master Interview, 68 ("Taylor Interview").

20. Inez Cavanaugh, liner notes to *Don Byas: A Night in Tunisia*, recorded January 13–14, 1963, at the Montmarte Jazzhus, Copenhagen.

21. Leo Mathisen, Little Beat Records 13001 (Denmark); *1946 Tour* Wordpress.

22. Boris Rabinowitch, liner notes to *For Europeans Only*, Steeplechase Classics 6020/21 (1983).

23. Leonard Feather, *The Encyclopedia of Jazz*, 391 (New York: Bonanza Books, 1960).

24. Tom Lord, The Jazz Discography, Alan Jeffreys.

25. *1946 Tour* Wordpress.

26. Steeplechase Classics 6020/21 (1983).

27. Dan Morgenstern NEA Jazz Master interview by Ed Berger, March 28–29, 2007, Archives Center, National Museum of American History, Smithsonian Institution.

28. *1946 Tour* Wordpress.

29. *1946 Tour* Wordpress.

30. *1946 Tour* Wordpress.

31. *1946 Tour* Wordpress.

32. Tom Lord Discography, Jackie Tunis.

33. Discogs says 1906 (https://www.discogs.com/artist/693035-Glyn-Paque); *Who's Who of Jazz* and Grove Music Online say 1907. John Chilton, *Who's Who of Jazz*, 253 (New York: Macmillan, 1972); "Paque, (Eric) Glyn, Otto Flückinger and Howard Rye, January 20, 2002. https://www.oxfordmusiconline.com/grovemusic/view/10.1093/gmo/9781561592630 .001.0001/omo-9781561592630-e-2000752600?rskey=OeYxeC&result=1.

34. *Basler Woche*, no. 31, November 8, 1946, cited in *1946 Tour* Wordpress.

35. November 4, 1946, *Neue Zürcher Zeitung*, cited in *1946 Tour* Wordpress.

36. Taylor Interview, 68.

37. Taylor Interview, 69.

38. Billy Taylor to Marc Myers. https://marcmyers.typepad.com/my_weblog/page/127/.

39. Jacq, "Les Cahiers d'un Alligator," *Hot Club Magazine*, June 18, 1947, 9.

40. "Don Byas et l'Accordéon," *L'Actualité Musicale et Artistique*, 1947.

Chapter 9. Don, Sam, Carlos

1. Teddy Reig, quoted in liner notes by Dan Morgenstern to *Savoy Jam Party: The Savoy Sessions*, Arista Records SJL 2213, 1976 (hereinafter "Morgenstern Liner Notes").

2. Glyn Paque, from Poplar Bluff, Missouri, moved to Switzerland in 1937. John Chilton, *Who's Who of Jazz*, 253 (New York: Macmillan, 1972).

3. Fred Coot and Els de Jong, interview of Jopie Byas, *Jazz/Press* no. 41: 17–18, July 8, 1977.

4. Wim Bossema, "Een Amerikaanse Saxophonist Die Te Goed Nederlands Sprak," *de Volkskrant*, February 16, 1996.

5. Conover, Willis. Bob LaPlante interview with Don Byas; unidentified audio recording, November 2, 1965. University of North Texas Libraries, UNT Digital Library (hereinafter "Conover/LaPlante"). https://digital.library.unt.edu/ark:/67531/metadc983758/m1/?q=byas: accessed November 6, 2022.

6. Conover/LaPlante.

7. Martin Davies, liner notes to *Don Byas, New York–Paris, 1938–1955*, Frémeaux & Associés FA 5622.

8. Inez Cavanaugh, liner notes to *Don Byas: A Night in Tunisia*, recorded at the Montmatre Jazzhus, Copenhagen, January 13–14, 1963 (hereinafter "Cavanaugh").

9. Bert Vuijsje, "Don Byas: Van Swing naar Bop," *Vrij Nederland*, July 11, 1964.

10. Jesper Thilo, *Man Ska' ku' Se Komikken* (Copenhagen: Lindhardt & Ringhof, 2000) (hereinafter "Thilo"). Thilo is a Danish saxophonist.

11. Conover/LaPlante.

12. Conover/LaPlante.

13. Igor Cornelissen, "Het Amsterdamse Leven van Don Byas," *Vrij Nederland*, January 2, 1993 (hereinafter "Cornelissen").

14. Marc Myers, "Don Byas in Paris, 1946–54, *Jazzwax*, April 2009.

15. Cavanaugh.

16. J. P. Meriadec, "Don Byas: Le Plus Grande Saxophoniste du Monde," *Le Petit Varois*, July 16, 1958.

17. Don Byas (live video) "Tea for Two." https://www.youtube.com/watch?v=jH6nVM_ep84.

18. Stuff Smith, *Pure at Heart: Anecdotes & Interviews*, edited by Anthony Barnett, 69 (Lewes, East Sussex: Allardyce, Barnett, 2002).

19. Hans Dulfer, *Jazzwereld* 40, no. 14, 1972 (hereinafter "Dulfer"); Cornelissen.

20. Dulfer.

21. Author interview of Han Bennink, April 3, 2023.

22. "Don Byas' Geluk," *Het Parool*, May 3, 1963.

23. Mike Hennessey, "Man Here Blows a Mean Tenor," *Melody Maker*, February 20, 1965, 6.

24. Pierre Christophe, "Le Saxophoniste Tenor Carlos Wesley 'Don' Byas." http://www.jazzhotclub-marennes-oleron.fr/donbyas.pdf (hereinafter "Pierre Christophe").

25. Steve Voce, "And Quiet Flows the Don," *Jazz Journal*, October 1972, 7 (hereinafter "Voce").

26. Thilo.

27. Thilo.

28. Voce.

29. Pierre Christophe.

30. J. P. Meriadec, "Don Byas Le Plus Grand Saxophoniste du Monde est Partie en Guerre contre les Poissons," *Le Petit Varois*, July 16, 1958.

31. *Meet Me Where They Play the Blues: Jack Teagarden und Seiner Musik*, Buchendorf, Oreos Verlag 1986; Georgia Land Lotteries, Wikipedia. https://www.quora.com/Was-Jack-Teagarden-a-Native-American.

32. Rex Stewart, *Jazz Masters of the 30s*, 147 (New York: Da Capo Press, 1972).

33. Bill Coleman, *Trumpet Story*, 203 (Boston: Northeastern University Press, 1989) (hereinafter "Coleman").

34. *Buck Clayton's Jazz World* by Buck Clayton assisted by Nancy Miller Elliott, 100–101 (Oxford: Bayou Press, 1986) (hereinafter "Clayton").

35. Clayton, 135–36.

36. Dulfer.

37. Interview by author of James Carter, February 17, 2023, in which Carter describes a gift of several cognac-soaked reeds of Byas's that Hans Dulfer gave him (hereinafter "Carter Interview"). Telephone interview with Hans Dulfer, March 31, 2023.

38. Morgenstern Liner Notes.

39. Dan Morgenstern, *Jazz People*, photographs by Ole Brask, 166 (New York: Da Capo Press, 1993).

40. The author draws no conclusions with respect to Byas's capacity for drink based on his genetic makeup.

41. Coleman, 203–4.

42. Jack van Poll, "Jack's Groove: Don Byas," *Jazzmozaiek* 9, no. 8: 29, 2009.

43. John Litwiler, "Art Blakey: Bu's Delights and Laments," *DownBeat*, November 2009, 33. ("Bu" was a nickname derived from "Buhaina," part of the Muslim name he took—Abdullah Ibn Buhaina—at one point during a 1947 sojourn in Africa.)

44. Thilo.

45. Mike Hennessey, "Don Byas: Emphatic Expatriate," *DownBeat*, July 27, 1967, 23 (hereinafter "Hennessey Expatriate").

Notes 205

46. Dizzy Gillespie with Al Fraser, *To BE, or not . . . to BOP*, 203 (Garden City, New York: Doubleday & Company Inc., 1979).

47. Pierre Christophe.

48. Cornelissen.

49. Cornelissen.

50. Hennessey Expatriate, 23.

51. Thilo.

52. Dulfer.

53. https://en.wikipedia.org/wiki/Teddy_Reig.

54. Morgenstern Liner Notes.

55. Steve Goodson, "Conn Saxophones: A History of Excellence and Innovation." https://www.saxgourmet.com/conn-saxophones-a-history-of-excellence-and-innovation/.

56. Selmer Balanced Action (1936–1947), Saxophone.org. https://www.saxophone.org/museum/saxophones/model/34.

57. Carter interview.

58. Arthur Taylor, *Notes and Tones*, 54, interview in Paris, November 11, 1969 (New York: Coward, McCann & Geoghegan, 1977) (hereinafter "Arthur Taylor").

59. *De Volkskrant*, March 1, 1970.

60. Todd Bryant Weeks, *Luck's in My Corner: The Life and Music of Hot Lips Page*, 137 (New York: Routledge, 2008).

61. Arthur Taylor, 54.

62. "Saxofonist Don Byas: Op Jazz-Muziek Moet Je Lekker Kunnen Dansen," *De Telegraaf*, July 30, 1964.

63. Cornelissen.

64. Gunther Schuller, *The Swing Era: The Development of Jazz, 1930–1945*, 588 (New York, Oxford: Oxford University Press, 1989).

65. Hennessey Expatriate, 23.

66. Chris Albertson, "Jelly Roll Morton: Biography and Notes on the Music," 6 (Time Life Records, 1979) (hereinafter "Albertson").

67. Alan Lomax, *Mister Jelly Roll*, 51–52 (Berkeley: University of California Press, 2001) (hereinafter "Lomax").

68. Lomax, 324.

69. Jack V. Buerkle and Danny Barker, *Bourbon Street Black: The New Orleans Black Jazzman*, 14 (New York: Oxford University Press, 1973).

70. Lomax, 4, 8.

71. Cornelissen.

72. Albertson, 5.

73. Lomax, 330.

74. Hampton Hawes with Don Asher, *Raise Up Off Me*, 126 (New York: Thunder's Mouth Press, 2001).

75. Arthur Taylor, 182.

Chapter 10. Spanish (and Portuguese) Tinge

1. Morton, "Jelly Roll" (1938: Library of Congress Recording), The Complete Recordings by Alan Lomax.

2. Cornelis J. Hazevoet, *Don Byas Chronology, 1946–1972*, 3 (hereinafter "Hazevoet Chronology 2"), citing André Hodeir, "Don Redman à Pleyel," *Jazz Hot*, 1946, 2nd series, no. 12: 6–7, and G. Montassut, "Redman au Beaulieu," *Jazz Hot*, 1946, 2nd series, no. 12: 7–8.

3. Billy Taylor to Marc Myers. https://marcmyers.typepad.com/my_weblog/page/127/.

4. John Chilton, *Who's Who of Jazz*, 123–24 (New York: Macmillan, 1972) (hereinafter "Chilton").

5. Leonard Feather, *The Encyclopedia of Jazz*, 228 (New York: Bonanza Books, 1960) (hereinafter "Feather").

6. Chilton, 152; Feather, 258.

7. Cornelius J. Hazevoet, *Don Byas Part 2: European Recordings, 1946–1972* (updated through January 14, 2023), 8 (hereinafter "Hazevoet 2").

8. Hazevoet 2, 8–13.

9. Harold Wentworth and Stuart Berg Flexner, *Dictionary of American Slang*, 423 (New York: Thomas Y. Crowell Company, 1975).

10. Cornelius J. Hazevoet, liner notes to *Don Byas Meets the Jacobs Brothers: Groovin' High*, Dutch Jazz Archives NJA 1603 (2016).

11. Hazevoet 2, 12.

12. Feather, 268.

13. Hazevoet Chronology 2, 4, citing wallonica.org/blog/2019/12/18/faisant-raoul-1917-1979.

14. Hazevoet Chronology 2, 5–8.

15. Armand Molinetti. https://www.discogs.com/artist/384816-Armand-Molinetti.

16. Hazevoet 2, 27.

17. Bernard Hilda. https://www.discogs.com/artist/1482530-Bernard-Hilda.

18. Jordi Pujol Baulenas, *Jazz in Barcelona 1920–1965* (Almendra Music, 2005) (hereinafter "Baulenas").

19. Baulenas.

20. Alfredo Papo, "Don Byas, el Musico . . ." *Ritmo y Melodia*, July 1947, no. 22 (hereinafter "Papo").

21. Baulenas.

22. Hazevoet Chronology 2, 5.

23. *JazzHot*, no. 29, January 1949.

24. Uncredited liner notes to *Lunch in LA*, Contemporary Records/Fantasy Inc., OJCCD-1953-2 (C-14004), 2003.

25. Tete Montoliu. https://en.wikipedia.org/wiki/Tete_Montoliu.

26. Baulenas; *Don Byas—George Johnson: Those Barcelona Days, 1947–1948*, Fresh Sound Records, FSR 3001 CD (hereinafter "Fresh Sound CD").

27. Jan Evensmo, *The Tenor Sax of Carlos Wesley Byas "Don," Part 2 (Europe 1946–1960)*, updated Feb. 17, 2021.

28. Hazevoet Chronology 2, 6.

29. Hazevoet Chronology 2, 6.

30. Advertisement, *La Vanguardia Esparola*, December 5, 1947, 10.

31. Baulenas.

32. Baulenas.

Notes

33. Fresh Sound CD.

34. Email from Cornelis Hazevoet, March 11, 2023. https://en.wikipedia.org/wiki/National _Union_(Portugal).

35. *Amália Rodrigues & Don Byas: Encontro*, Celluloid Records CELCD6147.

36. https://www.furious.com/perfect/amaliarodrigues.html.

37. "Fado," Salwa El-Shawan Castelo-Branco, Grove Music Online, January 20, 2001. https://www.oxfordmusiconline.com/grovemusic/view/10.1093/gmo/9781561592630 .001.0001/omo-9781561592630-e-0000009216?rskey=DN6PIF&result=1.

38. https://en.wikipedia.org/wiki/Fado.

39. Fred Coot and Els de Jong, *Jazz/Press*, no. 41: 17, July 8, 1977.

40. US Bureau of Labor Statistics CPI Inflation Calculator. https://www.historicalstatistics .org/Currencyconverter.html.

41. Advertisement, *La Vanguardia Espanola*, May 14, 1961; Hazevoet Chronology 2, 24.

42. Hazevoet Chronology 2, 6.

43. Alain Tomas, liner notes to *Don Byas: New York–Paris, 1938–1955*, Frémeaux & Associés FA5622; BASF MB 20658.

44. Bill Cranfield, "Don Byas," *Jazz News*, December 20, 1961, 13.

Chapter 11. Paris Years

1. Alain Tomas, liner notes to *Don Byas, New York–Paris: 1938–1955*, Frémeaux & Associés, FA5622 (hereinafter "Frémeaux").

2. "Paris is Liberated after Four Years of Nazi Occupation." https://www.history.com/this -day-in-history/paris-liberated.

3. Marc Myers, "Don Byas in Paris, 1946–54," Jazzwax, October 21, 2014. https://www.jazz wax.com/2014/10/don-byas-in-paris-1946-54.html.

4. Bill Coleman, *Trumpet Story*, 167 (Boston: Northeastern University Press, 1981) (hereinafter "Coleman").

5. Coleman; Cornelis J. Hazevoet, *Don Byas: Part 2, European Recordings, 1946–1972*, updated through January 14, 2023 (hereinafter "Hazevoet 2").

6. Coleman, 168.

7. Coleman, 169.

8. Frémeaux; Hazevoet 2, 20; Cornelis J. Hazevoet, *Don Byas Chronology 1946–1972*, updated through February 7, 2023, 12 (hereinafter "Hazevoet Chronology 2").

9. Coleman, 169–70.

10. Coleman, 167–68.

11. *DownBeat*, July 1, 1949, 3.

12. Coleman, 170.

13. "Le Ringside." It is unclear what Robinson's involvement in the restaurant was, and it is possible he was merely employed for publicity to attract patrons; in the most extensive biography of Robinson, *Sweet Thunder: The Life and Times of Sugar Ray Robinson* by Wil Haygood (New York: Alfred A. Knopf, 2009), no mention is made of the club under either of its two names. https://fr.wikipedia.org/wiki/Le_Ringside.

14. The *Baltimore Afro-American*, May 31, 1952, Magazine Section, 4.

15. Bill Cranfield, "Don Byas," *Jazz News* 5, no. 51: 13, December 20, 1961 (hereinafter "Cranfield").

16. Hazevoet Chronology 2, 12.

17. Buck Clayton, assisted by Nancy Miller Elliott, "Buck Clayton's Jazz World," 151 (Bayou Press Ltd, Oxford, 1986).

18. Art Buchwald, "Just Jazz," quoted in liner notes to *Jazz from Saint-Germain-des-Prés*, Verve Clef Series, MGV-8119.

19. Cranfield.

20. Hazevoet Chronology 2, 13.

21. Hazevoet 2, 22.

22. Klaus Stratemann, *Duke Ellington: Day by Day and Film by Film*, 321 (Copenhagen: JazzMedia ApS, 1992) (hereinafter "Stratemann"); Alun Morgan, "The Nineteen-Fifties," included in *Duke Ellington: His Life and Music*, edited by Peter Gammond, 105 (New York: Da Capo Press Inc., 1977). Trumpeter Bill Coleman makes the curious claim that Byas was hired by Ellington to replace trombonist Ted Kelly "who had taken sick and had to go back to the USA," Coleman, 176. Hazevoet clarifies that "[t]echnically speaking Rouse's replacement was Alva McCain" and that Byas was "an added star" attraction. Hazevoet Chronology 2, 14.

23. Stratemann, 322.

24. Email from Cornelis J. Hazevoet, February 20, 2023; the dates were April 19, 1950, at the Théâtre Municipal, Mulhouse, France, and April 25, 1950, at the Théâtre Municipal, Casablanca, Morocco.

25. *Jazz Hot*, no. 650, Winter 2009–10, February 16, 2010.

26. Stuart Nicholson, *Reminiscing in Tempo: A Portrait of Duke Ellington*, 279 (Boston: Northeastern University Press, 1999), citing Patricia Willard, interview with Lawrence Brown, July 1976, the Smithsonian Institution Jazz Oral History Program.

27. Al Monroe, "Swinging the News," *Chicago Defender*, September 9, 1950, 20.

28. Leonard Feather, *The Encyclopedia of Jazz*, 190 (New York: Bonanza Books, 1960).

29. IMDb https://www.imdb.com/title/tt6893170/; https://www.youtube.com/watch?v=ssxIy7hQ2LA.

30. Hazevoet 2, 28.

31. Hazevoet 2, 25–31.

32. Marc Myers, https://marcmyers.typepad.com/my_weblog/page/127/.

33. The *Baltimore Afro-American*, May 31, 1952, Magazine Section, 4.

34. Frémeaux.

35. *DownBeat*, December 2, 1953.

36. Hazevoet 2, 31–35.

37. Dizzy Gillespie with Al Fraser, *To Be, or Not . . . to Bop*, 64 (University of Minnesota Press, 2009).

38. Hazevoet 2, 29, 30, 31, 34, 36; Hazevoet Chronology 2, 16.

39. Hazevoet 2, 35; Schola cantorum, medieval music school, Britannica.

40. "Don Byas: 1912–1972," *DownBeat*, October 26, 1972, 10.

41. "Byas: the tenor in between Hawk and Pres," *Melody Maker*, August 21, 1965, 6 (hereinafter "Melody Maker").

42. Hugues Panassié and Madeleine Gautier, *The Dictionary of Jazz*, vii (London: The Jazz Book Club, 1959).

43. Melody Maker.

44. Inez Cavanaugh, liner notes to *Don Byas: A Night in Tunisia*, recorded at the Montmartre Jazzhus, Copenhagen, January 13–14, 1963.

Notes

45. Fred Coot/Els de Jong, "Remember . . . ! Don Byas 1912–1972, *JazzPress* 41, 1977, 18 (hereinafter "Coot/de Jong").

46. Coot/de Jong, 18.

47. *Jazz Jamboree Nos. 1, 2, 3*. https://www.imdb.com/title/tt7486636/fullcredits?ref_=tt_ ov_st_sm; Hazevoet 2, 37.

48. John Chilton, *Sidney Bechet: The Wizard of Jazz*, 83–84, 234, 241 (New York: Oxford University Press, 1987).

49. "New Orleans to Paris Pals Mourn Death of Jazz Star Sidney Bechet," *Chicago Defender*, May 23, 1959, 19.

50. Jan Evensmo, *The Tenor Sax of Carlos Wesley Byas "Don" Part 2 (Europe 1946–1960)*, updated through February 17, 2021.

51. Linda Dahl, *Morning Glory: A Biography of Mary Lou Williams*, 230–31 (New York: Pantheon Books, 1999).

52. Dave Dexter Jr., liner notes to *The Mary Lou Williams Quartet featuring Don Byas*, GNP Crescendo 9030, 1974.

53. Hazevoet 2, 38–43.

54. "Don Byas: 1912–1972," *DownBeat*, October 26, 1972, 10.

Chapter 12. Amsterdam Years

1. According to Alain Tomas, Byas met his second wife in 1951 (liner notes to *Don Byas: New York–Paris, 1938–1955*, Frémeaux & Associés FA 5622, adapted from the French text by Martin Davies). According to another, they met in 1952: Mike Hennessey, "Don Byas: Emphatic Expatriate," *DownBeat*, July 27, 1967, 26. Neither of these dates align with Byas's known performances in Europe or his addresses as listed on official Dutch documents beginning in February 1954.

2. Leonard Feather, *The Encyclopedia of Jazz*, 165 (New York: Bonanza Books, 1960).

3. Igor Cornelissen, "Het Amsterdamse Leven van Don Byas," *Vrij Nederland*, January 2, 1993 (hereinafter "Cornelissen"). https://www.discogs.com/artist/5439083-Orkest-Piet-van -Dijk; https://www.discogs.com/artist/692087-Ado-Broodboom.

4. Wim Bossema, "Een Amerikaanse Saxophonist Die Te Goed Nederlands Sprak," *de Volkskrant*, February 16, 1996 (hereinafter "Bossema").

5. Cornelissen.

6. Cornelissen.

7. Cornelissen.

8. Fred Coot and Els de Jong, "Remember . . . ! Don Byas 1912–1972, *Jazz/Press*, no. 41: 17–18, July 8, 1977 (hereinafter "Coot/de Jong").

9. Cornelissen.

10. Coot/de Jong.

11. Coot/de Jong.

12. Het Vrije Volk, February 25, 1965.

13. Mike Hennessey, "Don Byas: Emphatic Expatriate," *DownBeat*, July 17, 1967, 26 (hereinafter "Hennessey").

14. Persoonskaarten of Johanna Eksteen and Carlos Wesley Byas, on file with the Amsterdam Stadsarchief.

15. Cornelis J. Hazevoet, *Don Byas Chronology 1912–1946*, 19 (hereinafter "Hazevoet Chronology 2").

16. Ollie Stewart, "Report from Europe," the *Baltimore Afro-American*, October 29, 1955, 4.

17. Pop singer Johnny Jordaan (stage name of Johannes Hendricus van Musscher); folk singer Tante Leen (stage name of Helena Jansen-Polder); Manke Nelis (stage name of Cornelis Pieters), singer of *levenslied*, a subgenre of sentimental popular music; and accordionist Jan Cornelis "Johnny" Meijer. Pop singer Willy Alberti (stage name of Carel Verbrugge) is recognized by a memorial plaque on a church.

18. "Don Byas's Geluk," *Het Parool*, May 3, 1963.

19. Hennessey.

20. Ronnie Scott, *Some of My Best Friends Are Blues*, with Mike Hennessey, 64–66 (London: Northway Publications, 2004) (hereinafter "Scott").

21. Scott, 61.

22. Interview of Billy Taylor NEA Jazz Master (1988) by Anthony Brown and Eugene Holly, November 19, 1993, the Smithsonian Institution Jazz Oral History Program, NEA Jazz Master Interview, 44.

23. Coot/de Jong.

24. Cornelissen.

25. Coot/de Jong.

26. Email from John Engels to author, January 8, 2023.

27. Email from Eric Ineke to author, January 7, 2023.

28. The date of the job was November 8, 1968. Receipts provided by Cornelis J. Hazevoet. Rate of exchange of Dutch guilders to US dollars calculated in accordance with US Treasury Reporting Rates of Exchange as of March 31, 1968.

29. Cornelis J. Hazevoet, *Don Byas Part 2: European Recordings 1946–1972*, 42–44 (hereinafter "Hazevoet Discography 2").

30. Marc Myers. https://marcmyers.typepad.com/my_weblog/page/127/.

31. "Black Saxophonist to US under the Motto 'Don Byas Returns to the US after 25 years," *Nieuwsblad van het Noorden*, August 19, 1969.

32. *Combat*, "Les Lundis du Jazz," November 10, 1958.

33. Hazevoet Discography 2, 49.

34. Bossema.

35. Hazevoet Discography 2, 61.

36. Email to author from Cornelis Hazevoet, February 2, 2023, translating article in *de Volkskrant*, October 22, 1962.

37. Coot/de Jong.

38. Coot/de Jong.

39. Hennessey, 26.

40. "Don Byas's Happiness," *Het Parool*, May 3, 1963.

41. "Black Saxophonist to US with the Motto: 'Don Byas Returns to the State after 25 Years," *Nieuwsblad van het Noorden*, August 19, 1969.

42. "Byas: The Tenor in between Hawk and Pres," *Melody Maker*, August 21, 1965, 6.

43. Coot/de Jong.

44. Coot/de Jong.

45. Hans Dulfer, *Jazzwereld* 40, no. 14, 1972.

46. Cornelissen.

47. Hazevoet Discography 2, 8–41, 42–77.

Notes

48. An abbreviation for Société Pour l'Administration du Droit de Reproduction Mécanique des Auteurs, Compositeurs, Éditeurs Réalisateurs et Doubleurs Sous-Titreurs.

49. An abbreviation that stands for the combined organizations Vereniging Buma and Stichting Stemra.

50. Cornelis J. Hazevoet, *Don Byas, Part 1: American Recordings, 1938–1946*, 35–79, updated through March 8, 2022.

51. Rud Niemans, "Jazznomade Don Byas Vond Huis en Liefde in Amsterdam-West," De Telegraaf, July 3, 1964 (hereinafter "Niemans").

52. Hazevoet Chronology 2, 20.

53. Hazevoet Discography 2, 42–48.

54. John Litweiler, "Art Blakey: Bu's Delights and Laments," *DownBeat*, March 25, 1976, 33.

55. Cornelissen.

56. Hennessey.

57. Bossema.

58. Cornelissen.

59. Don Byas documentary *Don Byas Come Back*, Nick van den Bosom, Omroepvereniging VARA, 1970. https://www.youtube.com/watch?v=1sGQHsSzBgo.

60. Coot/de Jong.

61. Hennessey.

62. Niemans.

63. Hennessey.

64. Bob Snead's Jazz Corner, *Cleveland Call and Post*, February 21, 1959, 5C.

Chapter 13. The Sixties

1. C. J. Hazevoet, *Don Byas, Part 1: American Recordings, 1938–1946*, 8.

2. Clarke, Kenny. https://www.encyclopedia.com/arts/dictionaries-thesauruses-pictures -and-press-releases/clarke-kenny-actually-kenneth-spearman-aka-klook-klook-mop -salaamliaquat-ali.

3. https://www.cruiselinehistory.com/the-french-line-ss-liberte-1950s/.

4. Michael Zwerin, "Le Jazz Triste," *Esquire*, May 1968, 115 (hereinafter "Zwerin").

5. https://www.imdb.com/title/tt0051378/?ref_=fn_al_tt_3.

6. Zwerin.

7. Letter from Frans Elsen to Misha Mengelberg, June 1960.

8. Unpublished memoirs of Jopie Byas.

9. C. J. Hazevoet, *Don Byas, Part 2: European Recordings, 1946–1972*, 52–53, updated through January 14, 2023 (hereinafter "Hazevoet Discography 2").

10. Ollie Stewart, "Report from Europe," the *Baltimore Afro-American*, October 22, 1960, 4.

11. Dizzy Gillespie, interviewed for "Norman's Conquests," a history of JATP broadcast on BBC Radio, April–June 1994, cited in Alyn Shipton *A New History of Jazz*, 637 (London, New York: Continuum, 2001) (hereinafter "Shipton").

12. Shipton, 637–38.

13. Hazevoet Discography 2, 53–55.

14. Monroe Berger, Edward Berger, James Patrick, *Benny Carter: A Life in American Music* 1, 316 (Methuen, New Jersey, London: The Scarecrow Press and the Institute of Jazz Studies, Rutgers University, 1982).

15. John Chilton, *The Song of the Hawk: The Life and Recordings of Coleman Hawkins*, 322 (Ann Arbor: University of Michigan Press, 1990) (hereinafter "Chilton *Hawk*").

16. *Jazz News*, December 3, 1960, cited in Chilton *Hawk*, 323.

17. *Melody Maker*, August 21, 1965.

18. *Jazz Journal*, July 1983, cited in Chilton *Hawk*, 324.

19. Chilton *Hawk*, 191.

20. *Jazz News*, December 20, 1961.

21. Julian "Cannonball" Adderley, "Jazz at The Philharmonic," *New York Amsterdam News*, February 11, 1961, 13.

22. Hazevoet Discography 2, 56–57.

23. Bill Cranfield, "Clayton in Concert," *Jazz News*, May 17, 1961.

24. Scott Yanow, *AllMusic Guide to Jazz*, 165 (San Francisco: Miller Freeman, 1998).

25. George E. Pitts, "'Cannonball' Really Whales on Alto Sax," *Pittsburgh Courier*, A32, March 17, 1956.

26. Idrees Sulieman, *Cadence*, September 1979, 4, cited in http://www.jazzdiscography. com/Artists/Blakey/chron.htm.

27. Gary Giddins, liner notes to *Don Byas/Bud Powell—A Tribute to Cannonball*, Columbia Records 35755.

28. Bert Vuijsje, "De Come-Back van Don Byas, *Haagse Post*, April 29, 1970.

29. Valerie Wilmer, *As Serious as Your Life: The Story of the New Jazz*, 95, 100 (New York: Lawrence Hill & Co. Inc., 1980).

30. "Op Jazz-Muziek Moet Je Lekker Kunnen Dansen," Volkskrant, March 1, 1970.

31. Conversation between author and Han Bennink, April 3, 2023.

32. Hugues Panassié and Madeleine Gautier, *Dictionary of Jazz*, 70 (London: The Jazz Book Club, 1959).

33. Igor Cornelissen, "Het Amsterdamse Leven van Don Byas," *Vrij Nederland*, January 2, 1993, 70.

34. Bill Cranfield, "Don Byas," *Jazz News*, December 20, 1961, 13.

35. *Billboard Magazine*, April 28, 1962, 11.

36. Ronnie Scott with Mike Hennessey, *Some of My Best Friends Are Blues*, 56 (London: Northway Publications, 2004).

37. Mike Hennessey, "Don Byas: Emphatic Expatriate," *DownBeat*, July 27, 1967, 26 (hereinafter "Hennessey Expatriate").

38. Bob LaPlante interview with Don Byas, November 2, 1965, University of North Texas Libraries. https://digital.library.unt.edu/ark:67531/metadc983758/m1, accessed June 9, 2022.

39. Hennessey Expatriate, 26.

40. Exchange between author and Loek Hopstaken, December 13, 2023.

41. Anthony Barnett, "Don Byas; Tenor Saxophonist," *Jazz Monthly*, September 1965, 15.

42. Balder, Norse mythology. https://www.britannica.com/topic/Balder-Norse-mythology.

43. Hazevoet Discography 2, 58–61.

44. Hazevoet Discography 2, 61–2; Cornelis J. Hazevoet, *Don Byas Chronology 1946–1972*, updated through April 7, 2023, 24–25 ("Hazevoet Chronology 2").

45. John S. Wilson review of "April in Paris," *DownBeat*, September 12, 1963, 27.

46. Harvey Pekar, review of "Ballads for Swingers," *DownBeat*, November 3, 1966, 28.

47. Hazevoet Discography 2, 63; NJA CD 1603.

48. Hazevoet Chronology 2, 26.

Notes 213

49. Jazznomade Don Byas Vond Huis en Liefde in Amsterdam-West, *De Telegraaf*, July 3, 1964.

50. Richard Paul, "Louis Armstrong Knocks Out the Beatles," Voice of America News, May 9, 2014. https://www.voanews.com/a/louis-armstrong-knocks-out-the-beatles/1911617.html.

51. Mike Hennessey, "Man Here Blows Mean Tenor," *Melody Maker*, February 20, 1965, 6.

52. Les Tomkins, liner notes to *Autumn Leaves: The Stan Tracey Quartet with Don Byas*, JHAS 613 (hereinafter "Tomkins").

53. Hazevoet Discography 2, 64.

54. Tomkins.

55. Hazevoet Discography 2, 64–65. See also Anthony Barnett, *Desert Sands: The Recordings and Performances of Stuff Smith: An Annotated Discography and Biographical Source Book* (Lewes, East Sussex, Allardyce, Barnett, Publishers, 1995).

56. Hazevoet Discography 2, 65–66.

57. Hazevoet Chronology 2, 28. https://en.wikipedia.org/wiki/Stu_Martin_(drummer).

58. Hazevoet Chronology 2, 28.

59. Hazevoet Chronology 2, 28.

60. Vladimir Cosma, Tom Lord Discography.

61. "Don Byas na 25 jaar terug in de States," *Nieuwsblad van het Noorden*, August 19, 1969.

62. Hazevoet Discography 2, 66–68.

63. Hazevoet Discography 2, 73.

64. *Het Parool*, August 11, 1969; *Het Vrije Volk*, August 11, 1969; *De Nieuwe Limburger*, August 11, 1969.

65. "Negersaxofonist naar US onder Het Motto: 'Don Byas na 25 jaar terug in de States," *Nieuwsblad van het Noorden*, August 19, 1969.

66. Ken Vail, *Duke's Diary: The Life of Duke Ellington, 1950–1974*, 366 (Lanham, Maryland and Oxford: The Scarecrow Press, 2002); Hazevoet Discography 2, 73.

67. Mercer Ellington with Stanley Dance, *Duke Ellington in Person: A Personal Memoir*, 146–47 (New York: Da Capo Press Inc., 1978).

68. Hazevoet Discography 2, 74.

69. Shanachie, 6,333.

70. Inez Cavanaugh, Tom Lord Discography.

Chapter 14. With Ben, near the End

1. J. de Valk, *Ben Webster: His Life and Music*, 142 (Berkeley, California: Berkeley Hills Books, 2001) (hereinafter "de Valk").

2. Frank Büchmann-Møller, *Someone to Watch Over Me*, 236–37 (Ann Arbor: University of Michigan Press, 2006) (hereinafter "Büchmann-Møller").

3. Mrs. Hartlooper is usually referred to as seventy-two years old in 1966, when Webster first rented a room from her, but it appears she was born August 11, 1891, which would make her seventy-four years old in May 1966. Perhaps she was still sufficiently vain in her seventies to shave two years off her age.

4. de Valk, 151.

5. Hans Dulfer, *Jazzwereld* 40, no. 14, 1972.

6. Stuff Smith, *Pure at Heart: Anecdotes & Interviews*, edited by Anthony Barnett, 69 (Lewes, East Sussex: Allardyce, Barnett, 2002).

7. Michael Steinman, "His Grief, His Art: Ben Webster, 1970," *Jazz Lives*. https://jazzlives .wordpress.com/2009/04/28/his-grief-his-art-ben-webster-1970/.

8. Wim Bossema, "Een Amerikaanse Saxophonist Die Te Goed Nederlands Sprak," *de Volkskrant*, February 16, 1996 (hereinafter "Bossema").

9. Igor Cornelissen. "Het Amsterdamse Leven van Don Byas," *Vrij Nederland*, January 2, 1993 (hereinafter "Cornelissen").

10. Bossema.

11. Cornelissen.

12. Advertisements, *New York Amsterdam News*, April 7, 1945, 9B and May 26, 1945, 7B.

13. *New York Amsterdam News*, July 21, 1945, A14.

14. Michael Zwerin, "Le Jazz Triste," *Esquire*, May 1968, 120.

15. Büchmann-Møller, 111.

16. Büchmann-Møller, 94.

17. Dan Morgenstern, liner notes to *Don Byas, Savoy Jam Party: The Savoy Sessions* (Savoy SJL 2213, 1976).

18. Jim Burns, "Don Byas," *Jazz Journal* 18, no. 9: 5, September 5, 1965.

19. Whitney Balliett, *Collected Works: A Journal of Jazz, 1954–2000*, 640 (New York: St. Martin's Press, 2000).

20. Cornelis J. Hazevoet, *Don Byas, Part 2: European Recordings 1946–1972*, updated through January 14, 2023, 65 (hereinafter "Hazevoet Discography 2").

21. Büchmann-Møller, 245, citing review by Bert Vuijsje in *Jazzwereld*, January 1968.

22. de Valk, 156.

23. de Valk, 156, citing review by Bert Vuijsje in *Vrij Nederland*, April 1967.

24. Martin Williams, *The Jazz Tradition*, 82 (New York, Oxford: Oxford University Press, 1983).

25. de Valk, 156–57, citing review in *Vrij Nederland*, May 1967.

26. *Jazzwereld*, July/August 1967.

27. *Big Ben: Ben Webster in Europe*, Johan van der Keuken, 1967; Hazevoet Discography 2, 67–8.

28. "Berliner Jazztage met Schandaal Begonnen," *De Twentsche Courant Tubantia*, November 8, 1965 (hereinafter "*Tubantia*").

29. Büchmann-Møller, 233.

30. *Tubantia*.

31. Büchmann-Møller, 253.

32. de Valk, 230.

33. de Valk, 162.

34. *DownBeat*, September 3, 1970, 22.

35. Büchmann-Møller, 257.

36. Büchmann-Møller, 277, citing an interview with Eddie Barefield.

37. Fred Coot/Els de Jong, "Remember . . . ! Don Byas 1912–1972), *Jazz/Press*, July 8, 1977, 17.

38. Strata-East, SES-7410.

Notes   215

Chapter 15. The Out Chorus

1. Michael Zwerin, "Le Jazz Triste," *Esquire*, May 1968, 115.

2. "Negersaxofonist Naar US onder Het Motto: 'Don Byas na 25 jaar terug in de States,'" Nieuwsblad van het Noorden, August 19, 1969.

3. Hollie I. West, "Good Guys and Bad Guys," *Washington Post*, July 19, 1970, 147.

4. "Don Byas: 1912–1972," *DownBeat*, October 26, 1972, 10.

5. Dan Morgenstern, interview by Ed Berger, NEA Jazz Master interview, the Smithsonian Institution Jazz Oral History Program, March 28–29, 2007.

6. Dan Morgenstern, *Jazz People*, photographs by Ole Brask (New York: Da Capo Press, 1993).

7. Cornelis J. Hazevoet, *Don Byas Part 2: European Recordings, 1946–1972*, 73 (hereinafter "Hazevoet Discography 2").

8. Don Byas documentary *Don Byas Come Back*, Nick van den Boezem, Omroepvereniging VARA, 1970. https://www.youtube.com/watch?v=1sGQHsSzBgo (hereinafter "Don Byas Come Back").

9. Cornelis J. Hazevoet, *Don Byas Chronology, 1946–1972*, updated through April 7, 2023, 26 (hereinafter "Hazevoet Chronology 2").

10. *Don Byas Come Back*, translation by Eyla Jeschke.

11. Gary Giddins, *Visions of Jazz*, 182 (Oxford, New York: Oxford University Press, 182).

12. Fred Coot and Els de Jong, "Remember . . . ! Don Byas 1912–1972, *Jazz/Press*, no. 41: 17–18, July 8, 1977 (hereinafter "Coot/de Jong").

13. Mike Hennessey, "Don Byas: Emphatic Expatriate," *DownBeat*, July 27, 1967, 23.

14. Hollie I. West, "Good Guys and Bad Guys," *Washington Post*, July 19, 1970, H7; Hollie I. West, "Tina at Newport," *Washington Post*, July 13, 1970, C1, C6.

15. Hazevoet Chronology 2, 33; *DownBeat*, September 3, 1970, 40; *Chicago Daily Defender* TV Fare, July 10–16, 1971, 35.

16. "Don Byas: 1912–1972," *DownBeat*, October 26, 1972, 10.

17. Igor Cornelissen, "Het Amsterdamse Leven van Don Byas," *Vrij Nederland*, January 2, 1993 (hereinafter "Cornelissen").

18. Contract dated July 17, 1970, between Bernard Jackson and Don Byas.

19. Chicago *Daily Defender*, July 16–23, 1970.

20. John Litweiler, "Caught in the Act," *DownBeat*, October 1, 1970, 27 (hereinafter "Litweiler").

21. The club has had over sixty-three locations in its history. https://en.wikipedia.org/wiki/Jazz_Showcase.

22. Hazevoet Discography 2, 75; *DownBeat*, September 3, 1970, 40; October 1, 1970, 27.

23. Litweiler.

24. *Chicago Daily Defender*, July 16–25, 1970.

25. *Jazzwereld* 32, November/December 1970, 12.

26. Larry Kart, email to John Litweiler, private notes, collection of Cornelis J. Hazevoet.

27. Contract dated July 17, 1970, between Don Byas and Bernard Jackson; "Don Byas and Vi Redd give a 'Boss' Show, *Chicago Daily Defender*, July 23, 1970, 16.

28. John Litweiler, "Caught in the Act," *DownBeat*, October 1, 1970, 27 (hereinafter "Litweiler").

29. Hazevoet Chronology 2, 33; citing *Crescendo*, October 1970, 24, and November 1970, 14.

30. *DownBeat*, October 15, 1970, 39.

31. Jeffrey Taylor, "Brooklyn Rediscovers Cal Massey," *American Music Review* 39, no. 2, Spring 2010. http://www.brooklyn.cuny.edu/web/aca_centers_hitchcock/NewsS10.pdf.

32. *New York Times*, August 14, 1970, 24, and August 21, 1970, 20 (advertisements).

33. Photo by Neal Graham. Stanley Cowell on piano is not visible. An original was donated to the Netherlands Jazz Archive by Byas's widow. According to an October 1, 1970, *DownBeat* article, other musicians on the date were Rhan Burton and Stanley Cowell (piano), Jerry Griffin (drums), and Joe Texidor (percussion). Hazevoet Chronology 2, 33.

34. Jazzmobile, Wikipedia. https://en.wikipedia.org/wiki/Jazzmobile; Hazevoet Chronology 2, 32.

35. *DownBeat*, March 25, 1976, 16.

36. Hazevoet Chronology 2, 34.

37. Wim Bossema, "Een Amerikaanse Saxophonist Die Te Goed Nederlands Sprak," *de Volkskrant*, February 16, 1996 (hereinafter "Bossema").

38. Coot/de Jong.

39. Hazevoet Discography 2, 75; *Don Byas: Greatest on Tenor Sax—Trial in Mood*, Polydor MR 3171.

40. Steve Schwartz and Michael Fitzgerald, Art Blakey Chronology (and the Jazz Messengers), JazzMF. https://jazzmf.com/art-blakey-chronology-and-the-jazz-messengers/. *DownBeat*, April 29, 1971, photo caption; October 26, 1972, 10.

41. *DownBeat*, October 14, 1971, 38; Hazevoet Chronology 2, 35.

42. *Washington Post*, April 21, 1971, B7.

43. Klaus Stratemann, *Duke Ellington: Day by Day and Film by Film*, 616 (Copenhagen: JazzMedia ApS, 1991) (hereinafter "Stratemann").

44. Hazevoet Discography 2, 76.

45. "Davis, Wild Bill [William Strethen]," Andrew Jaffe, revised by Barry Kernfeld, Grove Music Online, January 20, 2002. https://www.oxfordmusiconline.com/grovemusic/view/10.1093/gmo/9781561592630.001.0001/omo-9781561592630-e-2000114700?rskey=Oty039&result=1.

46. Stratemann, 616.

47. Alain Tomas, liner notes, *Don Byas: New York–Paris, 1838–1955*, adapted by Martin Davies, Frémeaux & Associés, 2016; Hazevoet Chronology 2, 32–33.

48. Ben Kragting, review of *5 Jaar Jazz in Venlo* (1970–1975), *Doctor Jazz Magazine* 51, Summer 2013, 23–24 (translated from the Dutch by Cornelis Hazevoet).

49. Bossema; Cornelissen.

50. Bossema.

51. Coot/de Jong.

52. Keith Jarrett quoted in liner notes by Neil Tesser to *Mysteries: The Impulse Years 1975–1976*, Impulse! IMPD-189.

53. It is unclear what Jopie Byas meant by this; she may have used "brother" in a figurative sense, the way jazz musicians often refer to each other as "brother," or since the notice was intended as a group communication, she may have been speaking on behalf of Byas's two brothers, who were still alive. In other communications following her husband's death, she included "schoonzoon," the Dutch word for "son-in-law."

54. Coot/de Jong.

55. Bossema.

56. *Kansas City Star*, August 25, 1972, 23.

57. https://www.jazzmusicarchives.com/artist/daniele-dagaro.

58. Bossema.

59. Leonard Feather, *The Encyclopedia of Jazz*, 107 (New York: Bonanza Books, 1960) (hereinafter "Feather").

60. Bossema.

61. Bossema.

62. Bossema.

63. Cornelissen.

64. https://en.m.wikipedia.org/wiki/Claude_Nougaro.

65. Correspondence between Les Éditions du Chiffre Neuf and Johanna Eksteen-Byas, undated and March 3, 1975.

66. Cornelissen.

67. Hans Dulfer, *Jazzwereld* 40, no. 14, 1972.

68. The author is indebted for this background to Russel Gershon, saxophonist and founder of the Either/Orchestra. Any error or misstatement on the point is mine. https://en.wikipedia.org/wiki/Russ_Gershon.

69. Sean Little, Sax on the Web. https://www.saxontheweb.net/threads/berg-larsen-150.90815/.

70. Ira Gitler, *Jazz Masters of the 40's*, 215 (New York: Da Capo Press Inc., 1966).

71. Cornelissen.

72. Cornelissen.

73. Cornelissen.

74. Coot/de Jong, 17–18.

75. "Byas: the tenor in between Hawk and Pres," *Melody Maker*, August 21, 1965, Max Jones, 6.

76. Max Jones, 6.

77. Gary Giddins, liner notes to *Don Byas/Bud Powell—A Tribute to Cannonball*, Columbia Records 35755.

78. Dan Morgenstern, liner notes to *Savoy Jam Party: The Savoy Sessions*, Arista Records SJL 2213 (1976).

79. Letter from Dan Morgenstern to Jaap Lüdeke on letterhead of the Institute of Jazz Studies dated November 10, 1995.

80. Email from Cornelis J. Hazevoet to author, January 10, 2023.

81. Interview by author of James Carter, February 17, 2023.

82. *Jazz Journal*, January 1964, cited in John Chilton, *The Song of the Hawk: The Life and Recordings of Coleman Hawkins*, 323 (Ann Arbor: University of Michigan Press, 1990) (hereinafter "Chilton").

83. Feather, 229.

84. Stanley Dance, *The World of Duke Ellington*, 172 (New York: Da Capo Press Inc., 1970).

85. Jones, 77.

86. Mike Hennessey, "Man Here Blows a Mean Tenor," *Melody Maker*, February 20, 1965, 6 (hereinafter "Hennessey Tenor").

87. Jim Burns, "Don Byas," *Jazz Journal* 18, no. 9, September 1965.

88. Stanley Dance, *The World of Count Basie*, 90 (New York: Da Capo, 1980).

89. Feather, 229.

90. Chilton, 323.

91. Ted Panken, "A *DownBeat* Profile on Benny Golson and Several Interviews, on His 83rd Birthday," *Today is the Question: Ted Panken on Music, Politics and the Arts*, January 25, 2012. https://tedpanken.wordpress.com/tag/don-byas/.

92. Bob Snead's Jazz Corner, *Cleveland Call and Post*, March 7, 1959, 8.

93. Martin Williams, *The Jazz Tradition*, 193 (New York, Oxford: Oxford University Press, 1983) (hereinafter "Williams").

94. Larry Appelbaum, "Before & After: Sonny Rollins," *JazzTimes*, June 2011 (hereinafter "Appelbaum").

95. Aidan Levy, *Saxophone Colossus: The Life and Music of Sonny Rollins*, 318–19 (New York: Hachette Books, 2022) (hereinafter "Levy").

96. Appelbaum.

97. Levy, 318–19.

98. Levy, 318–19.

99. Appelbaum.

100. Levy, citing Larry Appelbaum, "Before & After: Sonny Rollins," *JazzTimes*, 2011.

101. Bill Kopp, "Sonny Rollins," *Record Collector*, January 22, 2019, cited in Levy, 251.

102. Whitney Balliett, *Collected Works: A Journal of Jazz 1954–2000*, 824 (New York: St. Martin's Press, 2000).

103. "The Music of Don Byas Featuring James Carter," NPR Music, September 27, 2007. https://www.npr.org/2007/09/27/15295550/the-music-of-don-byas-featuring-james-carter. Phillip Lutz, "James Carter Reimagines the Art of Django Reinhardt," *DownBeat*, August 30, 2019.

104. Count Basie, as told to Albert Murray, *Good Morning Blues*, 240 (New York: Primus/Donald I. Fine, 1985).

105. Interview of Billy Taylor by Marc Myers. https://www.jazzwax.com/2010/12/billy-taylor-1921-2010.html.

106. Ira Gitler, liner notes to John Coltrane's *Soultrane*, Prestige Records 7142.

107. Williams, 226, 228.

108. Arthur Taylor, *Notes and Tones*, 53 (New York: Coward, McCann & Geoghegan, 1977).

109. Rud Niemans, "Jazznomade Don Byas Vond Huis en Liefde in Amsterdam-West," *De Telegraaf*, July 3, 1964.

110. Hazevoet Chronology 2, 26.

111. Åke Abrahamsson, "*Den Gyllene Cirkeln; Jazzen På 1960-talet*. Prisma, Stockholm, 2002.

112. "Op jazz-muziek moet je lekker kunnen dansen," Volkskrant, March 1, 1970.

113. Mike Hennessey, "If You Can't Pat Your Foot to It, It's Not Jazz," *Melody Maker*, July 8, 1967.

114. Hennessey Tenor.

115. Williams, 143.

116. Williams, 193.

117. Inez Cavanaugh, liner notes to *Don Byas: A Night in Tunisia*, recorded at Montmarte Jazzhus, Copenhagen, January 13–14, 1963.

118. Bert Vuijsje, "De Come-Back van Don Byas," *Haagse Post*, April 29, 1970.

119. "Don Byas's Geluk," *Het Parool*, May 3, 1963.

120. Bossema.

Epilogue

1. Mike Hennessey, "Man Here Blows Mean Tenor," *Melody Maker*, February 20, 1965.

SELECTED BIBLIOGRAPHY

Balliett, Whitney. 1981. *Night Creature: A Journal of Jazz, 1975–1980*. New York: Oxford University Press.

Balliett, Whitney. 2000. *Collected Works: A Journal of Jazz 1954–2000*. New York: St. Martin's Press.

Barnett, Anthony. 1965. "Don Byas; Tenor Saxophonist." *Jazz Monthly*, September.

Barnett, Anthony. 2002. *Stuff Smith: Pure at Heart, Anecdotes & Interviews*. Lewes, East Sussex: Allardyce, Barnett, Publishers.

Basie, Count, as Told to Albert Murray. 1985. *Good Morning Blues: The Autobiography of Count Basie*. New York: Primus/Donald I. Fine Inc.

Bossema, Wim. 1996. "Een Amerikaanse Saxophonist Die Te Goed Nederlands Sprak Teruggenvonden Muziek van Don Byas Gereconstrueerd." *De Volkskrant*, February 16.

Büchmann-Møller, Frank. 2009. *Someone to Watch Over Me: The Life and Music of Ben Webster*. Ann Arbor, MI: University of Michigan Press.

Burns, Jim. 1965. "Don Byas." *Jazz Journal* 18, no. 9, September.

Burrows, George. 2019. *The Recordings of Andy Kirk and His Clouds of Joy*. New York: Oxford University Press.

Byas, Don. 1961. "In My Opinion." *Jazz Journal* 14, no. 3.

Chilton, John. 1972. *Who's Who of Jazz*. Revised ed. New York: Da Capo Press.

Chilton, John. 1990. *The Song of the Hawk: The Life and Recordings of Coleman Hawkins*. Ann Arbor, MI: University of Michigan Press.

Clare, John. 1999. "Don Byas Remembered." *Jazz Journal* 52, no. 12, December.

Clayton, Buck, assisted by Nancy Miller Elliott. 1986. *Buck Clayton's Jazz World*. Oxford: Bayou Press Ltd.

Coleman, Bill. 1991. *Trumpet Story*. Boston: Northeastern University Press.

Conover, Willis. 1965. Bob LaPlante interview with Don Byas; unidentified audio recording, November 2. University of North Texas Libraries, UNT Digital Library. https://digital .library.unt.edu/ark:/67531/metadc983758/m1/?q=byas: accessed November 6, 2022.

Coot, Fred and Els De Jong. 1977. Interview of Johanna Eksteen Byas. *Jazz/Press*, no. 41, July 8.

Coot, Fred and Els De Jong. 1977. "Remember . . . ! Don Byas 1912–1972. *Jazz/Press*, no. 41, July 8.

Cornelissen, Igor. 1993. "Het Amsterdamse Leven van Don Byas." *Vrij Nederland*, January 2.

Cranfield, Bill. 1961. "Don Byas." *Jazz News*, December 20.

Cunniffe, Thomas. 2009. "Timme Rosenkrantz and the Town Hall Concert (June 9, 1945)." Jazz History Online, March 15. https://jazzhistoryonline.com/town-hall-1945/.

Dahl, Linda. 1999. *Morning Glory: A Biography of Mary Lou Williams*. New York: Pantheon Books.

Dance, Stanley. 1980. *The World of Count Basie*. New York: Da Capo Press Inc.

Daniels, Douglas Henry. 2006. *One O'Clock Jump: The Unforgettable History of the Oklahoma City Blue Devils*. Boston, MA: Beacon Press.

Delannoy, Luc. 1993. *Pres: The Story of Lester Young*. Fayetteville, AR: University of Arkansas Press.

Delaunay, Charles. 1948. *New Hot Discography*. New York: Criterion.

De Valk, Jeroen. 2001. *Ben Webster: His Life and Music*. Berkeley, CA: Berkeley Hills Books.

Dexter, Dave Jr. 1974. Liner notes to *The Mary Lou Williams Quartet Featuring Don Byas*. GNP-9030.

Driggs, Frank, and Chuck Haddix. 2005. *Kansas City Jazz: From Ragtime to Bebop—A History*. Oxford, New York: Oxford University Press.

Dulfer, Hans. 1972. "In Memoriam Don Byas." *Jazzwereld* 40, no. 14.

Evensmo, Jan. 2021. *The Tenor Sax of Carlos Wesley Byas "Don," Part 1 (1938–1946) and Part 2 (Europe 1946–1960)*.

Feather, Leonard. 1960. *The Encyclopedia of Jazz*. New York: Bonanza Books.

Foley, Hugh W. Jr. 2000. *Jazz from Muskogee, Oklahoma: Eastern Oklahoma as a Hearth of Musical Culture*. PhD thesis, Oklahoma State University, May.

Foley, Hugh W. Jr. 2019. *Oklahoma Music Guide: Biographies, Big Hits & Annual Events*. Stillwater, OK: New Forums Press Inc.

Gelly, Dave. 2006. *Being Prez: The Life and Music of Lester Young*. Oxford: Oxford University Press.

Giddins, Gary. 1979. Liner notes to *Don Byas/Bud Powell—A Tribute to Cannonball*. Columbia 35755.

Giddins, Gary. 1998. *Visions of Jazz: The First Century*. New York, Oxford: Oxford University Press.

Gillespie, Dizzy, Al Fraser. 1979. *To BE, or not . . . to BOP*. Garden City, New York: Doubleday & Company Inc.

Gitler, Ira. 1966. *Jazz Masters of the 40's*. New York: Da Capo Press Inc.

Gitler, Ira. 1985. *Swing to Bop: An Oral History of the Transition in Jazz in the 1940s*. New York, Oxford: Oxford University Press.

Hampton, Lionel, with James Haskins. 1989. *Hamp: An Autobiography*. New York: Amistad Press Inc.

Hazevoet, Cornelis J. 2023. *Don Byas Chronology, 1912–1946 and 1946–1972*.

Hazevoet, Cornelis J. 2022. *Don Byas Part 1: American Recordings 1938–1946 and Part 2: European Recordings 1946–1972*.

Hennessey, Mike. 1965. "Man Here Blows Tenor." *Melody Maker*, February 20.

Hennessey, Mike. 1967. "Don Byas: Emphatic Expatriate." *DownBeat* 34, no. 14, July 27.

Hennessey, Mike. 1967. "If You Can't Pat Your Feet to It, It's Not Jazz." *Melody Maker*, July 8.

Hershorn, Tad. 2011. *Norman Granz: The Man Who Used Jazz for Justice*. Berkeley, CA: University of California Press.

Selected Bibliography

Kernodle, Tammy L. 2020. *Soul on Soul: The Life and Music of Mary Lou Williams*. Urbana, Chicago, and Springfield, IL: University of Illinois Press.

Kirk, Andy, As Told to Amy Lee. 1989. *Twenty Years on Wheels*. Ann Arbor, MI: University of Michigan Press.

Lester, James. 1994. *Too Marvelous for Words: The Life & Genius of Art Tatum*. New York, Oxford: Oxford University Press.

Lord, Tom. 2021. *The Jazz Discography*, version 21.0. Chilliwack, British Columbia: Lord Music Reference.

Mohr, Kurt. 1958. "Don Byas: Toujours au Premier Rang." *Jazz Hot*, no. 131, April.

Morgenstern, Dan. 1968. Liner notes to *Don Byas in Paris*. Prestige Records, 7598.

Morgenstern, Dan. 1970. "Newport '70: Back in Orbit." *DownBeat*, September 3.

Morgenstern, Dan. 1972. "Don Byas: 1912–1972." *DownBeat*, October 26.

Morgenstern, Dan. 1976. Liner notes to *Savoy Jam Party: The Savoy Sessions*. Savoy 2213.

Morgenstern, Dan. 1993. *Jazz People*. New York: Da Capo Press.

Morgenstern, Dan. 2007. NEA Jazz Master interview, the Smithsonian Institution Jazz Oral History Program. March 28–29.

Openneer, Herman. 1992. "Don Byas' Debuut in Nederland." *NJA/Jazz Archief Bulletin*, no. 6, December.

Panassié, Hughes, and Madeleine Gautier. 1959. *Dictionary of Jazz*. London: The Jazz Book Club.

Pearson, Nathan W. Jr. 1987. *Goin' to Kansas City*. Urbana and Chicago: University of Illinois Press.

Rosenkrantz, Timme. 2012. *Harlem Jazz Adventures: A European Baron's Memoir, 1934–1969*. Lanham, Maryland; Toronto, Canada; Plymouth, UK: The Scarecrow Press.

Russell, Ross. 1971. *Jazz Style in Kansas City and the Southwest*. Berkeley, Los Angeles: University of California Press.

Schoenberg, Loren. 2023. Liner notes to *Classic Don Byas Sessions 1944–1946*. Stamford, Connecticut: Mosaic Records LLC.

Schuller, Gunther. 1989. *The Swing Era: The Development of Jazz, 1930–1945*. New York, Oxford: Oxford University Press.

Shipton, Alyn. 2001. *A New History of Jazz*. London and New York: Continuum.

Shipton, Alyn. 1999. *Groovin' High: The Life of Dizzy Gillespie*. New York, Oxford: Oxford University Press.

Stebel, Paul. 1952. "Don Byas." *Swing Time*, no. 18, Summer.

Taylor, Arthur. 1977. *Notes and Tones: Musician to Musician Interviews*. New York: Coward, McCann & Geoghegan.

Tomas, Alain. 2016. Liner notes to *Don Byas: New York–Paris, 1938–1955*. Frémeaux & Associés FA 5622.

Vail, Ken. 1996. *Bird's Diary: The Life of Charlie Parker 1945–1955*. Chessington, Surrey: Castle Communications plc.

Voce, Steve. 1972. "And Quiet Flows the Don." *Jazz Journal* 25, no. 10. October.

Vuijsje, Bert. 1970. "De Come-Back van Don Byas," *Haagse Post*, April 29.

Vuijsje, Bert. 1964. "Don Byas: From Swing to Bop," *Vrij Nederland*, July 11.

Weeks, Todd Bryant. 2008. *Luck's in My Corner: The Life and Music of Hot Lips Page*. New York and London: Routledge.

INDEX

Adams, Pepper, 147
Adderley, Cannonball, 139–40
Adderley, Nat, 139
Agerbeek, Rob, 147
Aiken, Augustine "Gus," 108
Albert, Don (Albert Dominique), 37
Ali, Rashid, 163
Allen, Country, 15, 17
Allen, Henry "Red," 73
Allen, Jasper "Jap," 59
Almstedt, Gunnar, 144
Alvis, Hayes, 76
Ammons, Albert, 56
Ammons, Gene, 163
Anderson, Andy, 18
Anderson, William "Cat," 108
Armstrong, Louis, 18, 27, 83, 89, 177; in Bing
    Crosby movie, 16; Esquire All-American
    Award Winners recording, 80; first jazz
    artist to record "Body and Soul," 27;
    "Hello, Dolly!" success, 146
Arvanitas, George, 144
Asch, Moe, 57–58
Attenoux, Michel, 122
Auld, Georgie, 30, 45, 139
Axen, Bent, 144
Ayler, Albert, 141–42, 144

Bailey, Benny, 168
Bailey, Buster, 52, 59

Bailey, Mildred, 119
Bailey, Pearl, 60
Baker, Harold "Shorty," 23
Banks, Alvin "Buddy," 123, 125
Barclay, Eddie (Édouard Ruault), 61, 118,
    134, 135
Barefield, Bob, 15, 17, 18
Barefield, Eddie, 13, 78, 108; band breaks up,
    20; hires Byas, 17; Saints and Sinners
    band, 158
Barelli, Aimé, 116
Barker, Danny, 72
Barnet, Charlie, 30, 62, 139
Bascomb, Paul, 48
Basie, Count, 7, 8, 11, 12, 15, 19, 26, 28, 30,
    34, 37, 41, 42, 45, 51, 52, 56, 57, 80, 82, 83,
    84, 97, 98, 102, 130, 147, 173, 174, 176, 178;
    Carnegie Hall jam session, 50; fires Byas,
    53–54, 55, 62, 133, 154; fires Lester Young,
    47–48; hires Byas, 20, 48–49; Lucky
    Millinder band battle in Baltimore, 43;
    models dueling tenors of Jesse Stone, 36
Beason, Bill, 59
Bechet, Sidney, 86, 93, 106, 116, 119, 143; influ-
    ence on Johnny Hodges, 34; moves to
    Paris, 122; Paris jazz festival, 117
Bell, Aaron, 5, 8
Benjamin, Joe, 120
Bennett, Benny, 120, 124, 130
Bennett, Lou, 143

Index

Bennink, Han, 96
Berry, Emmet, 59, 140
Berry, Leon Brown "Chu," 27, 29, 30, 41, 42, 43, 52, 72, 139, 171, 176; link between Hawkins and Byas, 35–36; switches to tenor sax, 36
Bess, Druie, 7
Best, Denzil, 56
Bias, Michael (grandfather), 3
Big Chief Jazzband, 144
Bigard, Barney, 60
Bishop, Wally, 125
Bjørn, Atli, 147, 155
Blakey, Art, 100, 134, 164, 168, 171
Blanton, Jimmie, 19, 62
Blue Devils, 9, 50
Bolling, Claude, 119
Booker, Beryl, 85
Bostic, Earl, 59, 78, 79
Bouchéty, Jean, 91, 107, 109, 115
Bradley, Will, 52
Brannon, Teddy, 84
Brice, Pee Wee, 17
Bridgers, Aaron, 137
Broodboom, Ado, 126
Brooks, David, 16
Brooks, Dudley, 17
Broonzy, Big Bill, 63
Brown, Lawrence, 15, 118
Brown, Pete, 73
Brown, Ray, 76
Brown, Scoville, 61
Brown, Sonny, 163
Buckner, Teddy, 15
Burman, Anders, 144
Burrell, Kenny, 163
Burton, Ron, 159
Bush, Marjorie, 22–23
Bushell, Garvin, 47
Byas, Carlos Wesley (birth name), 3, 5, 7, 10, 12, 93, 166, 167, 170; early gigs with professional bands, 11; early music lessons, 4; first plays professionally, 9; parents' musical talent, 6
Byas, Carlos Wesley, Jr. (son), 24, 131
Byas, Carlotta (daughter), 98, 131, 167

Byas, Don, 25, 27, 28, 29, 30, 64, 68, 73, 78, 92, 159; adds nickname "Don," 12, 14, 93; affair with Mary Lou Williams, 24, 45; Art Tatum's influence, 31–33, 176–77; artistic talents outside music, 93, 178; becoming Dutch, 96; Ben Webster's influence, 35; blames rock as an economic threat to jazz, 145; cameo in *The Seven Lively Arts*, 70; Chu Berry's possible influence, 36; claims to have taught Charlie Parker, 178; Coleman Hawkins ranks as seventh-favorite tenor saxophonist, 30, 139; competitiveness in games, 95; contempt for drug users, 102; criticized for sentimentality in his playing, 171; death, 166–68; diagnosed with lung cancer, 166; dies without a will, 169; difficulty getting accepted as young freelancer in New York, 42; discrepancy over birth year, 46; dislike of free jazz, 141; dislike of Ornette Coleman's music, 180; dislike of playing with different European rhythm sections, 120–21; drinking problems, 53–54, 99–101, 111, 148–49, 154; drug use, 102; drunken night in Paris with Paul Gonsalves, 149–50; earns minimal royalties, 133; eclipses Gillespie at Monroe's, 74; enjoys life in Amsterdam, 135; European tour with Don Redman, 82, 84, 85; exercise fanaticism, 96–97; fails to secure US record contract, 164; featured in Charlie Parker's band, 78; fired by Andy Kirk, 45; fired by Count Basie, 52–55; first hears Duke Ellington in person, 40; first record as a leader, 58–59; fluency in several languages, 94; focus on using local rhythm sections, 174; forms quartet with Erroll Garner, 55; Herschel Evans's influence, 36; high asking price costs work, 130; hired by Cozy Cole, 70–71; hired by Eddie Barefield, 17–18; hired instead of Gillespie and Pettiford at Onyx Club, 74; hired to record by Benny Carter, 80; hospitalized for physical exam, 165; influence on Benny Golson, 175; influence on James

Carter, 176; influence on Johnny Griffin, 35; influences on, 26, 31; informal blowing session with Sonny Rollins, 175–76; inspired by Benny Carter, 37; Johnny Hodges's influence, 35; joins Bernard Hilda orchestra, 110; joins Count Basie, 47–48; joins Lionel Hampton, 14, 16; lack of financial savvy, 134; leaves for California, 13, 15; leaves for New York, 20; loses gigs to Dixieland revival bands, 141; love of cooking, 97–98, 178; love of fishing, 95–96, 122, 132, 178–79; marriage to Marjorie Bush, 22–23; mastery of ballads, 119–20; meets and marries Johanna Ecksteen, 125–28; money tightens with children, 131–32; mouthpiece used, 37, 169, 177; moves to New York, 39; need for eyeglasses, 94; obituaries, 168; as prankster, 98–99; racial background, 106; receives Esquire silver "Esky" Award, 68; relocates to Spain, 109; remains in Paris after Redman band dissolves, 91; relationship with John Coltrane, 176–77; resentment of comparisons to Coleman Hawkins, 170; returns to the Netherlands, 165; returns to Paris, 114; rivalry with Ben Webster, 154; Spanish tinges in his music, 107; stormy friendship with Ben Webster, 151–53; subs for Charlie Parker at Town Hall, 68; switches to tenor saxophone, 13, 15; tenor saxophone models used, 103, 171–72; tenor saxophonists influenced by, 173; use of difficult-to-play mouthpieces, 169–70; viewed as a native in the Netherlands, 131, 142; views on protest in music, 104–5; working as a single on the road, 124; works as mailman to supplement income, 143

Byas, Don, jam sessions: battles, 102–3, 111, 117; in Belgium, 109; bests other tenor saxophonists at Minton's, 72; with Charlie Parker, 75–76; with Gerry Mulligan, 77; with Jerry Thomas and Glyn Paque, 89; joins, 51–52; with Julio Pamies, 118; with tenor sax greats, 28

Byas, Don, performances: Art Blakey's Jazz Messengers, 164; Ben Webster and Brew Moore in Copenhagen, 147, 155; Berliner Jazzstage with Ben Webster, 156–57; bests Coleman Hawkins on tour, 139; bests Lucky Thompson while playing drunk, 174; Billy Taylor's Jazzmobile workshop, 163–64; Bud Powell, 144; Calvin Massey, 163; Chicago, 162–63; cutting contests with Webster on stage, 155–56; Duke Ellington, 24, 118, 149, 164; freelancing as leader, 119; Edgar Hayes, 47; Guy Willox, 91; homecoming tour of US, 160–61; Hot Lips Page (co-leads septet), 116–17; last, 165; Lucky Millinder in film, 42–43; Luis Rovira, 112; Milt Jackson, 163; Molde Jazz Festival, 147; Newport Jazz Festival, 161–62, 168; radio with Kurt Edelhagen, 137, 140; Ronnie Scott's with Stan Tracey, 146; Roy Eldridge, 118–19; subs for Gerry Mulligan with Earl Hines, 146–47; Tete Montoliu, 111; Timme Rosenkrantz Memorial Concert, 150, 158; Thad Jones-Mel Lewis Band, 161; Town Hall with Slam Stewart, 66–67, 173; tours Europe with Bill Coleman, 115–16; tours with Benny Carter, 84; tours with Jazz at the Philharmonic, 38, 138; two concerts at Times Hall, 80; US, 161–65, 168; Village Vanguard, 161, 163

Byas, Don, recordings with/recordings of: Albert Ammons, 56; Albinia Jones, 63; Amália Rodrigues, 112–13; Andy Kirk's orchestra, 43, 44; Ben Webster, 156–58; Ben Webster and Tete Montoliu, 113; Benny Carter, 38, 60; Benny Goodman, 58; Billy Eckstine, 61; Buck Clayton Sextet, 118; Bud Powell (co-leads), 140–41; Carnegie Hall, 52; Clyde Hart, 61; Coleman Hawkins, 30, 31, 56–57; Columbia in Spain and Portugal, 112; Count Basie, 20, 49–50; Cozy Cole, 63; Dizzy Gillespie, 62, 120; Don Redman, 83–84, 86–90; Duke Ellington, 35; Earl Bostic, 79; Eddie Heywood Jr., 57; Emmet Berry, 59; Esquire All-American

Award Winners, 80; George Williams, 79–80; Gotham label (as leader), 85; Guarneri Quartet, 79; "Harvard Blues" record, 50, 84; John Kirby, 59; Kenny Clarke and Oscar Pettiford, 137; "Laura," 68–69, 70; Las Estrellas de Ritmo y Melodia (The Stars of Rhythm and Melody), 111; Leo Mathisen, 85; live recordings in 1963, 144; Mary Lou Williams, 57–58, 123; Minton's jam sessions, 71; Oran "Hot Lips" Page, 58; Oscar Pettiford, 61–62; Paris, 130; Polydor in Japan, 164, 171; Savoy (as leader), 84; Savoy Records all-star session, 59; studio recordings 1962–1964, 144–45; Swing label, 108; Switzerland, 147; Teddy Wilson Octet, 84; Timmie Rosenkrantz, 41–42, 65; Woody Herman, 63

Byas, Dottie Mae (daughter), 131, 167

Byas, Dottie Mae (mother), 3, 170

Byas, Ellie Mae (daughter), 131, 167

Byas, Jopie (second wife), 106, 131–32, 133, 134, 135; death, 170; not husband's primary heir, 169; sells husband's tenor saxophone, 171–72; unwanted visit by Ben Webster, 152–53, 158, 164, 165, 166, 167, 168

Byas, Vincent Weaver "Vint" (brother), 5

Byas, Walter Jackson "Jack" (brother), 5, 167, 170

Byas, Walter Wesley (father), 3, 4, 106

Byas, Polly (grandmother), 3

Byrd, Donald, 109

Caceres, Ernie, 59

Caldwell, Albert "Happy," 71

Calloway Cab, 17

Campbell, Wilbur, 162

Capitaine, George, 111

Carlsson, Jan, 161

Carman, Jack, 85, 86

Carmichael, Hoagy, 46

Carney, Harry, 57, 78

Carroll, Robert, 45, 47

Carter, Benny, 36, 37–38, 57, 60, 80, 108, 138; cuts Jimmy Dorsey, 45

Carter, James, 103, 172–73, 176

Carter, Ron, 68

Casey, Al, 74

Catlett, Big Sid, 28, 57

Cavanaugh, Inez, 42, 55, 66, 82, 85, 88, 96, 97, 99, 107, 111, 150, 178

Cherry, Don, 144

Christian, Charlie, 19, 51, 71, 178

Christian, Jodie, 162

Churchill, Savannah, 38, 63

Clark, Bill, 120

Clark, Pete, 85

Clark Monroe's Uptown House, 52, 72, 74, 76

Clarke, Kenny "Klook," 45, 72, 116, 119, 135; appears at Grand Semaine du Jazz, 116; joins Bud Powell "Three Bosses" trio, 140; member of Minton's house band, 51–52, 71; origin of nickname, 136; moves to France to work with Michel Legrand, 136–37; records album with Byas and Bud Powell, 147; works in Edgar Hayes's band, 46–47

Clayton, Wilbur "Buck," 36, 39, 76; baited by Byas into fight with Ed Lewis, 98; first plays in band with Byas, 19; hires Byas for sextet recording, 118; jam session recording at Carnegie Hall, 52; leads brief tour of Europe, 140; plays at the Blue Note in Paris with Byas, 117; plays two concerts at Times Hall, 80; victim of Byas's language prank, 99

Cobb, Arnett, 37, 48

Cole, Cozy, 59, 60, 63, 70, 71

Cole, Nat "King," 19, 21, 125

Coleman, Bill, 65, 69, 80, 98, 100, 115–16

Coleman, Ornette, 141, 178

Collins, John, 45, 125

Collins, Kyle, 9

Collins, Shad, 59

Coltrane, John, 33, 48, 167, 171, 173, 176, 177, 178, 180

Commodore Records, 41, 56

Condon, Eddie, 65

Connie's Inn, 83

Cosma, Vladimir, 147

Crawford, James, 76

Crombie, Tony, 146

Daly, Georges "Geo," 115
Dameron, Tadd, 86
D'Agaro, Daniele, 168
D'Amico, Hank, 59
Dandridge, Hugo, 17
Darville, John, 86
Davern, Kenny, 158
Davis, Art, 38, 138
Davis, Eddie "Lockjaw," 139
Davis, Harvey, 47
Davis, Miles, 8, 109, 116, 117, 137, 167, 180
Davis, William Strethen "Wild Bill," 164
Dawson, Alan, 146
de Fatto, Guy, 119
de Jong, Henk, 125
de Ruiter, Leo, 148
de Villers, Michel, 115
Denjean, Jacques, 144, 145
Dickinson, Vic, 58
Diéval, Jacques "Jack," 115, 116
do Carmo, Carlos, 147
Dodds, Johnny, 89
Doggett, Bill, 79
Dolphy, Eric, 61
Dorsey, Jimmy, 37, 83
Drew, Kenny, 102, 146, 156–57
Dulfer, Hans, 37, 96, 98, 102, 131, 132, 151, 169
Durham, Eddie, 28, 47, 79–80
Dylag, Roman, 148

Echols, Charlie, 19, 36, 108
Eckinger, Isla, 147
Eckstine, Billy, 60–61, 74, 134
Edelhagen, Kurt, 137, 140
Edison, Harry "Sweets," 43
Edwards, Al "Fats," 117
Edward's Jazz Band, 115–16, 117
Eksteen, Johanna "Jopie," 25, 125–27. *See also* Byas, Jopie
Eldridge, Roy, 38, 45, 62, 71–72, 76, 110; adds Byas to his band, 118–19; tours with Earl Hines, 146; tours with JATP, 138
Ellington, Duke, 5, 8, 19, 24, 29, 34, 40, 41, 45, 56, 57, 62, 69, 70, 73, 78, 80, 82, 89, 94, 98, 108, 110, 116, 138, 147, 154, 165, 173; adds Byas as featured soloist for tour, 118; features Byas in benefit concert,

164; features Byas in Paris concert, 35, 149; features Byas in Zurich concert, 35; praise for Byas's composition "Orgasm," 168; praises Coleman Hawkins, 27
Ellington, Mercer, 149–50
Elsen, Frans, 70, 137
Elstak, Nedly, 145
Engels, John, 129, 145
Engström, Nils, 144
Ervin, Booker, 156, 163
Esquire All-American Award Winners, 35, 80
Evans, Bill, 109
Evans, Herschel, 19, 26, 36, 174; influence on Byas, 15; part of jam session at the Cherry Blossom, 28; tenor saxophonists influenced by, 37
Ezell, Ellis, 8, 10

Faisant, Raoul, 109
Farmer, Art, 147, 165
Feld, Morey, 78
Fenton, Nick, 5, 52
Fields, Kansas, 117, 122
Finch, Candy, 99
Fitzgerald, Ella, 8
Flagstad, Mikkel, 137
Fleagle, Brick, 42
Flennoy, Lorenz, 18, 19
Floyd, Troy, 36–37
Fol, Hubert, 117
Fol, Raymond, 115, 117, 122
Frazier, George, 50
Freeman, Bud, 30, 139
Freeman, Lawrence, 11
Frost, Richie, 116, 120
Fuentes, Luis, 138
Fuller, Curtis, 163

Gabler, Milt, 40–41, 83
Gaillard, Slim, 67, 68
Gaines, Otto Lee, 12
Garbaek, Jan, 161
Garner, Erroll, 66, 74, 77, 78, 80; joins Byas quartet, 55; learns "Laura" from Byas, 70; moves to New York, 56; records with Byas, 68; shares bill with Byas and Stuff Smith, 60

Garrison, Jimmy, 177
Garros, Christian, 144
Gaskin, Leonard, 61, 84
Gaudry, Michel, 129
Geller, Herb, 165
George, Karl, 11, 12
Getz, Stan, 137
Gibson, Andy, 43
Gillespie, Dizzy, 31, 36, 47, 56, 60, 68, 69, 72, 73, 76, 77, 78, 80, 81, 120, 123, 129, 136, 176; co-leads band with Oscar Pettiford, 74–75; co-leads combo with Charlie Parker, 76–77; complains about release of Jerry Newman's recordings, 51–52; disgust with Byas's drinking, 101; hires Paul Gonsalves, 173; plays in Minton's House band, 71; praises Norman Granz's treatment of musicians, 138; records famous version of "A Night in Tunisia," 84; records with Clyde Hart, 61–62; reunion with Byas at Newport, 161; use of pseudonyms, 63
Glenn, William "Tyree," 15, 17, 19, 20, 39, 58, 59, 107, 108; impresses Timme Rosenkrantz, 40, 41; tours with Don Redman, 85, 89, 91, 107, 108
Gold, Sanford, 84
Golson, Benny, 173
Gonsalves, Paul, 101, 149, 174, 175; acknowledges Byas influence, 173; drunken night in Paris with Byas, 150
Goodman, Benny, 16, 48, 58, 67, 71, 83, 119
Gordon, Dexter, 78, 80, 101, 103, 144, 162, 163, 165, 169, 177, 180
Grammy Hall of Fame, 84
Grant, Alton, 15
Granz, Norman, 21, 130, 138
Grappelli, Stephane, 147
Green, Bennie, 60
Green, Claude, 58
Green, Freddie, 50, 52
Green, Oliver, 3
Greenber, Rowland, 137
Griffin, Johnny, 33–34, 96, 174
Grimes, Herman, 15
Grimes, Tiny, 68, 71
Gruntz, George, 165

Guarneri, Johnny, 57, 63, 68, 79
Guarneri, Leo, 78
Gustafsson, Rune, 144
Guy, Joe, 52

Haig, Al, 77, 80
Hall, Al, 45
Hamilton, Jimmy, 45
Hampton, Lionel, 12, 14, 15, 17, 36, 48, 79, 111, 148, 168, 174
Hancock, Herbie, 160–61, 164
Handy, W. C., 42
Hanna, Roland, 161
Hansen, Ole Jacob, 145
Harper, Buddy, 17
Harrington, John, 11
Harris, Benny, 56
Harris, Charlie, 125
Harris, Joe, 144
Harris, Wynonie, 79
Harrison, Jimmy, 98
Hart, Clyde, 58, 59, 61, 62, 74, 76, 103
Haughton, Chauncey "Shorty," 85
Hausser, Michel, 100
Haverhoek, Henk, 165–66
Hawes, Hampton, 61, 106
Hawkins, Coleman, 8, 21, 36, 37, 41, 42, 45, 48, 49, 57, 61, 70, 72, 74, 77, 78, 80, 87, 89, 103, 138, 154, 155, 168, 170, 171, 173, 174, 175, 176, 177, 178; influence on Byas, 26; inspires Byas to switch to tenor sax, 13, 26; jam session battles, 27–29; make of tenor sax played, 172; ratings of other tenor saxophonists, 30, 139; recordings with Byas, 30–31, 38; sextet with Byas, 56; wins Esquire gold, 68
Hawkins, Erskine, 48
Hawkins, Leonard, 61
Hayes, Edgar, 45, 46–47, 78, 80, 136
Hayes, Thamon, 47
Haynes, Cyril, 60, 63
Heard, J. C., 68, 79
Heath, Al, 102
Heath, Albert "Tootie," 157
Henderson, Fletcher, 13, 18, 27, 28, 29, 49, 80, 82, 118, 119
Henderson, Horace, 118

Index

Hendricks, Jon, 139, 173
Herman, Woody, 56, 63, 69, 86
Heywood, Eddie, Jr., 57
Hicks, Billy, 42
Hilda, Bernard, 110, 111
Hill, Teddy, 36, 51, 71, 72, 119, 136
Hines, Earl, 43, 60, 74, 76, 146–47, 148
Hite, Les, 16
Hodeir, André, 118
Hodges, Johnny, 34, 35, 37, 48, 80, 85, 86, 98, 110, 138, 165
Holder, Terence "T," 7, 11
Holiday, Billie, 8, 29, 45, 61, 66, 74, 85, 136
Holland, Dave, 68
Holland, Herbert Lee "Peanuts," 85, 89, 107, 108, 109
Howard, Paul, 15, 16, 17, 18
Hughes, Spike, 72

Ineke, Eric, 129
Inge, Edward, 45
Inzalaco, Tony, 165
Iversen, Einar, 144

Jackson, Milt, 163
Jackson, Oliver, 140
Jackson, Quentin, 85, 91
Jacobs, Pim, 145, 148
Jacobs, Ruud, 96, 145, 148
Jacquet, Illinois, 29, 37, 48, 103
Jaffe, Nat, 60, 64
Jami, Hakim, 163
Jarrett, Keith, 161, 166–67
Jaspar, Bobby, 92, 109
Jazz at the Philharmonic (JATP), 69, 78, 98, 130, 138, 139, 140
Jazzhus Montmartre, 144, 155
Jeffreys, Alan, 85, 86
Johansen, Egil, 148
Johnson, Albert "Budd," 18, 56, 57, 74, 84; replaces Byas in Gillespie-Pettiford group, 62
Johnson, Bert, 13, 14–15, 18
Johnson, Charlie, 119
Johnson, Eddie, 70
Johnson, George "Happy," 17, 59, 111, 156
Johnson, J. J., 109

Johnson, Pete, 47, 52, 63
Jones, Elvin, 177
Jones, Jimmy, 66
Jones, Jo, 28, 38, 42, 50, 52, 54, 135, 138, 139, 161
Jones, Quincy, 135, 147
Jones, Slick, 63
Jones, Thad, 161
Jordan, Clifford, 148
Jordan, Louis, 79

Karlsen, Kjell, 137
Kersey, Ken, 52, 76
Kessel, Barney, 7
Keynote Records, 57, 63
Kid Dynamite (Lodewijk Rudolf Arthur Parisius), 126
Killian, Al, 78
King, Paul, 15
Kirby, John, 28, 61
Kirk, Andy, 7, 11, 15, 24, 43, 44, 102
Kirk, Rahsaan Roland, 161, 163, 173
Kruger, Irv, 62
Krupa, Gene, 66, 119
Kyle, Billy, 42, 43

Lafitte, Guy, 138
Laird, Rick, 146
Lallemand, "Fats" Sadi Pol, 124, 130
Langereis, Rob, 129, 147, 156
Lawrence, Elliot, 77
Lee, George E., 37
Leeman, Cliff, 74
Legrand, Michel, 136
Lermarchand, Pierre, 123–24
Levey, Stan, 77
Levy, John, 63
Lewis, Bill, 7
Lewis, Ed, 49, 98
Lewis, Frank, 77
Lewis, John, 159
Lewis, Mel, 161
Lind, Ove, 144
Lindberg, Gören, 161
Loeb, Peter Arthur, 163
Lovano, Joe, 176
Love, Clarence, 7
Lucas, Al, 57, 58, 74

Lüdeke, Jaap, 172
Luter, Claude, 122

Madna, Rob, 145
Mallory, Eddie, 20, 39–40, 41, 108
Manne, Shelly, 62, 176
Marsh, Warne, 68
Martin, Bobby, 89
Martin, Stu, 147
Massey, Calvin, 163
Mathiesen, Leo "The Lion," 42, 85
Mavounzy, Robert, 86
McKinney's Cotton Pickers, 12, 59, 83, 119
McLaughlin, John, 160
McLure, Morris "Red Mack," 17
McPartland, Marian, 117
McShann, James Columbus "Jay," 12, 46, 75, 76, 83; plays gigs with Byas as teens, 9–10
McVea, Jack, 17
Methany, Pat, 161
Meyers, Arnvid, 148
Michelot, Pierre, 118, 123, 130, 140
Mikkelborg, Palle, 102
Miller, Glenn, 107
Miller, Johnny, 16, 21
Millinder, Lucky, 42–43, 148, 174
Mills Blue Rhythm Band, 39, 46
Mingus, Charles, 18, 69
Minton, Henry, 31, 71
Minton's Playhouse, 36, 51, 52, 55, 62, 71, 154
Mitchell, Red, 68
Mölgaard, Torolf, 102
Molinetti, Armand, 109, 119
Monk, Thelonious, 62, 72, 73, 75, 84, 136–37, 167, 168, 173; jam sessions at Minton's, 51, 71; plays in Coleman Hawkins's sextet, 56
Montoliu, Tete (Vicenç Montoliu i Massana), 94, 111, 165–66; records with Webster and Byas, 157; works with Byas, 113, 140
Moody, James, 99, 116, 118, 119
Moore, Brew, 144, 146, 147, 155, 156–57
Moore, Oscar, 21
Morales, Humberto "Canto," 120
Morgan, Al, 17, 18
Morgan, Jane, 110
Morris, Ramon, 164

Morton, Ferdinand "Jelly Roll," 7, 15, 63, 105, 106, 107
Moseholm, Erik, 144
Moten, Bennie, 9, 11, 36, 37, 47, 49, 50, 58, 78, 83, 152
Muldoon, Oliver, 119
Mulligan, Gerry, 77, 146–47
Murray, Sunny, 141
Myers, Bump, 21

Nance, Ray, 57, 78
Nanton, Joe "Tricky Sam," 108
Netherlands Jazz Archive, 168
Newman, Jerry, 51, 71
Newport Jazz Festival, 161, 168, 173
Newton, Frankie, 59, 80
Nicholas, Albert, 7, 64
Nordin, Sture, 161
Norvo, Red, 59, 66, 67, 68
Nougaro, Claude, 108, 169

Oliver, Buford, 85, 88, 91, 107, 109
Onyx Club, 54, 62, 73, 74, 75, 84, 101, 173

Palmieri, Remo, 59
Page, Oran "Hot Lips," 76, 78, 104, 174; co-leads septet with Byas, 116–17; hires Byas for his band, 47, 58
Page, Walter, 11, 14, 42, 49, 52, 58, 135, 152
Paque, Glyn, 89
Pamies, Jules "Julio," 118
Paraboschi, Roger, 115, 124, 130
Parker, Charlie "Yardbird" or "Bird," 9, 36, 60, 69, 72, 74, 80, 101, 116, 117, 123, 137, 141, 144, 171, 176, 178; invites Gerry Mulligan to sit in, 77; late for Town Hall concert, 68; plays with Byas, 75–77, 78; plays with Clyde Hart, 61
Parker, Jack "The Bear," 58
Paul, Les, 21
Payne, Sylvester "Sonny," 61
Pearson, Henry Mattathias, 163
Peck, Nathan "Nat," 91, 107
Pedersen, Bjørn, 144
Pedersen, Niels-Henning Ørsted, 68, 146; plays with Byas, Webster, and Moore, 147, 155; records with Byas, 144

Peiffer, Bernard, 115, 188
Perry, Ray, 67
Persiany, André "Pepé," 99, 138
Person, Houston, 68
Pettiford, Oscar, 31, 73, 76, 84, 101, 117, 135, 137; forms group with Dizzy Gillespie, 74–75; hires Byas for record date, 61–62
Phillips, Flip, 66, 80
Phillips, Gene, 19
Pochonet, Gérard "Dave," 123
Poindexter, Pony, 150
Powell, Bud, 69, 75, 137, 167; co-leads record date with Byas, 140–41; plays with Byas in Denmark, 144; plays in Don Byas Orchestra, 61
Powell, Gordon "Specs," 80
Price, Sammy, 15
Prima, Louis, 56
Procope, Russell, 41, 80
Proteau, Tony, 118, 122–23

Quersin, Benoît, 130

Rabinowitch, Boris, 85–86
Radcliffe, Fred, 84, 85
Raeburn, Boyd, 84, 86
Ramey, Gene, 140
Ramos, Miguel, 111
Rasmussen, Hugo, 102
Rasmussen, Peter, 85
Redd, Vi, 162
Redman, Dewey, 166–67
Redman, Don, 45, 61, 69, 78, 92, 103, 107, 108, 110, 150, 152, 168; European tour, 82–91; includes Byas on record dates, 42, 81, 82, 83–84
Reid, Rufus, 162
Reig, Teddy, 103
Réwéliotty, André, 122
Reys, Rita, 148
Rivers, Sam, 68
Roach, Max, 31, 69, 116, 117; first bop quintet at the Onyx, 75; records with Byas, 84
Robertson, Eddie, 56
Rodrigues, Amália, 112, 113, 148
Rogers, Shorty, 66
Rogers, Timmie, 38, 63

Rollins, Sonny, 156, 175
Rose, Hillary, 45
Rosenkrantz, Timme, 39–42, 55–56, 77, 81–83, 88, 111, 150, 152, 158; promotes Town Hall concert with Byas, 65–67
Ross, Theodore "Doc," 9
Rostaing, Hubert, 117
Rouse, Charlie, 118
Rousseau, Charlie, 16
Rovira, Luis, 112
Rowles, Jimmy, 21
Rushing, Jimmy, 50–51, 130
Russell, Curley, 77

Sampson, Deryck, 74
Sannes, Elvin, 145
Saratoga Jazz Hounds, 119
Savoy Records, 58
Schifrin, Lalo, 38, 138
Schiöpffe, William, 144
Schmidlin, Peter, 147
Schoenberg, Loren, 50
Schuller, Gunther, 50, 79, 105
Scott, Cecil, 36, 119
Scott, Mabel, 19
Scott, Tony, 148
Sears, Al, 34
See, Cees, 145, 146
Shavers, Charlie, 43, 52, 58, 59, 63, 64
Shaw, Artie, 119
Shaw, Arvell, 134
Shepp, Archie, 68, 142, 150
Shorter, Wayne, 147
Sim, Pierre, 144
Simmons, Art, 120, 125
Simmons, John, 85
Singer, Hal, 78, 154
Sjøsten, Lars, 148
Skeete, Frank, 84
Slinger, Cees, 125, 129, 148, 156, 168
Smith, Cladys "Jabbo," 108
Smith, Hezekiah Leroy Gordon "Stuff," 60, 61, 73, 78, 96, 146, 152; death and memorial concert, 148; describes Byas's love for fishing, 96; jam session at Times Hall, 80; plays Town Hall concert, 65
Smith, Mamie, 27

Smith, Tab, 43, 52, 57, 176
Snowden, Elmer, 119
Solal, Martial, 123, 130
Spieler, Bernard, 117
Spirits of Rhythm, 73
Stewart, Rex, 29, 41, 98, 116
Stewart, Sammy, 36
Stewart, Slam, 28, 55, 58, 66, 67, 68, 77, 102, 155, 176; joins Don Byas quartet, 55; records with Byas, 59, 68; Town Hall duet with Byas, 33, 155, 173, 179
Stitt, Sonny (Edward Hammond Boatner Jr.), 72, 167
Stone, Jesse, 26, 27, 36
Strayhorn, Billy, 12
Sturgis, Ted, 65, 74, 85
Sulieman, Idrees (Leonard Graham), 140–41, 144
Sullivan, Joe, 73
Sweatman, Wilbur, 27, 63

Tate, Buddy, 37, 44, 52, 53, 167
Tatum, Art, 18, 31–33, 66, 67, 73, 176–77
Taylor, Arthur, 26, 104
Taylor, Billy (bassist), 63, 70
Taylor, Billy (pianist), 30, 40, 71, 74, 75, 95, 163; brings wife on Don Redman's European tour, 85; on Byas hearing David Raksin's "Laura" in film, 69–70; perceives Art Tatum's impact on Byas, 33, 176; plays Town Hall with Stuff Smith, 65; praises Byas for accepting him as young musician, 129; records with Byas, 63; remains in Europe to play after tour ends, 91, 107, 109
Taylor, Theodora "Teddy," 85
Teagarden, Jack, 98
Thielemans, Toots, 117
Thilo, Jesper, 97
Thomas, Joe, 7, 63
Thomas, T. B. "Turk," 11
Thomas, Walter "Foots," 7, 70
Thompson, Lucky, 122, 128, 137, 139, 173–74
Thompson, Sir Charles, 68, 140, 147–48
Thunus, Vicky, 111
Tilché, J. J., 107
Times Hall, 60, 80

Tizol, Juan, 69
Tomas, Alain, 12, 15
Torin, "Symphony Sid" (Sidney Tarnopol), 66, 77
Town Hall, 33, 65–66, 67, 68, 77, 80, 83, 102, 173
Tracey, Stan, 146
Trent, Alphonso, 7, 11
Trumbauer, Frankie, 158
Trunk, Peter, 146, 157
Turner, Bruce, 146
Turner, Joe, 63
Tyner, McCoy, 164, 177

Ulanov, Barry, 80

van Dijk, Piet, 126
van Poll, Jack, 100
Vance, Dick, 58
Vander, Maurice, 123, 130
Varne, Per, 145
Vaughan, Sarah, 60, 61, 84, 130
V-Disc, 60
Venuti, Joe, 73
Viale, Jean-Louis, 130
Village Vanguard, 161
Vogue label, 114, 119, 123
Voice of America, 52
Voumard, Géo, 123, 129, 134

Wallington, George, 62, 75, 84
Ware, Wilbur, 161, 163
Warne, Selwyn, 56
Warren, Earle, 31–32, 52, 140
Warren, Fran, 67
Warwick, Carl, 43
Washington, Dinah, 60, 61
Washington, Jack, 11
Waters, Benny, 37
Waters, Ethel, 20, 39–40, 56
Watts, Kenny, 63
Weather Report, 160
Webb, Speed, 119
Weber, Eberhard, 161
Webster, Ben, 21, 28, 37, 53, 72, 96, 113, 132, 139, 141, 146, 154, 155–56, 159, 166, 168, 173, 175; affair with Mary Lou Williams, 23; alcohol problems, 152; co-leads record date

with Byas, 35, 115, 148, 156, 157; friendship and rivalry with Byas, 152–53; jam sessions with Byas, 78, 154; Johnny Hodges's influence, 34; last live date with Byas, 158; part of three tenor date in Copenhagen, 147; ranked at top by Coleman Hawkins, 30; returns to Copenhagen, 158; temporarily relocates to Amsterdam, 151–52; unannounced visits to the Byas home, 152–53

Wells, Dicky, 80, 140, 174–75

Wess, Frank, 12–13

West, Harold "Doc," 55, 62, 68, 74

Whitby, Francis "Doc," 20

White, Leroy "Snake," 17

Whyte, Zach, 119

Williams, Bob, 85

Williams, Claude "Fiddler," 7

Williams, Cootie, 43, 75

Williams, Elmer, 29

Williams, George, 79–80

Williams, John, 11, 23, 43

Williams, Louis, 112

Williams, Mary Lou, 11, 44, 66, 123, 153, 178; affair with Byas, 23–24, 45, 153; Cherry Blossom cutting contest, 28–29; hires Byas for record dates, 57–58, 123; jams with Byas in Paris, 117; leaves Andy Kirk, 43

Williams, Nelson, 119

Williams, Rudy, 42, 59

Willox, Guy (Guy Dirickx), 91

Wilson, Buster, 16

Wilson, Dick, 29, 44

Wilson, Garland, 123

Wilson, Teddy, 12, 45, 59, 61, 66, 67, 81, 84, 94, 136, 146

Wijkamp, Ton, 145

Wöhrmann, Nicke, 144

Woode, Jimmy, 144, 146

Woodyard, Sam, 147

Young, James "Trummy," 60, 61, 84

Young, John, 162

Young, Lee, 17, 19, 20, 21, 125

Young, Lester "Prez," 9, 17, 21, 30, 37, 42, 45, 49, 72, 125, 129, 139, 148, 171, 174, 175, 177,

178; bests Coleman Hawkins at Cherry Blossom, 28–29; leaves Count Basie, 47–48; replaces Byas in Count Basie's band, 62; returns to Count Basie, 52–54, 62

Ypma, Peter, 129, 147, 156

Zacharias, Bernard, 122

ABOUT THE AUTHOR

Con Chapman is a Boston-area writer, author of *Rabbit's Blues: The Life and Music of Johnny Hodges*, winner of the 2019 Book of the Year Award by Hot Club de France, and Kansas City *Jazz: A Little Evil Will Do You Good*, nominee for 2023 Book of the Year Award by the Jazz Journalists Association. His work has appeared in *The Atlantic*, the *Boston Globe*, the *Boston Herald*, and other publications.

www.ingramcontent.com/pod-product-compliance
Lightning Source LLC
Chambersburg PA
CBHW020811260325
24008CB00002B/8